𝔉𝔞𝔲𝔰𝔱

A TRAGEDY

By Johann Wolfgang von Goethe

Translated, in the original meters,

by Bayard Taylor

INTRODUCTION BY

VICTOR LANGE

Professor of German Language and Literature,
Chairman of German Studies,
Cornell University

THE MODERN LIBRARY · NEW YORK

THE MODERN LIBRARY
is published by RANDOM HOUSE, INC.

BENNETT CERF • DONALD S. KLOPFER

Manufactured in the United States of America

Begun before
Kant's Critique of Pure Reason

INTRODUCTION

By VICTOR LANGE

Concern for man !!!

L IKE Dante and Milton, Goethe is often identified
with one central achievement. His *Faust* crowns and
symbolizes a long life of incomparable scope and variety
which encompasses the space of nearly a century, from
1749 to 1832, and which illuminates with extraordinary
brilliance the features of an age that was decisive in the
making of the modern mind. In every one of his works,
from *The Sorrows of Young Werther* to the serenely
elegiac poems of his old age, Goethe is concerned with
the nature of modern man and the special moral and
intellectual challenges with which he finds himself con-
fronted. And it is characteristic of Goethe's sense of the
relevance of poetic symbols that, prompted by his experiences as man of letters, scientist and social philosopher, he should again and again have turned to the figure
of the great magus of the Renaissance.

Even as a child in Frankfurt he must have come upon
representations in prose or crudely dramatic form of the
history of Doctor Georg Faust, a contemporary of
Luther's and a figure of remarkable independence of
thought and belief, typical of the revolutionary spiritual
climate of the sixteenth century. Faust's classical and
alchemistic learning, his defiance of the then current
modes of salvation and, even more important, his hyp-
notic personality made him, soon after his death in 1540,
the subject of popular imagination. In the Frankfurt
Faust-Book of 1587 and in Marlowe's *Tragical History of*

v

Doctor Faustus, written only a few years later, he emerged
as a definite poetic character: the magician and necromancer who sold his soul to the Devil became the
symbol of an all-consuming greed for power and a ruthless, superhuman desire to be the "great emperor of the
world." But by the early eighteenth century the Christian theme of the sufferings of the heretic which had sus-
tained the earlier treatments of the Faust saga had lost
much of its compelling appeal. When Goethe first saw a
melodramatic version of it on the puppet stage, he can
no longer have been struck by the specifically Christian
implications of the story. In the rationalistic climate of
that enlightened century, the problem of Faust, his re-
jection of orthodoxy, had become, if not wholly secular-
ized, at least subject to the scrutiny of worldly skepticism.

Goethe's years of study at the Universities of Leipzig
and Strasbourg may have reinforced in his mind the contemporary view of Faust as a rebel not against Christian
dogma only, but against any sort of categorical system
of values. His interest in the great representatives of the
nature philosophy of the Renaissance, in Paracelsus,
Campanella, and Giordano Bruno became increasingly
alive and, moved by a new enthusiasm for the Shake-
spearean tragic hero, he planned a number of dramatic
portraits of the "titanic" man, of Caesar, Mohammed,
Prometheus, Goetz von Berlichingen. It may have been
at that time, shortly after 1770, that the figure of Faust
offered itself to Goethe as a representative symbol not
only of greed for power, or of superhuman intelligence,
but of a type of perception which, indicative of the
modern mind, sought to penetrate the paradoxes of
knowledge and life. Even before 1775 when he went to
Weimar to accept a court position that was to grow more
demanding and more responsible as the years went by,
he appears to have completed the *Urfaust*, a dramatic

sketch, unpublished at the time, in which the core of
Faust's story, his association (not his pact) with Mephistopheles, his love for Margaret, and his eventual
doom are represented in a rapid sequence of picturesque
scenes, some in verse, some in prose.

Goethe's first ten years in Weimar were years of ad-
justment; his interests were divided between public service, an increasing devotion to science, and philosophical
and poetic exercises that indicate his growing desire for
inner stability. His journey to Italy in 1786–88 represents a decisive turn in his development. In the light of
his deepened attachment to the world of forms and to a
sense of personal discipline, he could now complete some
of his best poetic projects that had for long remained
fragmentary. The so-called *Faust-Fragment* of 1790
shows the result of this self-scrutiny: Goethe recast
several of the familiar scenes, and added a number of
significant passages that give further reality to Faust's
moral situation. During the years between 1794 and
1805, Schiller's friendship and encouragement were of in-
estimable importance to Goethe; it was he who suggested
a reconsideration of the whole Faust scheme, and in
June, 1797, Goethe once again turned his full attention
to *Faust,* composed the "Dedication," the "Prelude on
the Stage" and the "Prologue in Heaven," and thus
placed the familiar incidents of Faust's life in a larger
ethical context—the tension between the creative energies
of the Lord and the destructive forces of Mephistopheles.
Faust, in the form in which we know it, did not appear
until 1808.

Goethe was then nearly sixty years old, at the height
of a distinguished life and in full mastery of his poetic
powers. In a rich philosophical novel, *Wilhelm Meister's
Apprenticeship,* he had set forth his idea of a fruitful life,
and in *Hermann and Dorothea* he had elaborated his

central theme of the interplay of chaos and order. No
less revealing of the diversity of his interests were the
published results of his studies in optics and botany. Indeed, his scientific and historical knowledge provided
essential elements for the First Part of *Faust*, and when
he contemplated a continuation of it, he did so because
he hoped that an imaginative treatment of Faust's later
career might offer a poetic vehicle for an even more impressive representation of modern philosophical ideas.

As early as 1800 he had begun the "Helen" episode,
which was later to evolve into the third act of the Second
Part, but for some time work on *Faust* was again suspended. Two novels, *Elective Affinities* (1809) and *Wilhelm Meister's Travels* (1821), another major scientific
work, *The Science of Color* (1810), his autobiography,
Poetry and Truth, and the splendid series of *Divan* poems
give to the years between 1808 and 1825 their unmistak-
able character: all these works are the products of a cir-
cumspect and skeptical mind, who with all his deliberate
detachment from the literary fashions of his romantic
contemporaries and from the political demands of the
day, remains the dominant figure of his time. In 1825,
seventy-six years of age, he resumed *Faust* and the poem
remained his "Hauptgeschaeft," his main business, until
it was completed in July, 1831, eight months before his
death.

II

It is not surprising that a work of such slow and irregular
growth as *Faust* should not easily reveal its unity, indeed
that it should prove most rewarding when tested with a
variety of critical tools. We must, first of all, remember
that it is a product of imagination and that before in-
quiring into its philosophical meaning we should recognize the power of its poetic effects. Even in the English
translation, we can feel that each scene is filled with a

special atmosphere and that each uses the sort of language, imagery, and rhythm appropriate to it: the sweeping lines of the "Prologue in Heaven" are followed by the tense and throbbing verse of the study scenes. The "Easter Walk" with its solid figures and its bright colors offers a beautiful combination of promise and recollection; the Gretchen episodes develop swiftly in purely lyrical terms; and for the incidents of nature magic in the "Witches' Kitchen" and at the "Walpurgis-night" revels, Goethe uses a curiously suggestive kind of speech by which he anticipates the unrealistic devices of the Second Part. There the symbolic and metaphorical intentions are far more deliberate but they are also, we must admit, not always fully realized. In the company of the earlier Faust, of Gretchen, Mephistopheles, and perhaps especially of the minor figures such as the students, neighbor Martha, and Valentine, we are touched, moved, elevated or shocked. The Second Part stirs our feelings less immediately; it challenges our intellectual perception in a more oblique and demanding manner. But by the continued presence of his whole poetic personality Goethe sustains throughout the play a remarkably powerful imaginative energy.

This is not, of course, to say that the full force of the poem can be felt on its surface; it is a calculated work of art and the organizing mind behind it has made use of many resources. We should recognize the suitability of the free arrangement of the scenes in the First Part and of the more spacious architecture of the five acts of the Second. We must be aware of the associations of symbols such as the Earth Spirit or the setting of "Forest and Cavern" and relate them to particular philosophical impulses. We must bring knowledge as well as feeling to the play, especially to the Second Part, which is, in a comprehensive sense, concerned with knowledge itself.

But while the reader of *Faust* cannot miss the beauty or profundity of detail, he may find himself puzzled by the problem of the unity, of the central meaning, that holds this enormously suggestive poem together. The simple moral of the old Faust plot is here no longer adequate. If it had been Goethe's intention merely to retell the case history of a man who loses his soul, he would not have needed the intricate machinery of human involvement and superhuman guidance, he would not have given Faust the extraordinary dimensions of thought and passion, nor matched him against the brilliantly cynical intelligence of Mephistopheles. He could have made certain that any doubt as to the purpose of this spectacle should be resolved in the mind of the reader. Instead, Goethe himself was careful not to prejudice the interpretation of the work. In one of the many revealing conversations with Eckermann, he said, on May 6, 1827: "They come and ask what idea I meant to embody in my *Faust;* as if I knew myself, and could inform them. From heaven, through the world, to hell, would indeed be something; but this is no idea, only a course of action. And further: that the devil loses the wager, and that a man continually struggling from difficult errors towards something better, should be redeemed, is an effective—and, to many, a good enlightening—thought; but it is no idea at the foundation of the whole, or of every individual scene. It would have been a fine thing indeed if I had strung so rich, varied, and highly diversified a life as I have brought to view in *Faust* upon the slender string of one pervading idea." We may perhaps reach a more certain conclusion as to Goethe's purpose if we summarize briefly the successive phases of the plot.

III

Neither the "Dedication" nor the "Prelude on the

Stage" contains anything that is related to the action of the play: the first states the poet's attitude toward the material he is about to present, the second indicates the special nature of the spectacle to be produced. But the bearing of the "Prologue in Heaven" upon the subsequent plot cannot be overemphasized—it is the key to everything that is to come. Among the angelic host praising the Lord and His Creation, there appears Mephistopheles, one of the Lord's servants, whose function it is, like that of Satan in *Job*, to question and, where he can, to undermine all evidences of creative life. He cannot praise nor be wholly indifferent; his detachment makes him the supremely ironic spirit, for whom all efforts, especially those of man, seem ludicrous, pointless and absurd. The Lord insists that the sense of discrimination between good and evil, even though it may not easily be realized in a life of positive action, represents the true character of the human being. As long as this perception of values is active, it should entitle man to eventual salvation. This is the meaning of the term "striving" which the Lord recognizes as the essence of man's character and which, not in the sense of aggressive and amoral ruthlessness, but of a persistent power of moral judgment, Goethe offers as the central concept of Faust's career. Mephistopheles dares to test this divine assumption and hopes to disprove the validity of the Lord's thesis by destroying the sense of good and evil in one conspicuous specimen, Faust. The Lord agrees; he knows that as long as man lives, he is in any case immersed in the destructive element, but that his unceasing awareness of the great moral issues will preserve his human integrity.

When we first meet Faust he is a man of incomparable learning who has mastered every field of knowledge without, however, having found anywhere the reassurance of insight into ultimate meanings. As he speculates upon

the symbols of cosmic significance, he must admit his
human limitations; he can only hope, through the Earth
Spirit, to reach an understanding at least of all earthly
experience. But that, too, is shown to be impossible.
His despair is profound—the scene with his obtuse,
rationalistic assistant Wagner gives to it dramatic emphasis—and he contemplates suicide. At the moment of
surrender he is held back by a sudden welling-up of
childhood memories, which now, at the sound of the
Easter bells, restore his determination to live. Before
the city gates in the company of the townspeople he longs
again for a rich and meaningful life: no matter what aid
may offer itself, natural or supernatural, he will not reject it. When Mephistopheles emerges from his disguise,
ironically present at Faust's attempt to translate the
beginning of the Gospel of St. John, he finds Faust ready
to come to terms. He can give him satisfaction and
hopes that by extinguishing Faust's "striving," he may
demonstrate not only Faust's but God's failure.

Faust is not easily deceived. He insists that his desires
are not the obvious ones; they are superhuman in kind,
and above all, in intensity; they may baffle and perhaps
even defeat Mephistopheles. But the tempter can only
smile at Faust's peculiarities; they seem to him no more
than human; he knows that the weakness of reason which
they seem to imply will only serve his own ends. This
theme, the paradoxical nature of reason, is the subject
matter of many of Mephistopheles' speculations, and
especially of the interview with the naïve student.

What Mephistopheles now has to offer Faust is not
sufficiently seductive: the banal amusements of the
drinking students leave the mature man indifferent and
the tricks and gestures by which his youth is to be restored in the Witches' Kitchen strike Faust as childish
and repulsive. Before Mephistopheles can provide a

experience of still cruder physical satisfaction, Faust, himself, without assistance or prompting, meets Margaret. Their love, maudlin and commonplace to Mephistopheles, draws them together in a genuine but incongruous attachment. Margaret's simple, circumscribed world cannot survive under the torrential force of Faust's passion. As soon as Mephistopheles recognizes the evolving tragedy, he seizes upon it as a further test of Faust's moral energies. Through him, Faust becomes the cause of Valentine's death. They must flee, and in the satanic frenzy of the Walpurgis-night, Faust seems for a brief moment close to a total suspension of moral perception. But the most powerful means of seduction cannot destroy Faust's memory of Margaret; as he comes to rescue her, he is overwhelmed by the spectacle of a moral decision in Margaret that is clearer and, in spite of her madness, more resolute than he himself can achieve. She refuses to be freed by Mephistophelian devices and submits to the judgment of God. Faust, most deeply stirred and here, perhaps, farthest from the kind of amorality that Mephistopheles hopes to achieve, is forcibly reminded of his attachment to his servant; as a voice from above promises Margaret forgiveness, Mephistopheles disappears with Faust.

Impressive in its dramatic sweep though the First Part may be, readers have always felt that the fate of Faust, undoubtedly the main unifying element in this phase of the poem, is at the end left in abeyance. If Goethe wished to continue the story of Faust's life and death, to complete it along the lines of the old *Faust-Book*, he had much episodic material that was as yet unused—Faust's appearance at the emperor's court and his evocation of Helen of Troy were certainly promising dramatic episodes. And that, in continuing his work on *Faust* (even before the First Part was published) he turned first of all to the Helen episode, seems to suggest that he hoped to find there a logical extension and perhaps even the conclusion of Faust's history.

But when, twenty-five years later, he resumed work on *Faust*, his perspectives, poetic as well as philosophical, had changed, and the Second Part was to derive its coherence not from the figure of Faust but from the unity of Goethe's own view of life, and especially of civilization, attached to Faust's experience but frequently enough independent of it.

"The first part is almost entirely subjective," Goethe remarked to Eckermann in February, 1831. "It all issues from a more confused, more passionate individual, and this twilight may well explain its great appeal. But in the Second Part there is scarcely anything subjective, here there appears a higher, broader, brighter, less passionate world, and those who have not knocked about a bit and gathered experience will not be able to make much of it."

The five acts of the Second Part contain Goethe's most moving comments on the culture of his time. We find Faust, in a magnificent opening scene, restored (though not morally exonerated) by the impartial forces of nature. With an unexpectedly clear realization of the limits of experience, but still devoted to the pursuit of the "highest form of life," he decides to live resolutely within this world. He appears at court, where Mephistopheles, disguised as the jester, has promised relief to the pleasure-loving but bankrupt emperor. As a frivolous stunt Faust undertakes to produce the apparition of Helen, and he must venture alone to the timeless and spaceless realm of the "Mothers," where Helen dwells—a descent into the area of purest beauty, which to Mephistopheles is no more than a journey into nothing. Faust appears at court with the image which is not the true Helen but only an idol; and when in a moment of blinding desire he reaches for her, she disappears, striking him to the ground.

In the second act Mephistopheles has carried the unconscious Faust back to his old study where Wagner has meanwhile come close to the successful production of an artificial "homunculus." This wraithlike creature has extraordinary powers of perception; he recognizes Faust's longing for Helen and offers to guide him from the murky North to Greece where in that night the spirits of classical demons are about to assemble. Mephistopheles, eager to be present at this "Classical Walpurgis-night," hides his devilish—northern—features, which would have no place in that world of beauty, behind the mask of Phorcyas, one of the ugliest creatures of Greek mythology. While Faust searches for Helen, Homunculus, a mere bodiless abstraction, attempts to achieve reality, but during the orgies of the nature elements he destroys himself.

The scene in which Faust was to find Helen and plead for her release was never written. At the beginning of the third act we find Helen returned to the palace at Sparta, terrified and insulted by Phorcyas-Mephistopheles and eventually persuaded to accept the protection of Faust, now the powerful lord of a neighboring castle. In a scene of superb poetry the wedding between Helen and Faust, between the classical and romantic sensibilities, takes place. Their child, Euphorion, cannot live: like Icarus he attempts to fly and crashes at the feet of his parents. "We imagine," say the stage directions, "that in the dead body we perceive a well-known form; yet the corporeal part vanishes at once, and the aureole rises like a comet toward heaven. The garment, mantle and lyre remain upon the ground." With this image, and the splendid dirge that follows, Goethe paid his tribute to Byron. Helen must follow Euphorion; only her garment and veil remain in Faust's arms.

What this enormously ramified search for Helen and her eventual loss mean for Faust can hardly be defined by one single set of criteria: it is a spiritual crisis that rests upon religious as well as aesthetic experiences and that reflects Goethe's own maturest view of the classical ideal. The union with Helen reminds Faust of the precarious meaning of all existence: early in the fourth act, he recalls "the grand significance of fleeting days," *fluechtger Tage grossen Sinn*. But he recognizes the vision of Helen as a deceptive dream in which he cannot acquiesce. Another vision points to what seems a more substantial form of spiritual beauty crystallizing the memory of Margaret.

Mephistopheles once again offers Faust the satisfactions of lust and passion. But Faust brushes these suggestions aside. Even fame seems insubstantial to him: "the Deed is everything, the Glory naught." The encounter with Helen has made him impatient for heroic action; he will now conquer "the aimless force of elements unruly" and compel the useless ocean to yield fertile soil. The true motive for this titanic project has been variously interpreted. It is certainly, in contrast to Mephistopheles' temptation, an affirmation of a creative desire and his determination to assume social responsibilities; but it is a decision that is not yet free of selfish will to power. Aided by Mephistopheles' magic he wins a crucial war for the emperor and is given as a reward the right to reclaim a barren stretch of swamp. He is now a hundred years old. Early in the fifth act, he surveys from the terrace of his palace the lands that he has claimed from the sea. Only one small settlement within his property is not yet in his control. With the same ruthless impatience that has so often jeopardized his actions, he orders Mephistopheles to remove the old couple living there. Mephistopheles soon returns to report, not their resettlement, but their destruction, and Faust, horrified at his own dependence upon Mephistopheles' demonic cynicism, turns away from him. As he faces his death he has come to realize the futility of his association with "magic."

> "Not yet have I my liberty made good:
> If I could banish Magic's fell creations,
> And totally unlearn the incantation,—
> Stood I, O Nature! Man alone in thee,
> Then were it worth one's while a man to be!
> Ere in the Obscure I sought it, such was I,—
> Ere I had cursed the world so wickedly."

In a superb scene in which Anguish, *die Sorge*, nearly overwhelms him, he remembers his resolve to free himself of supernatural help and, although Anguish blinds him, it cannot destroy him. Mistaking the chatter of lemures digging his grave for the noise of workmen, he envisages his community of free people on free soil. But "the highest moment" which was to be his last is not an achievement, it is a mere anticipatory vision.

> "Then dared I hail the Moment fleeing:
> Ah, still delay, thou art so fair!"

With these last words "Faust sinks back: the lemures take him and lay him upon the ground." The sepulcher scene which follows is no more than a dramatic concession. Mephistopheles has, in effect, long ago lost all chance of winning the wager and his last, theatrical attempt to snatch Faust's body from the angels cannot succeed.

IV

It is sometimes asked whether Faust's end is not curiously incongruous, whether a life so violent and so little exemplary ought not by rights to have fallen to Mephistopheles, whether it is not merely a poetic or perhaps we may even say a divine trick that Faust should be saved. This is a crucial test of interpretation and it must be faced most seriously.

The critics of the nineteenth century were agreed that Faust's pursuit of meaning was fraught with error and hubris, but they felt justified to read into Faust's later life—beginning at the emperor's court—a clearer recognition of human obligations, culminating in the attainment of the highest form of social responsibility. Faust's salvation represented from this point of view a deserved reward for his persistent striving from darkness to clarity.

But this optimistic and liberal reading of the poem offers countless difficulties and it was bound to disturb those in our own day who remembered Goethe's use of the word "tragedy" in the title of both parts, a term which otherwise he seldom used, and never in a casual sense. Faust's active life, his commendable if intermittent striving for any sort of security of action or knowledge, cannot serve as a key to the play. It is charged with error and confusion. Indeed, Faust's problem is insoluble in the course of life itself: he is forever torn between faith and despair and whenever he seems to be close to the attainment of spiritual patience, he is plunged again into the element of insecurity. His own extravagant passion and—almost as another aspect of his own self—Mephistopheles' cynicism, never cease to threaten his chances, not of a just compensation but of redemption and forgiveness. It is not until his end that he succeeds in freeing himself of the deceptive magic which tends to obscure the infinite magnitude of man's task to maintain himself between cosmos and chaos. His titanic wavering between superhuman longing and radical self-debasement, between his will to transcend and his suicidal paralysis, between his curse of all faith, hope, love and patience at one time and his ecstatic praise of a pantheistic Godhead at another—these are the extremes of experience between which Faust must go his way.

We should, for instance, remember Faust's attitude, throughout the play, toward the "word." It is to him the metaphor of all life, the unfathomable vehicle of an inexpressible substance. And we must in comparison listen to the cynical ease with which Mephistopheles— not only in his interview with the student—offers the word as the ready and effective device of confusion and deceit. What is tragically ambivalent to Faust is to Mephistopheles a sardonic comedy of errors. Ambiguity is for Faust—and in the opposite sense for Mephistopheles—the essence of all experience. His concern once he is associated with Mephistopheles is not merely with finding satisfaction, but with transcending, in finding it, the ever-present conflict between elation and dejection, between hope and despair. The Lord's confident assumption is that Faust has the power, if not to eliminate this conflict, at least to subordinate it to a compelling vision of man's moral responsibilities. That he may be tricked into forgetting the elemental force of this conflict and that trivial satisfactions may dull his moral sense and lead Faust to spiritual stagnation, that is Mephistopheles' hope.

The pivot upon which the meaning of the poem turns is the wager between the Lord and Mephistopheles. If this is fully realized, the pact between Faust and Mephistopheles assumes its proper—and secondary—function. It amounts to little more than the joining of the two partners in an enterprise in which Faust will dramatically demonstrate his powers of spiritual judgment and Mephistopheles his ingenuity as a provider of physical and intellectual distractions.

Still, we may find it disquieting, and perhaps incompatible with our more realistic predilections, that Faust's sense of discrimination should remain so speculative, that it is never translated into the practical evidence of beneficial action. Faust does little if any good; he becomes, on the contrary, increasingly involved in guilt and violence. What are we to think, for instance, of his love for Margaret? However touching its poetic rendering may be, is it not for Faust essentially a means of self-expansion? His divided nature makes it impossible for him to establish an ordered and satisfying relationship and his complexity is not relieved but only made more terrifying by contrast with the simple and clearly-defined feelings of Margaret, her orthodox belief and her eventual surrender to the judgment of God. We may be moved by the pathos of Margaret's fate, but it is Faust, not she, who is the truly tragic figure. No matter how much Mephistopheles may wish to trivialize this love, to exploit its elements of sensuality and crime, Faust remains aware of the deep and irreconcilable conflicts which are inherent in his passion. The scene "Forest and Cavern" is the most telling instance of Faust's inner rallying, but the introspection of that moment forces him again into despair and nihilism. His fall is deepest during the sexual orgies of the Walpurgis-night; yet even there, his conscience, his powers of distinction between sense and madness awaken, and the spectacle of Margaret's agony in the dungeon and her acceptance, enviable enough from Faust's point of view, of the categorical verdict of the Church move him most deeply. His departure with Mephistopheles suggests not his surrender to the element of evil, but an awareness of his continued tragic involvement in it. Throughout the five acts of the Second Part, the integrity of Faust's actions can often be questioned. He is still, and perhaps even more recklessly so, the romantic striver after the certainty that only fatal self-delusion could ever hope to achieve.

To his very end Faust is not a "good man." What Goethe has represented in the person of Faust and in the poem as a whole is not, after all, a model either of excellence or of depravity. It is rather an account, rendered with compassion as well as critical intelligence, of modern man. Faust's "two souls," his extremes of effusion and action, are the source of his highest as well as his lowest aspirations. But between ultimate knowledge of good and evil and unexceptionable, virtuous deeds, there lies, for Faust, a gulf which is, in the pursuit of our earthly life, unbridgeable. His last speeches acknowledge the tragic, the ultimately ambiguous nature of all human effort. There can be no other reason for the final scene which resumes and completes the religious theme of the "Prologue in Heaven." Faust's quest on earth is given its true meaning only within the frame of "divine reconciliation": the forgiveness that is commensurate with his striving must come from above; it can be shown only poetically in symbols of extremely rarefied spirituality. "You must admit," Goethe said in 1831, "that the conclusion where the redeemed soul is carried up, was difficult to manage; and that, amid such supersensual, scarcely conceivable matters, I might easily have lost myself in the void—if I had not, by means of sharply-defined figures, and images from the Christian Church, given my poetical design a desirable form and substance." Classical mythology would hardly have conveyed the full meaning of the essentially modern, Christian transfiguration of Faust—the radical experience of inadequacy that must remain insubstantial without the constant "striving" for an awareness of good and evil and that can be resolved, not in secular justice, but only in divine grace. In stages of extraordinarily rich meaning and poetic power Faust's earthly remains are at last transformed into pure perception, and Margaret, Mephistopheles' great metaphysical antagonist, can now lead Faust to clarity. Her unselfish love merges with that of the Blessed Virgin to elevate him to forgiveness.

> "Earth's insufficiency—Here grows to Event;
> The Indescribable—Here it is done."

BIBLIOGRAPHY

GOETHE

Biermann, B. *Goethe's World*. Norfolk (Conn.), 1949.

Curtius, L., and Weigand, H. J. *Wisdom and Experience*. New York, 1949. Selections from Goethe's prose.

Eckermann's Conversations with Goethe. New York, 1931.

Fairley, B. *Goethe as Revealed in His Poetry*. Chicago, 1932.

Fairley, B. *A Study of Goethe*. Oxford, 1947.

Lewes, G. H. *The Life and Works of Goethe*. London and New York, 1930.

Lewisohn, L. *Goethe, the Story of a Man*. 2 vols. New York, 1949.

Rose, W. (ed.) *Essays on Goethe*. London, 1949.

Thomas, C. *Goethe*. New York, 1917.

Viëtor, Karl. *Goethe the Poet*. Cambridge (Mass.), 1949.

Willoughby, L. A. *Unity and Continuity in Goethe*. Oxford, 1947.

FAUST

Goethe's Faust. ed. C. Thomas. 2 vols. Boston, 1892–97. German text with English notes and introduction.

Goethes Faust. Herausgegeben von G. Witkowski. Leiden, 1939. Best German edition.

Butler, E. M. *The Myth of the Magus*. Cambridge, 1948.

Enright, D. J. *Commentary on Goethe's Faust*. Norfolk (Conn.), 1949.

Frantz, A. I. *Half a Hundred Thralls to Faust*. Chapel Hill, 1949.

Miller, R. D. *The Meaning of Goethe's Faust*. Cambridge, 1939.

Palmer, P. M. and More, R. P. *Sources of the Faust Tradition*. New York, 1936.

Santayana, George. *Three Philosophical Poets*. Cambridge (Mass.), 1910.

Stawell, F. M. and Dickinson, G. L. *Goethe and Faust*. London, 1928.

CONTENTS OF THE
FIRST PART OF THE TRAGEDY

DEVIL'S DEAL

SKETCHED (MARGARET)

CONTENTS.

DEDICATION.

AGAIN ye come, ye hovering Forms! I find ye,
As early to my clouded sight ye shone!
Shall I attempt, this once, to seize and bind ye?
Still o'er my heart is that illusion thrown?
Ye crowd more near! Then, be the reign assigned ye,
And sway me from your misty, shadowy zone!
My bosom thrills, with youthful passion shaken,
From magic airs that round your march awaken.

Of joyous days ye bring the blissful vision;
The dear, familiar phantoms rise again,
And, like an old and half-extinct tradition,
First Love returns, with Friendship in his train.
Renewed is Pain: with mournful repetition
Life tracks his devious, labyrinthine chain,
And names the Good, whose cheating fortune tore them
From happy hours, and left me to deplore them.

They hear no longer these succeeding measures,
The souls, to whom my earliest songs I sang:
Dispersed the friendly troop, with all its pleasures,
And still, alas! the echoes first that rang!
I bring the unknown multitude my treasures;
Their very plaudits give my heart a pang,
And those beside, whose joy my Song so flattered,
If still they live, wide through the world are scattered.

1

And grasps me now a long-unwonted yearning
For that serene and solemn Spirit-Land:
My song, to faint Æolian murmurs turning,
Sways like a harp-string by the breezes fanned.
I thrill and tremble; tear on tear is burning,
And the stern heart is tenderly unmanned.
What I possess, I see far distant lying,
And what I lost, grows real and undying.

PRELUDE ON THE STAGE.

MANAGER. DRAMATIC POET. MERRY-ANDREW.

MANAGER

YOU two, who oft a helping hand
        Have lent, in need and tribulation,
Come, let me know your expectation
Of this, our enterprise, in German land!
I wish the crowd to feel itself well treated,
Especially since it lives and lets me live;
The posts are set, the booth of boards completed,
And each awaits the banquet I shall give.
Already there, with curious eyebrows raised,
They sit sedate, and hope to be amazed.
I know how one the People's taste may flatter,
Yet here a huge embarrassment I feel:
What they're accustomed to, is no great matter.
But then, alas! they've read an awful deal.
How shall we plan, that all be fresh and new,—
Important matter, yet attractive too?
For 't is my pleasure to behold them surging,
When to our booth the current sets apace,
And with tremendous, oft-repeated urging,
Squeeze onward through the narrow gate of grace:
By daylight even, they push and cram in
To reach the seller's box, a fighting host,
And as for bread, around a baker's door, in famine,
To get a ticket break their necks almost.
This miracle alone can work the Poet
On men so various: now, my friend, pray show it.

POET.

Speak not to me of yonder motley masses,
Whom but to see, puts out the fire of Song!

Hide from my view the surging crowd that passes,
And in its whirlpool forces us along!
No, lead me where some heavenly silence glasses
The purer joys that round the Poet throng,—
Where Love and Friendship still divinely fashion
The bonds that bless, the wreaths that crown his
      passion!

Ah, every utterance from the depths of feeling
The timid lips have stammeringly expressed,—
Now failing, now, perchance, success revealing,—
Gulps the wild Moment in its greedy breast;
Or oft, reluctant years its warrant sealing,
Its perfect stature stands at last confessed!
What dazzles, for the Moment spends its spirit:
What's genuine, shall Posterity inherit.

MERRY-ANDREW.

Posterity! Don't name the word to me!
If *I* should choose to preach Posterity,
Where would you get cotemporary fun?
That men *will* have it, there's no blinking:
A fine young fellow's presence, to my thinking,
Is something worth, to every one.
Who genially his nature can outpour,
Takes from the People's moods no irritation;
The wider circle he acquires, the more
Securely works his inspiration.
Then pluck up heart, and give us sterling coin
Let Fancy be with her attendants fitted,—
Sense, Reason, Sentiment, and Passion join,—
But have a care, lest Folly be omitted!

MANAGER.

Chiefly, enough of incident prepare!
They come to look, and they prefer to stare.
Reel off a host of threads before their faces,
So that they gape in stupid wonder: then
By sheer diffuseness you have won their graces,
And are, at once, most popular of men.

Only by mass you touch the mass; for any
Will finally, himself, his bit select:
Who offers much, brings something unto many,
And each goes home content with the effect.
If you've a piece, why, just in pieces give it:
A hash, a stew, will bring success, believe it!
'T is easily displayed, and easy to invent.
What use, a Whole compactly to present?
Your hearers pick and pluck, as soon as they receive
    it!

POET.

You do not feel, how such a trade debases;
How ill it suits the Artist, proud and true!
The botching work each fine pretender traces
Is, I perceive, a principle with you.

MANAGER.

Such a reproach not in the least offends;
A man who some result intends
Must use the tools that best are fitting.
Reflect, soft wood is given to you for splitting,
And then, observe for whom you write!
If one comes bored, exhausted quite,
Another, satiate, leaves the banquet's tapers,
And, worst of all, full many a wight
Is fresh from reading of the daily papers.
Idly to us they come, as to a masquerade,
Mere curiosity their spirits warming:
The ladies with themselves, and with their finery, aid,
Without a salary their parts performing.
What dreams are yours in high poetic places?
You're pleased, forsooth, full houses to behold?
Draw near, and view your patrons' faces!
The half are coarse, the half are cold.
One, when the play is out, goes home to cards;
A wild night on a wench's breast another chooses:
Why should you rack, poor, foolish bards,
For ends like these, the gracious Muses?
I tell you, give but more—more, ever more, they ask:
Thus shall you hit the mark of gain and glory.

Seek to confound your auditory!
To satisfy them is a task.—
What ails you now? Is 't suffering, or pleasure?

POET.

Go, find yourself a more obedient slave!
What! shall the Poet that which Nature gave,
The highest right, supreme Humanity,
Forfeit so wantonly, to swell your treasure?
Whence o'er the heart his empire free?
The elements of Life how conquers he?
Is 't not his heart's accord, urged outward far and dim,
To wind the world in unison with him?
When on the spindle, spun to endless distance,
By Nature's listless hand the thread is twirled,
And the discordant tones of all existence
In sullen jangle are together hurled.
Who, then, the changeless orders of creation
Divides, and kindles into rhythmic dance?
Who brings the One to join the general ordination,
Where it may throb in grandest consonance?
Who bids the storm to passion stir the bosom?
In brooding souls the sunset burn above?
Who scatters every fairest April blossom
Along the shining path of Love?
Who braids the noteless leaves to crowns, requiting
Desert with fame, in Action's every field?
Who makes Olympus sure, the Gods uniting?
The might of Man, as in the Bard revealed.

MERRY-ANDREW.

So, these fine forces, in conjunction,
Propel the high poetic function,
As in a love-adventure they might play!
You meet by accident; you feel, you stay,
And by degrees your heart is tangled;
Bliss grows apace, and then its course is jangled;
You're ravished quite, then comes a touch of woe,
And there's a neat romance, completed ere you know!
Let us, then, such a drama give!
Grasp the exhaustless life that all men live!

Each shares therein, though few may comprehend:
Where'er you touch, there's interest without end.
In motley pictures little light,
Much error, and of truth a glimmering mite,
Thus the best beverage is supplied,
Whence all the world is cheered and edified.
Then, at your play, behold the fairest flower
Of youth collect, to hear the revelation!
Each tender soul, with sentimental power,
Sucks melancholy food from your creation;
And now in this, now that, the leaven works,
For each beholds what in his bosom lurks.
They still are moved at once to weeping or to laughter,
Still wonder at your flights, enjoy the show they see:
A mind, once formed, is never suited after;
One yet in growth will ever grateful be.

POET.

Then give me back that time of pleasures,
While yet in joyous growth I sang,—
When, like a fount, the crowding measures
Uninterrupted gushed and sprang!
Then bright mist veiled the world before me,
In opening buds a marvel woke,
As I the thousand blossoms broke,
Which every valley richly bore me!
I nothing had, and yet enough for youth—
Joy in Illusion, ardent thirst for Truth.
Give, unrestrained, the old emotion,
The bliss that touched the verge of pain,
The strength of Hate, Love's deep devotion,—
O, give me back my youth again!

MERRY-ANDREW.

Youth, good my friend, you certainly require
When foes in combat sorely press you;
When lovely maids, in fond desire,
Hang on your bosom and caress you;
When from the hard-won goal the wreath
Beckons afar, the race awaiting;
When, after dancing out your breath,

You pass the night in dissipating:—
But that familiar harp with soul
To play,—with grace and bold expression,
And towards a self-erected goal
To walk with many a sweet digression,—
This, aged Sirs, belongs to you,
And we no less revere you for that reason:
Age childish makes, they say, but 't is not true;
We're only genuine children still, in Age's season!

MANAGER.

The words you've bandied are sufficient;
'T is deeds that I prefer to see:
In compliments you're both proficient,
But might, the while, more useful be.
What need to talk of Inspiration?
'T is no companion of Delay.
If Poetry be your vocation,
Let Poetry your will obey!
Full well you know what here is wanting;
The crowd for strongest drink is panting,
And such, forthwith, I'd have you brew.
What's left undone to-day, To-morrow will not do.
Waste not a day in vain digression:
With resolute, courageous trust
Seize every possible impression,
And make it firmly your possession;
You'll then work on, because you must.
Upon our German stage, you know it,
Each tries his hand at what he will;
So, take of traps and scenes your fill,
And all you find, be sure to show it!
Use both the great and lesser heavenly light,—
Squander the stars in any number,
Beasts, birds, trees, rocks, and all such lumber,
Fire, water, darkness, Day and Night!
Thus, in our booth's contracted sphere,
The circle of Creation will appear,
And move, as we deliberately impel,
From Heaven, across the World, to Hell!

PROLOGUE IN HEAVEN.

The Lord.   The Heavenly Hosts.   *Afterwards*

Mephistopheles.

(*The* Three Archangels *come forward.*)

RAPHAEL.

THE sun-orb sings, in emulation,
  'Mid brother-spheres, his ancient round:
His path predestined through Creation
He ends with step of thunder-sound.
The angels from his visage splendid
Draw power, whose measure none can say;
The lofty works, uncomprehended,
Are bright as on the earliest day.

GABRIEL.

And swift, and swift beyond conceiving,
The splendor of the world goes round,
Day's Edenbrightness still relieving
The awful Night's intense profound:
The ocean-tides in foam are breaking,
Against the rocks' deep bases hurled,
And both, the spheric race partaking,
Eternal, swift, are onward whirled!

MICHAEL.

And rival storms abroad are surging
From sea to land, from land to sea.
A chain of deepest action forging
Round all, in wrathful energy.
There flames a desolation, blazing
Before the Thunder's crashing way:

Yet, Lord, Thy messengers are praising
The gentle movement of Thy Day.

THE THREE.

Though still by them uncomprehended,
From these the angels draw their power,
And all Thy works, sublime and splendid,
Are bright as in Creation's hour.

MEPHISTOPHELES.

Since Thou, O Lord, deign'st to approach again
And ask us how we do, in manner kindest,
And heretofore to meet myself wert fain,
Among Thy menials, now, my face Thou findest.
Pardon, this troop I cannot follow after
With lofty speech, though by them scorned and
      spurned,
My pathos certainly would move Thy laughter,
If Thou hadst not all merriment unlearned.
Of suns and worlds I've nothing to be quoted;
How men torment themselves, is all I've noted.
The little god o' the world sticks to the same old way,
And is as whimsical as on Creation's day.
Life somewhat better might content him,
But for the gleam of heavenly light which Thou hast
      lent him:
He calls it Reason—thence his power's increased,
To be far beastlier than any beast.
Saving Thy Gracious Presence, he to me
A long-legged grasshopper appears to be,
That springing flies, and flying springs,
And in the grass the same old ditty sings.
Would he still lay among the grass he grows in!
Each bit of dung he seeks, to stick his nose in.

THE LORD.

Hast thou, then, nothing more to mention?
Com'st ever, thus, with ill intention?
Find'st nothing right on earth, eternally?

MEPHISTOPHELES.

No, Lord! I find things, there, still bad as they can be.
Man's misery even to pity moves my nature;
I've scarce the heart to plague the wretched creature.

THE LORD.

Know'st Faust?

MEPHISTOPHELES.
The Doctor Faust?

THE LORD.

My servant, he!

MEPHISTOPHELES.

Forsooth! He serves you after strange devices:
No earthly meat or drink the fool suffices:
His spirit's ferment far aspireth;
Half conscious of his frenzied, crazed unrest,
The fairest stars from Heaven he requireth,
From Earth the highest raptures and the best,
And all the Near and Far that he desireth
Fails to subdue the tumult of his breast.

THE LORD.

Though still confused his service unto Me,
I soon shall lead him to a clearer morning.
Sees not the gardener, even while buds his tree,
Both flower and fruit the future years adorning?

MEPHISTOPHELES.

What will you bet? There's still a chance to gain him,
If unto me full leave you give,
Gently upon *my* road to train him!

THE LORD.

As long as he on earth shall live,
So long I make no prohibition.
While Man's desires and aspirations stir,
He cannot choose but err.

MEPHISTOPHELES.

My thanks! I find the dead no acquisition,
And never cared to have them in my keeping.
I much prefer the cheeks where ruddy blood is leap-
    ing,
And when a corpse approaches, close my house:
It goes with me, as with the cat the mouse.

THE LORD.

Enough! What thou hast asked is granted.
Turn off this spirit from his fountain-head;
To trap him, let thy snares be planted,
And him, with thee, be downward led;
Then stand abashed, when thou art forced to say:
A good man, through obscurest aspiration,
Has still an instinct of the one true way.

MEPHISTOPHELES.

Agreed! But 't is a short probation.
About my bet I feel no trepidation.
If I fulfil my expectation,
You'll let me triumph with a swelling breast:
Dust shall he eat, and with a zest,
As did a certain snake, my near relation.

THE LORD.

Therein thou 'rt free, according to thy merits;
The like of thee have never moved My hate.
Of all the bold, denying Spirits,
The waggish knave least trouble doth create.
Man's active nature, flagging, seeks too soon the level;
Unqualified repose he learns to crave;
Whence, willingly, the comrade him I gave,
Who works, excites, and must create, as Devil.
But ye, God's sons in love and duty,
Enjoy the rich, the ever-living Beauty!
Creative Power, that works eternal schemes,
Clasp you in bonds of love, relaxing never,
And what in wavering apparition gleams
Fix in its place with thoughts that stand forever!

(*Heaven closes: the* ARCHANGELS *separate.*)

MEPHISTOPHELES (*solus*).

I like, at times, to hear The Ancient's word,
And have a care to be most civil:
It's really kind of such a noble Lord
So humanly to gossip with the Devil!

FIRST PART OF THE TRAGEDY.

I.

NIGHT.

(A lofty-arched, narrow, Gothic chamber. FAUST, in a chair at his desk, restless.)

FAUST.

I'VE studied now Philosophy
  And jurisprudence, Medicine,—
And even, alas! Theology,—
From end to end, with labor keen;
And here, poor fool! with all my lore
I stand, no wiser than before:
I 'm Magister—yea, Doctor—hight,
And straight or cross-wise, wrong or right,
These ten years long, with many woes,
I 've led my scholars by the nose,—
And see, that nothing can be known!
That knowledge cuts me to the bone.
I 'm cleverer, true, than those fops of teachers,
Doctors and Magisters, Scribes and Preachers;
Neither scruples nor doubts come now to smite me,
Nor Hell nor Devil can longer affright me.
For this, all pleasure am I foregoing;
I do not pretend to aught worth knowing,
I do not pretend I could be a teacher
To help or convert a fellow-creature.
Then, too, I 've neither lands nor gold,
Nor the world's least pomp or honor hold—
No dog would endure such a curst existence!
Wherefore, from Magic I seek assistance,
That many a secret perchance I reach

Through spirit-power and spirit-speech,
And thus the bitter task forego
Of saying the things I do not know,—
That I may detect the inmost force
Which binds the world, and guides its course;
Its germs, productive powers explore,
And rummage in empty words no more!

O full and splendid Moon, whom I
Have, from this desk, seen climb the sky
So many a midnight,—would thy glow
For the last time beheld my woe!
Ever thine eye, most mournful friend,
O'er books and papers saw me bend;
But would that I, on mountains grand,
Amid thy blessed light could stand,
With spirits through mountain-caverns hover,
Float in thy twilight the meadows over,
And, freed from the fumes of lore that swathe me,
To health in thy dewy fountains bathe me!

Ah, me! this dungeon still I see,
This drear, accursed masonry,
Where even the welcome daylight strains
But duskly through the painted panes.
Hemmed in by many a toppling heap
Of books worm-eaten, gray with dust,
Which to the vaulted ceiling creep,
Against the smoky papers thrust,—
With glasses, boxes, round me stacked,
And instruments together hurled,
Ancestral lumber, stuffed and packed—
Such is my world: and what a world!

And do I ask, wherefore my heart
Falters, oppressed with unknown needs?
Why some inexplicable smart
All movement of my life impedes?
Alas! in living Nature's stead,
Where God His human creature set,

In smoke and mould the fleshless dead
And bones of beasts surround me yet!

Fly! Up, and seek the broad, free **land!**
And this one Book of Mystery
From Nostradamus' very hand,
Is 't not sufficient company?
When I the starry courses know,
And Nature's wise instruction seek,
With light of power my soul shall **glow,**
As when to spirits spirits speak.
'T is vain, this empty brooding here,
Though guessed the holy symbols be:
Ye, Spirits, come—ye hover near—
Oh, if you hear me, answer me!

(*He opens the Book, and perceives the sign of the
Macrocosm.*)

Ha! what a sudden rapture leaps from this
I view, through all my senses swiftly **flowing!**
I feel a youthful, holy, vital bliss
In every vein and fibre newly glowing.
Was it a God, who traced this sign,
With calm across my tumult stealing,
My troubled heart to joy unsealing,
With impulse, mystic and divine,
The powers of Nature here, around **my path,** re-
vealing?
Am I a God?—so clear mine eyes!
In these pure features I behold
Creative Nature to my soul unfold.
What says the sage, now first I recognize:
"The spirit-world no closures fasten;
Thy sense is shut, thy heart is dead:
Disciple, up! untiring, hasten
To bathe thy breast in morning-red!"

(*He contemplates the sign.*)
How each the Whole its substance gives,

Each in the other works and lives!
Like heavenly forces rising and descending,
Their golden urns reciprocally lending,
With wings that winnow blessing
From Heaven through Earth I see them pressing,
Filling the All with harmony unceasing!
How grand a show! but, ah! a show alone.
Thee, boundless Nature, how make thee my own?
Where you, ye breasts? Founts of all Being, shining,
Whereon hang Heaven's and Earth's desire,
Whereto our withered hearts aspire,—
Ye flow, ye feed: and am I vainly pining?

(*He turns the leaves impatiently, and perceives the
sign of the Earth-Spirit.*)

How otherwise upon me works this sign!
Thou, Spirit of the Earth, art nearer:
Even now my powers are loftier, clearer;
I glow, as drunk with new-made wine:
New strength and heart to meet the world incite me,
The woe of earth, the bliss of earth, invite me,
And though the shock of storms may smite me,
No crash of shipwreck shall have power to fright me!
Clouds gather over me—
The moon conceals her light—
The lamp's extinguished!—
Mists rise,—red, angry rays are darting
Around my head!—There falls
A horror from the vaulted roof,
And seizes me!
I feel thy presence, Spirit I invoke!
Reveal thyself!
Ha! in my heart what rending stroke!
With new impulsion
My senses heave in this convulsion!
I feel thee draw my heart, absorb, exhaust me:
Thou must! thou must! and though my life it cost
me!

(*He seizes the book, and mysteriously pronounces the sign of the Spirit. A ruddy flame flashes: the Spirit appears in the flame.*)

SPIRIT.

Who calls me?

FAUST (*with averted head*).
Terrible to see!

SPIRIT.

Me hast thou long with might attracted,
Long from my sphere thy food exacted,
And now—

FAUST.
Woe! I endure not thee!

SPIRIT.

To view me is thine aspiration,
My voice to hear, my countenance to see;
Thy powerful yearning moveth me,
Here am I!—what mean perturbation
Thee, superhuman, shakes? Thy soul's high calling,
    where?
Where is the breast, which from itself a world did
    bear,
And shaped and cherished—which with joy expanded,
To be our peer, with us, the Spirits, banded?
Where art thou, Faust, whose voice has pierced to me,
Who towards me pressed with all thine energy?
He art thou, who, my presence breathing, seeing,
Trembles through all the depths of being,
A writhing worm, a terror-stricken form?

FAUST.
Thee, form of flame, shall I then fear?
Yes, I am Faust: I am thy peer!

SPIRIT.

In the tides of Life, in Action's storm,
A fluctuant wave,
A shuttle free,
Birth and the Grave,
An eternal sea,
A weaving, flowing
Life, all-glowing,
Thus at Time's humming loom 't is my hand prepares
The garment of Life which the Deity wears!

FAUST.

Thou, who around the wide world wendest,
Thou busy Spirit, how near I feel to thee!

SPIRIT.

Thou 'rt like the Spirit which thou comprehendest,
Not me!

(*Disappears.*)

FAUST (*overwhelmed*).

Not thee!
Whom then?
I, image of the Godhead!
Not even like thee!

(*A knock.*)

O Death!—I know it—'t is my Famulus!
My fairest luck finds no fruition:
In all the fulness of my vision
The soulless sneak disturbs me thus!

(*Enter* WAGNER, *in dressing-gown and night-cap, a
lamp in his hand.* FAUST *turns impatiently.*)

WAGNER.

Pardon, I heard your declamation;
'T was sure an old Greek tragedy you read?
In such an art I crave some preparation,

Since now it stands one in good stead.
I 've often heard it said, a preacher
Might learn, with a comedian for a teacher.

FAUST.

Yes, when the priest comedian is by nature,
As haply now and then the case may be.

WAGNER.

Ah, when one studies thus, a prisoned creature,
That scarce the world on holidays can see,—
Scarce through a glass, by rare occasion,
How shall one lead it by persuasion?

FAUST.

You 'll ne'er attain it, save you know the feeling,
Save from the soul it rises clear,
Serene in primal strength, compelling
The hearts and minds of all who hear.
You sit forever gluing, patching;
You cook the scraps from others' fare;
And from your heap of ashes hatching
A starveling flame, ye blow it bare!
Take children's, monkeys' gaze admiring,
If such your taste, and be content;
But ne'er from heart to heart you'll speak inspiring,
Save your own heart is eloquent!

WAGNER.

Yet through delivery orators succeed;
I feel that I am far behind, indeed.

FAUST.

Seek thou the honest recompense!
Beware, a tinkling fool to be!
With little art, clear wit and sense
Suggest their own delivery;
And if thou 'rt moved to speak in earnest,
What need, that after words thou yearnest?
Yes, your discourses, with their glittering show,
Where ye for men twist shredded thought like paper,

Are unrefreshing as the winds that blow
The rustling leaves through chill autumnal vapor!

WAGNER.

Ah, God! but Art is long,
And Life, alas! is fleeting.
And oft, with zeal my critic-duties meeting,
In head and breast there's something wrong.
How hard it is to compass the assistance
Whereby one rises to the source!
And, haply, ere one travels half the course
Must the poor devil quit existence.

FAUST.

Is parchment, then, the holy fount before thee,
A draught wherefrom thy thirst forever slakes?
No true refreshment can restore thee,
Save what from thine own soul spontaneous breaks.

WAGNER.

Pardon! a great delight is granted
When, in the spirit of the ages planted,
We mark how, ere our time, a sage has thought,
And then, how far his work, and grandly, we have
        brought.

FAUST.

O yes, up to the stars at last!
Listen, my friend: the ages that are past
Are now a book with seven seals protected:
What you the Spirit of the Ages call
Is nothing but the spirit of you all,
Wherein the Ages are reflected.
So, oftentimes, you miserably mar it!
At the first glance who sees it runs away.
An offal-barrel and a lumber-garret,
Or, at the best, a Punch-and-Judy play,
With maxims most pragmatical and hitting,
As in the mouths of puppets are befitting!

WAGNER.

But then, the world—the human heart and brain!
Of these one covets some slight apprehension.

FAUST.

Yes, of the kind which men attain!
Who dares the child's true name in public mention?
The few, who thereof something really learned,
Unwisely frank, with hearts that spurned concealing,
And to the mob laid bare each thought and feeling,
Have evermore been crucified and burned.
I pray you, Friend, 't is now the dead of night;
Our converse here must be suspended.

WAGNER.

I would have shared your watches with delight,
That so our learned talk might be extended.
To-morrow, though, I 'll ask, in Easter leisure,
This and the other question, at your pleasure.
Most zealously I seek for erudition:
Much do I know—but to know all is my ambition.

[*Exit.*

FAUST (*solus*).

That brain, alone, not loses hope, whose choice is
To stick in shallow trash forevermore,—
Which digs with eager hand for buried ore,
And, when it finds an angle-worm, rejoices!

Dare such a human voice disturb the flow,
Around me here, of spirit-presence fullest?
And yet, this once my thanks I owe
To thee, of all earth's sons the poorest, dullest!
For thou hast torn me from that desperate state
Which threatened soon to overwhelm my senses:
The apparition was so giant-great,
It dwarfed and withered all my soul's pretences!

I, image of the Godhead, who began—
Deeming Eternal Truth secure in nearness—
To sun myself in heavenly light and clearness,

And laid aside the earthly man;—
I, more than Cherub, whose free force had planned
To flow through Nature's veins in glad pulsation,
To reach beyond, enjoying in creation
The life of Gods, behold my expiation!
A thunder-word hath swept me from my stand.

With thee I dare not venture to compare me.
Though I possessed the power to draw thee near me,
The power to keep thee was denied my hand.
When that ecstatic moment held me,
I felt myself so small, so great;
But thou hast ruthessly repelled me
Back upon Man's uncertain fate.
What shall I shun? Whose guidance borrow?
Shall I accept that stress and strife?
Ah! every deed of ours, no less than every sorrow,
Impedes the onward march of life.
Some alien substance more and more is cleaving
To all the mind conceives of grand and fair;
When this world's Good is won by our achieving,
The Better, then, is named a cheat and snare.
The fine emotions, whence our lives we mould,
Lie in the earthly tumult dumb and cold.
If hopeful Fancy once, in daring flight,
Her longings to the Infinite expanded,
Yet now a narrow space contents her quite,
Since Time's wild wave so many a fortune stranded.
Care at the bottom of the heart is lurking:
Her secret pangs in silence working,
She, restless, rocks herself, disturbing joy and rest:
In newer masks her face is ever drest,
By turns as house and land, as wife and child, pre-
    sented,—
As water, fire, as poison, steel:
We dread the blows we never feel,
And what we never lose is yet by us lamented!
I am not like the Gods! That truth is felt too deep:
The worm am I, that in the dust doth creep,—
That, while in dust it lives and seeks its bread,
Is crushed and buried by the wanderer's tread.

Is not this dust, these walls within them hold,
The hundred shelves, which cramp and chain me,
The frippery, the trinkets thousand-fold,
That in this mothy den restrain me?
Here shall I find the help I need?
Shall here a thousand volumes teach me only
That men, self-tortured, everywhere must bleed,—
And here and there one happy man sits lonely?
What mean'st thou by that grin, thou hollow skull,
Save that thy brain, like mine, a cloudy mirror,
Sought once the shining day, and then, in twilight
    dull,
Thirsting for Truth, went wretchedly to Error?
Ye instruments, forsooth, but jeer at me
With wheel and cog, and shapes uncouth of wonder;
I found the portal, you the keys should be;
Your wards are deftly wrought, but drive no bolts
    asunder!
Mysterious even in open day,
Nature retains her veil, despite our clamors:
That which she doth not willingly display
Cannot be wrenched from her with levers, screws, and
    hammers.
Ye ancient tools, whose use I never knew,
Here, since my father used ye, still ye moulder:
Thou, ancient scroll, hast worn thy smoky hue
Since at this desk the dim lamp wont to smoulder.
'T were better far, had I my little idly spent,
Than now to sweat beneath its burden, I confess it!
What from your fathers' heritage is lent,
Earn it anew, to really possess it!
What serves not, is a sore impediment:
The Moment's need creates the thing to serve and bless
    it!
Yet, wherefore turns my gaze to yonder point so
    lightly?
Is yonder flask a magnet for mine eyes?
Whence, all around me, glows the air so brightly,
As when in woods at night the mellow moonbeam lies?

I hail thee, wondrous, rarest vial!

I take thee down devoutly, for the trial:
Man's art and wit I venerate in thee.
Thou summary of gentle slumber-juices,
Essence of deadly finest powers and uses,
Unto thy master show thy favor free!
I see thee, and the stings of pain diminish;
I grasp thee, and my struggles slowly finish:
My spirit's flood-tide ebbeth more and more.
Out on the open ocean speeds my dreaming;
The glassy flood before my feet is gleaming,
A new day beckons to a newer shore!

A fiery chariot, borne on buoyant pinions,
Sweeps near me now! I soon shall ready be
To pierce the ether's high, unknown dominions,
To reach new spheres of pure activity!
This godlike rapture, this supreme existence,
Do I, but now a worm, deserve to track?
Yes, resolute to reach some brighter distance,
On Earth's fair sun I turn my back!
Yes, let me dare those gates to fling asunder,
Which every man would fain go slinking by!
'T is time, through deeds this word of truth to thun-
der:
That with the height of Gods Man's dignity may vie!
Nor from that gloomy gulf to shrink affrighted,
Where Fancy doth herself to self-born pangs com-
pel,—
To struggle toward that pass benighted,
Around whose narrow mouth flame all the fires of
Hell,—
To take this step with cheerful resolution,
Though Nothingness should be the certain, swift con-
clusion!

And now come down, thou cup of crystal clearest!
Fresh from thine ancient cover thou appearest,
So many years forgotten to my thought!
Thou shon'st at old ancestral banquets cheery,
The solemn guests thou madest merry,
When one thy wassail to the other brought.

The rich and skilful figures o'er thee wrought,
The drinker's duty, rhyme-wise to explain them,
Or in one breath below the mark to drain them,
From many a night of youth my memory caught.
Now to a neighbor shall I pass thee never,
Nor on thy curious art to test my wit endeavor:
Here is a juice whence sleep is swiftly born.
It fills with browner flood thy crystal hollow;
I chose, prepared it: thus I follow,—
With all my soul the final drink I swallow,
A solemn festal cup, a greeting to the morn!

> [*He sets the goblet to his mouth*

(*Chime of bells and choral song.*)

CHORUS OF ANGELS.
Christ is arisen!
Joy to the Mortal One,
Whom the unmerited,
Clinging, inherited
Needs did imprison.

FAUST.
What hollow humming, what a sharp, clear stroke,
Drives from my lip the goblet's, at their meeting?
Announce the booming bells already woke
The first glad hour of Easter's festal greeting?
Ye choirs, have ye begun the sweet, consoling chant,
Which, through the night of Death, the angels minis-
    trant
Sang, God's new Covenant repeating?

CHORUS OF WOMEN.
With spices and precious
Balm, we arrayed him;
Faithful and gracious,
We tenderly laid him:
Linen to bind him
Cleanlily wound we:
Ah! when we would find him,
Christ no more found we!

CHORUS OF ANGELS.

Christ is ascended
Bliss hath invested him,
Woes that molested him,
Trials that tested him,
Gloriously ended!

FAUST.

Why, here in dust, entice me with your spell,
Ye gentle, powerful sounds of Heaven?
Peal rather there, where tender natures dwell.
Your messages I hear, but faith has not been given;
The dearest child of Faith is Miracle.
I venture not to soar to yonder regions
Whence the glad tidings hither float;
And yet, from childhood up familiar with the note,
To Life it now renews the old allegiance.
Once Heavenly Love sent down a burning kiss
Upon my brow, in Sabbath silence holy;
And, filled with mystic presage, chimed the church-
    bell slowly,
And prayer dissolved me in a fervent bliss.
A sweet, uncomprehended yearning
Drove forth my feet through woods and meadows free,
And while a thousand tears were burning,
I felt a world arise for me.
These chants, to youth and all its sports appealing,
Proclaimed the Spring's rejoicing holiday;
And Memory holds me now, with childish feeling,
Back from the last, the solemn way.
Sound on, ye hymns of Heaven, so sweet and mild!
My tears gush forth: the Earth takes back her child!

CHORUS OF DISCIPLES.

Has He, victoriously,
Burst from the vaulted
Grave, and all-gloriously
Now sits exalted?
Is He, in glow of birth,
Rapture creative near?
Ah! to the woe of earth

Still are we native here.
We, his aspiring
Followers, Him we miss;
Weeping, desiring,
Master, Thy bliss!

CHORUS OF ANGELS.
Christ is arisen,
Out of Corruption's womb:
Burst ye the prison,
Break from your gloom!
Praising and pleading him,
Lovingly needing him,
Brotherly feeding him,
Preaching and speeding him.
Blessing, succeeding Him,
Thus is the Master near,—
Thus is He here!

II.

BEFORE THE CITY-GATE.

(Pedestrians of all kinds come forth.)

SEVERAL APPRENTICES.
WHY do you go that way?

OTHERS.
We 're for the Hunter's-lodge, to-day.

THE FIRST.
We'll saunter to the Mill, in yonder hollow.

AN APPRENTICE.
Go to the River Tavern, I should say.

SECOND APPRENTICE.
But then, it 's not a pleasant way.

THE OTHERS.

And what will *you?*

A THIRD.

As goes the crowd, I follow.

A FOURTH.

Come up to Burgdorf? There you 'll find good cheer,
The finest lasses and the best of beer,
And jolly rows and squabbles, trust me!

A FIFTH.

You swaggering fellow, is your hide
A third time itching to be tried?
I won't go there, your jolly rows disgust me!

SERVANT-GIRL.

No,—no! I'll turn and go to town again.

ANOTHER.

We'll surely find him by those poplars yonder.

THE FIRST.

That's no great luck for me, 't is plain.
You'll have him, when and where you wander:
His partner in the dance you'll be,—
But what is all your fun to me?

THE OTHER.

He's surely not alone to-day:
He'll be with Curly-head, I heard him say.

A STUDENT.

Deuce! how they step, the buxom wenches!
Come, Brother! we must see them to the benches.
A strong, old beer, a pipe that stings and bites,
A girl in Sunday clothes,—these three are my delights.

CITIZEN'S DAUGHTER.

Just see those handsome fellows, there!
It's really shameful, I declare;—

To follow servant-girls, when they
Might have the most genteel society to-day!

SECOND STUDENT (*to the First*).

Not quite so fast! Two others come behind,—
Those, dressed so prettily and neatly.
My neighbor's one of them, I find,
A girl that takes my heart, completely.
They go their way with looks demure,
But they'll accept us, after all, I'm sure.

THE FIRST.

No, Brother! not for me their formal ways.
Quick! lest our game escape us in the press:
The hand that wields the broom on Saturdays
Will best, on Sundays, fondle and caress.

CITIZEN.

He suits me not at all, our new-made Burgomaster!
Since he's installed, his arrogance grows faster.
How has he helped the town, I say?
Things worsen,—what improvement names he?
Obedience, more than ever, claims he,
And more than ever we must pay!

BEGGAR (*sings*).

Good gentlemen and lovely ladies,
So red of cheek and fine of dress,
Behold, how needful here your aid is,
And see and lighten my distress!
Let me not vainly sing my ditty;
He's only glad who gives away:
A holiday, that shows your pity,
Shall be for me a harvest-day!

ANOTHER CITIZEN.

On Sundays, holidays, there's naught I take delight in,
Like gossiping of war, and war's array,
When down in Turkey, far away,
The foreign people are a-fighting.
One at the window sits, with glass and friends,

And sees all sorts of ships go down the river gliding:
And blesses then, as home he wends
At night, our times of peace abiding.

THIRD CITIZEN.

Yes, Neighbor! that's my notion, too:
Why, let them break their heads, let loose their pas-
    sions,
And mix things madly through and through,
So, here, we keep our good old fashions!

OLD WOMAN (*to the Citizen's Daughter*).

Dear me, how fine! So handsome, and so young!
Who wouldn't lose his heart, that met you?
Don't be so proud! I'll hold my tongue,
And what you'd like I'll undertake to get you.

CITIZEN'S DAUGHTER.

Come, Agatha! I shun the witch's sight
Before folks, lest there be misgiving:
'T is true, she showed me, on Saint Andrew's Night,
My future sweetheart, just as he were living.

THE OTHER.

She showed me mine, in crystal clear,
With several wild young blades, a soldier-lover:
I seek him everywhere, I pry and peer,
And yet, somehow, his face I can't discover.

SOLDIERS.

Castles, with lofty
Ramparts and towers,
Maidens disdainful
In Beauty's array,
Both shall be ours!
Bold is the venture,
Splendid the pay!
Lads, let the trumpets
For us be suing,—
Calling to pleasure,
Calling to ruin.

Stormy our life is;
Such is its boon!
Maidens and castles
Capitulate soon.
Bold is the venture,
Splendid the pay!
And the soldiers go marching
Marching away!

FAUST AND WAGNER.

FAUST.

Released from ice are brook and river
By the quickening glance of the gracious Spring;
The colors of hope to the valley cling,
And weak old Winter himself must shiver,
Withdrawn to the mountains, a crownless king:
Whence, ever retreating, he sends again
Impotent showers of sleet that darkle
In belts across the green o' the plain.
But the sun will permit no white to sparkle;
Everywhere form in development moveth;
He will brighten the world with the tints he loveth,
And, lacking blossoms, blue, yellow, and red,
He takes these gaudy people instead.
Turn thee about, and from this height
Back on the town direct thy sight.
Out of the hollow, gloomy gate,
The motley throngs come forth elate:
Each will the joy of the sunshine hoard,
To honor the Day of the Risen Lord!
They feel, themselves, their resurrection:
From the low, dark rooms, scarce habitable;
From the bonds of Work, from Trade's restriction;
From the pressing weight of roof and gable;
From the narrow, crushing streets and alleys;
From the churches' solemn and reverend night,
All come forth to the cheerful light.
How lively, see! the multitude sallies,
Scattering through gardens and fields remote,
While over the river, that broadly dallies,

Dances so many a festive boat;
And overladen, nigh to sinking,
The last full wherry takes the stream.
Yonder afar, from the hill-paths blinking,
Their clothes are colors that softly gleam.
I hear the noise of the village, even;
Here is the People's proper Heaven;
Here high and low contented see!
Here I am Man,—dare man to be!

WAGNER.

To stroll with you, Sir Doctor, flatters;
'T is honor, profit, unto me.
But I, alone, would shun these shallow matters,
Since all that's coarse provokes my enmity.
This fiddling, shouting, ten-pin rolling
I hate,—these noises of the throng:
They rave, as Satan were their sports controlling,
And call it mirth, and call it song!

PEASANTS, UNDER THE LINDEN-TREE.

(*Dance and Song.*)

All for the dance the shepherd dressed,
In ribbons, wreath, and gayest vest
    Himself with care arraying:
Around the linden lass and lad
Already footed it like mad:
      Hurrah! hurrah!
      Hurrah—tarara-la!
    The fiddle-bow was playing.

He broke the ranks, no whit afraid,
And with his elbow punched a maid,
    Who stood, the dance surveying:
The buxom wench, she turned and said:
"Now, you I call a stupid-head!"
      Hurrah! hurrah!
      Hurrah—tarara-la!
    "Be decent while you're staying!"

Then round the circle went their flight,

They danced to left, they danced to right:
 Their kirtles all were playing.
They first grew red, and then grew warm,
And rested, panting, arm in arm,—
  Hurrah! hurrah!
  Hurrah—tarara-la!
 And hips and elbows straying.

Now, don't be so familiar here!
How many a one has fooled his dear,
 Waylaying and betraying!
And yet, he coaxed her soon aside,
And round the linden sounded wide:
  Hurrah! hurrah!
  Hurrah—tarara-la!
 And the fiddle-bow was playing.

OLD PEASANT.

Sir Doctor, it is good of you,
That thus you condescend, to-day,
Among this crowd of merry folk,
A highly-learned man, to stray.
Then also take the finest can,
We fill with fresh wine, for your sake:
I offer it, and humbly wish
That not alone your thirst it slake,—
That, as the drops below its brink,
So many days of life you drink!

FAUST.

I take the cup you kindly reach,
With thanks and health to all and each.

(*The People gather in a circle about him.*)

OLD PEASANT.

In truth, 't is well and fitly timed,
That now our day of joy you share,
Who heretofore, in evil days,
Gave us so much of helping care.
Still many a man stands living here,

Saved by your father's skilful hand,
That snatched him from the fever's rage
And stayed the plague in all the land.
Then also you, though but a youth,
Went into every house of pain:
Many the corpses carried forth,
But you in health came out again.
No test or trial you evaded:
A Helping God the helper aided.

ALL.

Health to the man, so skilled and tried,
That for our help he long may bide!

FAUST.

To Him above bow down, my friends,
Who teaches help, and succor sends!

(*He goes on with* WAGNER.)

WAGNER.

With what a feeling, thou great man, must thou
Receive the people's honest veneration!
How lucky he, whose gifts his station
With such advantages endow!
Thou 'rt shown to all the younger generation:
Each asks, and presses near to gaze;
The fiddle stops, the dance delays.
Thou goest, they stand in rows to see,
And all the caps are lifted high;
A little more, and they would bend the knee
As if the Holy Host came by.

FAUST.

A few more steps ascend, as far as yonder stone!—
Here from our wandering will we rest contented.
Here, lost in thought, I've lingered oft alone,
When foolish fasts and prayers my life tormented.
Here, rich in hope and firm in faith,
With tears, wrung hands and sighs, I've striven,
The end of that far-spreading death
Entreating from the Lord of Heaven!
Now like contempt the crowd's applauses seem:

Couldst thou but read, within mine inmost spirit,
How little now I deem
That sire or son such praises merit!
My father's was a sombre, brooding brain,
Which through the holy spheres of Nature groped and
      wandered,
And honestly, in his own fashion, pondered
With labor whimsical, and pain:
Who, in his dusky work-shop bending,
With proved adepts in company,
Made, from his recipes unending,
Opposing substances agree.
There was a Lion red, a wooer daring,
Within the Lily's tepid bath espoused,
And both, tormented then by flame unsparing,
By turns in either bridal chamber housed.
If then appeared, with colors splendid,
The young Queen in her crystal shell,
This was the medicine—the patient's woes soon ended,
And none demanded: who got well?
Thus we, our hellish boluses compounding,
Among these vales and hills surrounding,
Worse than the pestilence, have passed.
Thousands were done to death from poison of my
      giving;
And I must hear, by all the living,
The shameless murderers praised at last!

WAGNER.

Why, therefore, yield to such depression?
A good man does his honest share
In exercising, with the strictest care,
The art bequeathed to his possession!
Dost thou thy father honor, as a youth?
Then may his teaching cheerfully impel thee:
Dost thou, as man, increase the stores of truth?
Then may thine own son afterwards excel thee.

FAUST.

O happy he, who still renews
The hope, from Error's deeps to rise forever!

That which one does not know, one needs to use;
And what one knows, one uses never.
But let us not, by such despondence, so
The fortune of this hour embitter!
Mark how, beneath the evening sunlight's glow,
The green-embosomed houses glitter!
The glow retreats, done is the day of toil,
It yonder hastes, new fields of life exploring;
Ah, that no wing can lift me from the soil,
Upon its track to follow, follow soaring!
Then would I see eternal Evening gild
The silent world beneath me glowing,
On fire each mountain-peak, with peace each valley
     filled,
The silver brook to golden rivers flowing.
The mountain-chain, with all its gorges deep,
Would then no more impede my godlike motion;
And now before mine eyes expands the ocean
With all its bays, in shining sleep!
Yet, finally, the weary god is sinking;
The new-born impulse fires my mind,—
I hasten on, his beams eternal drinking,
The Day before me and the Night behind,
Above me heaven unfurled, the floor of waves beneath
     me,—
A glorious dream! though now the glories fade.
Alas! the wings that lift the mind no aid
Of wings to lift the body can bequeath me.
Yet in each soul is born the pleasure
Of yearning onward, upward and away,
When o'er our heads, lost in the vaulted azure,
The lark sends down his flickering lay,—
When over crags and piny highlands
The poising eagle slowly soars,
And over plains and lakes and islands
The crane sails by to other shores.

WAGNER.

I've had, myself, at times, some odd caprices,
But never yet such impulse felt, as this is.
One soon fatigues, on woods and fields to look,

Nor would I beg the bird his wing to spare us:
How otherwise the mental raptures bear us
From page to page, from book to book!
Then winter nights take loveliness untold,
As warmer life in every limb had crowned you;
And when your hands unroll some parchment rare and
   old,
All Heaven descends, and opens bright around you!

FAUST.

One impulse art thou conscious of, at best;
O, never seek to know the other!
Two souls, alas! reside within my breast,
And each withdraws from, and repels, its brother.
One with tenacious organs holds in love
And clinging lust the world in its embraces;
The other strongly sweeps, this dust above,
Into the high ancestral spaces.
If there be airy spirits near,
'Twixt Heaven and Earth on potent errands fleeing,
Let them drop down the golden atmosphere,
And bear me forth to new and varied being!
Yea, if a magic mantle once were mine,
To waft me o'er the world at pleasure,
I would not for the costliest stores of treasure—
Not for a monarch's robe—the gift resign.

WAGNER.

Invoke not thus the well-known throng,
Which through the firmament diffused is faring,
And danger thousand-fold, our race to wrong,
In every quarter is preparing.
Swift from the North the spirit-fangs so sharp
Sweep down, and with their barbéd points assail you;
Then from the East they come, to dry and warp
Your lungs, till breath and being fail you:
If from the Desert sendeth them the South,
With fire on fire your throbbing forehead crowning,
The West leads on a host, to cure the drouth
Only when meadow, field, and you are drowning.
They gladly hearken, prompt for injury,—

Gladly obey, because they gladly cheat us;
From Heaven they represent themselves to be,
And lisp like angels, when with lie they meet us
But, let us go! 'T is gray and dusky all:
The air is cold, the vapors fall.
At night, one learns his house to prize:—
Why stand you thus, with such astonished eyes?
What, in the twilight, can your mind so trouble?

FAUST.

Seest thou the black dog coursing there, through corn
     and stubble?

WAGNER.

Long since: yet deemed him not important in the least.

FAUST.

Inspect him close: for what tak'st thou the beast?

WAGNER.

Why, for a poodle who has lost his master,
And scents about, his track to find.

FAUST.

Seest thou the spiral circles, narrowing faster,
Which he, approaching, round us seems to wind?
A streaming trail of fire, if I see rightly,
Follows his path of mystery.

WAGNER.

It may be that your eyes deceive you slightly;
Naught but a plain black poodle do I see.

FAUST.

It seems to me that with enchanted cunning
He snares our feet, some future chain to bind.

WAGNER.

I see him timidly, in doubt, around us running,
Since, in his master's stead, two strangers doth he find.

FAUST.

The circle narrows : he is near!

WAGNER.

A dog thou seest, and not a phantom, here!
Behold him stop—upon his belly crawl—
His tail set wagging : canine habits, all!

FAUST.

Come, follow us!   Come here, at least!

WAGNER.

'T is the absurdest, drollest beast.
Stand still, and you will see him wait;
Address him, and he gambols straight;
If something's lost, he'll quickly bring it,—
Your cane, if in the stream you fling it.

FAUST.

No doubt you're right : no trace of mind, I own,
Is in the beast : I see but drill, alone.

WAGNER.

The dog, when he's well educated,
Is by the wisest tolerated.
Yes, he deserves your favor thoroughly,—
The clever scholar of the students, he!
        (*They pass in the city-gate.*)

III.

THE STUDY.

FAUST.

(*Entering, with the poodle.*)
BEHIND me, field and meadow sleeping,
    I leave in deep, prophetic night,
Within whose dread and holy keeping
The better soul awakes to light.

The wild desires no longer win us,
The deeds of passion cease to chain;
The love of Man revives within us,
The love of God revives again.

Be still, thou poodle! make not such racket and riot!
Why at the threshold wilt snuffing be?
Behind the stove repose thee in quiet!
My softest cushion I give to thee.
As thou, up yonder, with running and leaping
Amused us hast, on the mountain's crest,
So now I take thee into my keeping,
A welcome, but also a silent, guest.

Ah, when, within our narrow chamber
The lamp with friendly lustre glows,
Flames in the breast each faded ember,
And in the heart, itself that knows.
Then Hope again lends sweet assistance,
And Reason then resumes her speech:
One yearns, the rivers of existence,
The very founts of Life, to reach.

Snarl not, poodle! To the sound that rises,
The sacred tones that my soul embrace,
This bestial noise is out of place.
We are used to see, that Man despises
What he never comprehends,
And the Good and the Beautiful vilipends,
Finding them often hard to measure:
Will the dog, like man, snarl *his* displeasure?

But ah! I feel, though will thereto be stronger,
Contentment flows from out my breast no longer.
Why must the stream so soon run dry and fail us,
And burning thirst again assail us?
Therein I've borne so much probation!
And yet, this want may be supplied us;
We call the Supernatural to guide us;
We pine and thirst for Revelation,
Which nowhere worthier is, more nobly sent,

Than here, in our New Testament.
I feel impelled, its meaning to determine,—
With honest purpose, once for all,
The hallowed Original
To change to my beloved German.

(*He opens a volume, and commences.*)

'T is written: "In the Beginning was the *Word*."
Here am I balked: who, now, can help afford?
The *Word?*—impossible so high to rate it;
And otherwise must I translate it,
If by the Spirit I am truly taught.
Then thus: "In the Beginning was the *Thought*."
This first line let me weigh completely,
Lest my impatient pen proceed too fleetly.
Is it the *Thought* which works, creates, indeed?
"In the Beginning was the *Power*," I read.
Yet, as I write, a warning is suggested,
That I the sense may not have fairly tested.
The Spirit aids me: now I see the light!
"In the Beginning was the *Act*," I write.

If I must share my chamber with thee,
Poodle, stop that howling, prithee!
Cease to bark and bellow!
Such a noisy, disturbing fellow
I'll no longer suffer near me.
One of us, dost hear me!
Must leave, I fear me.
No longer guest-right I bestow;
The door is open, art free to go.
But what do I see in the creature?
Is that in the course of nature?
Is't actual fact? or Fancy's shows?
How long and broad my poodle grows!
He rises mightily:
A canine form that cannot be!
What a spectre I've harbored thus!
He resembles a hippopotamus.
With fiery eyes, teeth terrible to see:

O, now am I sure of thee!
For all of thy half-hellish brood
The Key of Solomon is good.

SPIRITS (*in the corridor*).
Some one, within, is caught!
Stay without, follow him not!
Like the fox in a snare,
Quakes the old hell-lynx there.
Take heed—look about!
Back and forth hover,
Under and over,
And he'll work himself out.
If your aid can avail him,
Let it not fail him;
For he, without measure,
Has wrought for our pleasure.

FAUST.
First, to encounter the beast,
The Words of the Four be addressed:
Salamander, shine glorious!
Wave, Undine, as bidden!
Sylph, be thou hidden!
Gnome, be laborious!

Who knows not their sense
(These elements),—
Their properties
And power not sees,—
No mastery he inherits
Over the Spirits.

Vanish in flaming ether,
Salamander!
Flow foamingly together,
Undine!
Shine in meteor-sheen,
Sylph!
Bring help to hearth and shelf,
Incubus! Incubus!
Step forward, and finish this!

Of the Four, no feature
Lurks in the creature.
Quiet he lies, and grins disdain:
Not yet, it seems, have I given him pain.
Now, to undisguise thee,
Hear me exorcise thee!
Art thou, my gay one,
Hell's fugitive stray-one?
The sign witness now,
Before which they bow,
The cohorts of Hell!

With hair all bristling, it begins to swell.

Base Being, hearest thou?
Knowest and fearest thou
The One, unoriginate,
Named inexpressibly,
Through all Heaven impermeate,
Pierced irredressibly!

Behind the stove still banned,
See it, an elephant, expand!
It fills the space entire,
Mist-like melting, ever faster.
'T is enough: ascend no higher,—
Lay thyself at the feet of the Master!
Thou seest, not vain the threats I bring thee:
With holy fire I'll scorch and sting thee!
Wait not to know
The threefold dazzling glow!
Wait not to know
The strongest art within my hands!

MEPHISTOPHELES
(*while the vapor is dissipating, steps forth from behind the stove in the costume of a Travelling Scholar*).

Why such a noise? What are my lord's commands?

FAUST.

This was the poodle's real core,
A traveling scholar, then? The *casus* is diverting.

MEPHISTOPHELES.

The learned gentleman I bow before:
You've made me roundly sweat, that's certain!

FAUST.

What is thy name?

MEPHISTOPHELES.

      A question small, it seems,
For one whose mind the Word so much despises;
Who, scorning all external gleams,
The depths of being only prizes.

FAUST.

With all you gentlemen, the name's a test,
Whereby the nature usually is expressed.
Clearly the latter implies
In names like Beelzebub, Destroyer, Father of Lies.
What art thou, then?

MEPHISTOPHELES.

      Part of that Power, not understood,
Which always wills the Bad, and always works the
    Good.

FAUST.

What hidden sense in this enigma lies?

MEPHISTOPHELES.

I am the Spirit that Denies!
And justly so: for all things, from the Void
Called forth, deserve to be destroyed:
'T were better, then, were naught created.
Thus, all which you as Sin have rated,—
Destruction,—aught with Evil blent,—
That is my proper element.

FAUST.

Thou nam'st thyself a part, yet show'st complete to
    me?

MEPHISTOPHELES.

The modest truth I speak to thee.
If Man, that microcosmic fool, can see
Himself a whole so frequently,
Part of the Part am I, once All, in primal Night,—
Part of the Darkness which brought forth the Light,
The haughty Light, which now disputes the space,
And claims of Mother Night her ancient place.
And yet, the struggle fails; since Light, howe'er it
    weaves,
Still, fettered, unto bodies cleaves:
It flows from bodies, bodies beautifies;
By bodies is its course impeded;
And so, but little time is needed,
I hope, ere, as the bodies die, it dies!

FAUST.

I see the plan thou art pursuing:
Thou canst not compass general ruin,
And hast on smaller scale begun.

MEPHISTOPHELES.

And truly 'tis not much, when all is done.
That which to Naught is in resistance set,—
The Something of this clumsy world,—has yet,
With all that I have undertaken,
Not been by me disturbed or shaken:
From earthquake, tempest, wave, volcano's brand,
Back into quiet settle sea and land!
And that damned stuff, the bestial, human brood,—
What use, in having that to play with?
How many have I made away with!
And ever circulates a newer, fresher blood.
It makes me furious, such things beholding:
From Water, Earth, and Air unfolding,
A thousand germs break forth and grow,
In dry, and wet, and warm, and chilly;

And had I not the Flame reserved, why, really,
There's nothing special of my own to show!

FAUST.

So, to the actively eternal
Creative force, in cold disdain
You now oppose the fist infernal,
Whose wicked clench is all in vain!
Some other labor seek thou rather,
Queer Son of Chaos, to begin!

MEPHISTOPHELES.

Well, we'll consider: thou canst gather
My views, when next I venture in.
Might I, perhaps, depart at present?

FAUST.

Why thou shouldst ask, I don't perceive.
Though our acquaintance is so recent,
For further visits thou hast leave.
The window's here, the door is yonder;
A chimney, also, you behold.

MEPHISTOPHELES.

I must confess that forth I may not wander,
My steps by one slight obstacle controlled,—
The wizard's-foot, that on your threshold made is.

FAUST.

The pentagram prohibits thee?
Why, tell me now, thou Son of Hades,
If that prevents, how cam'st thou in to me?
Could such a spirit be so cheated?

MEPHISTOPHELES.

Inspect the thing: the drawing's not completed.
The outer angle, you may see,
Is open left—the lines don't fit it.

FAUST.

Well,—Chance, this time, has fairly hit it!

And thus, thou'rt prisoner to me?
It seems the business has succeeded.

MEPHISTOPHELES.

The poodle naught remarked, as after thee he speeded;
But other aspects now obtain:
The Devil can't get out again.

FAUST.

Try, then, the open window-pane!

MEPHISTOPHELES.

For Devils and for spectres this is law:
Where they have entered in, there also they withdraw.
The first is free to us; we're governed by the second.

FAUST.

In Hell itself, then, laws are reckoned?
That's well! So might a compact be
Made with you gentlemen—and binding,—surely?

MEPHISTOPHELES.

All that is promised shall delight thee purely;
No skinflint bargain shalt thou see.
But this is not of swift conclusion;
We'll talk about the matter soon.
And now, I do entreat this boon—
Leave to withdraw from my intrusion.

FAUST.

One moment more I ask thee to remain,
Some pleasant news, at least, to tell me.

MEPHISTOPHELES.

Release me, now! I soon shall come again;
Then thou, at will, mayst question and compel me.

FAUST.

I have not snares around thee cast;
Thyself hast led thyself into the meshes.
Who traps the Devil, hold him fast!
Not soon a second time he'll catch a prey so precious.

MEPHISTOPHELES.

An't please thee, also I'm content to stay,
And serve thee in a social station;
But stipulating, that I may
With arts of mine afford thee recreation.

FAUST.

Thereto I willingly agree,
If the diversion pleasant be.

MEPHISTOPHELES.

My friend, thou 'lt win, past all pretences,
More in this hour to soothe thy senses,
Than in the year's monotony.
That which the dainty spirits sing thee,
The lovely pictures they shall bring thee,
Are more than magic's empty show.
Thy scent will be to bliss invited;
Thy palate then with taste delighted,
Thy nerves of touch ecstatic glow!
All unprepared, the charm I spin:
We're here together, so begin!

SPIRITS.

Vanish, ye darkling
Arches above him!
Loveliest weather,
Born of blue ether,
Break from the sky!
O that the darkling
Clouds had departed!
Starlight is sparkling,
Tranquiller-hearted
Suns are on high.
Heaven's own children
In beauty bewildering,
Waveringly bending,
Pass as they hover;
Longing unending
Follows them over.
They, with their glowing
Garments, out-flowing,
Cover, in going,

Landscape and bower,
Where, in seclusion,
Lovers are plighted,
Lost in illusion.
Bower on bower!
Tendrils unblighted!
Lo! in a shower
Grapes that o'ercluster
Gush into must, or
Flow into rivers
Of foaming and flashing
Wine, that is dashing
Gems, as it boundeth
Down the high places,
And spreading, surroundeth
With crystalline spaces,
In happy embraces,
Blossoming forelands,
Emerald shore-lands!
And the winged races
Drink, and fly onward—
Fly ever sunward
To the enticing
Islands, that flatter,
Dipping and rising
Light on the water!
Hark, the inspiring
Sound of their quiring!
See, the entrancing
Whirl of their dancing!
All in the air are
Freer and fairer.
Some of them scaling
Boldly the highlands,
Others are sailing,
Circling the islands;
Others are flying;
Life-ward all hieing,—
All for the distant
Star of existent
Rapture and Love!

MEPHISTOPHELES.

He sleeps! Enough, ye fays! your airy number
Have sung him truly into slumber:
For this performance I your debtor prove.—
Not yet art thou the man, to catch the Fiend and hold
    him!—
With fairest images of dreams infold him,
Plunge him in seas of sweet untruth!
Yet, for the threshold's magic which controlled him,
The Devil needs a rat's quick tooth.
I use no lengthened invocation:
Here rustles one that soon will work my liberation.

The lord of rats and eke of mice,
Of flies and bed-bugs, frogs and lice,
Summons thee hither to the door-sill,
To gnaw it where, with just a morsel
Of oil, he paints the spot for thee:—
There com'st thou, hopping on to me!
To work, at once! The point which made me craven
Is forward, on the ledge, engraven.
Another bite makes free the door:
So, dream thy dreams, O Faust, until we meet once
    more!

FAUST (*awaking*).

Am I again so foully cheated?
Remains there naught of lofty spirit-sway,
But that a dream the Devil counterfeited,
And that a poodle ran away?

IV.

THE STUDY.

FAUST. MEPHISTOPHELES.

FAUST.

A KNOCK? Come in! Again my quiet broken?

MEPHISTOPHELES.

'T is I!

FAUST.

Come in!

MEPHISTOPHELES.
Thrice must the words be spoken.

FAUST.
Come in, then!

MEPHISTOPHELES.
Thus thou pleasest me.
I hope we'll suit each other well;
For now, thy vapors to dispel,
I come, a squire of high degree,
In scarlet coat, with golden trimming,
A cloak in silken lustre swimming,
A tall cock's-feather in my hat,
A long, sharp sword for show or quarrel,—
And I advise thee, brief and flat,
To don the self-same gay apparel,
That, from this den released, and free,
Life be at last revealed to thee!

FAUST.
This life of earth, whatever my attire,
Would pain me in its wonted fashion.
Too old am I to play with passion;
Too young, to be without desire.
What from the world have I to gain?
Thou shalt abstain—renounce—refrain!
Such is the everlasting song
That in the ears of all men rings,—
That unrelieved, our whole life long,
Each hour, in passing, hoarsely sings.
In very terror I at morn awake,
Upon the verge of bitter weeping,
To see the day of disappointment break,
To no one hope of mine—not one—its promise keep-
　　ing:—
That even each joy's presentiment
With wilful cavil would diminish,
With grinning masks of life prevent

My mind its fairest work to finish!
Then, too, when night descends, how anxiously
Upon my couch of sleep I lay me:
There, also, comes no rest to me,
But some wild dream is sent to fray me.
The God that in my breast is owned
Can deeply stir the inner sources;
The God, above my powers enthroned,
He cannot change external forces.
So, by the burden of my days oppressed,
Death is desired, and Life a thing unblest!

MEPHISTOPHELES.

And yet is never Death a wholly welcome guest.

FAUST.

O fortunate, for whom, when victory glances,
The bloody laurels on the brow he bindeth!
Whom, after rapid, maddening dances,
In clasping maiden-arms he findeth!
O would that I, before that spirit-power,
Ravished and rapt from life, had sunken!

MEPHISTOPHELES.

And yet, by some one, in that nightly hour,
A certain liquid was not drunken.

FAUST.

Eavesdropping, ha! thy pleasure seems to be.

MEPHISTOPHELES.

Omniscient am I not; yet much is known to me.

FAUST.

Though some familiar tone, retrieving
My thoughts from torment, led me on,
And sweet, clear echoes came, deceiving
A faith bequeathed from Childhood's dawn,
Yet now I curse whate'er entices
And snares the soul with visions vain;

With dazzling cheats and dear devices
Confines it in this cave of pain!
Cursed be, at once, the high ambition
Wherewith the mind itself deludes!
Cursed be the glare of apparition
That on the finer sense intrudes!
Cursed be the lying dream's impression
Of name, and fame, and laurelled brow!
Cursed, all that flatters as possession,
As wife and child, as knave and plow!
Cursed Mammon be, when he with treasures
To restless action spurs our fate!
Cursed when, for soft, indulgent leisures,
He lays for us the pillows straight!
Cursed be the vine's transcendent nectar,—
The highest favor Love lets fall!
Cursed, also, Hope!—cursed Faith, the spectre!
And cursed be Patience most of all!

CHORUS OF SPIRITS (*invisible*).

Woe! woe!
Thou hast it destroyed,
The beautiful world,
With powerful fist:
In ruin 't is hurled,
By the blow of a demigod shattered!
The scattered
Fragments into the Void we carry,
Deploring
The beauty perished beyond restoring.
Mightier
For the children of men,
Brightlier
Build it again,
In thine own bosom build it anew!
Bid the new career
Commence,
With clearer sense,
And the new songs of cheer
Be sung thereto!

MEPHISTOPHELES.

These are the small dependants
Who give me attendance.
Hear them, to deeds and passion
Counsel in shrewd old-fashion!
Into the world of strife,
Out of this lonely life
That of senses and sap has betrayed thee,
They would persuade thee.
This nursing of the pain forego thee,
That, like a vulture, feeds upon thy breast!
The worst society thou find'st will show thee
Thou art a man among the rest.
But 't is not meant to thrust
Thee into the mob thou hatest!
I am not one of the greatest,
Yet, wilt thou to me entrust
Thy steps through life, I'll guide thee,—
Will willingly walk beside thee,—
Will serve thee at once and forever
With best endeavor,
And, if thou art satisfied,
Will as servant, slave, with thee abide.

FAUST.

And what shall be my counter-service therefor?

MEPHISTOPHELES.

The time is long: thou need'st not now insist.

FAUST.

No—no! The Devil is an egotist,
And is not apt, without a why or wherefore,
"For God's sake," others to assist.
Speak thy conditions plain and clear!
With such a servant danger comes, I fear.

MEPHISTOPHELES.

Here, an unwearied slave, I'll wear thy tether,
And to thine every nod obedient be:
When *There* again we come together,
Then shalt thou do the same for me.

FAUST.

The *There* my scruples naught increases.
When thou hast dashed this world to pieces,
The other, then, its place may fill.
Here, on this earth, my pleasures have their sources;
Yon sun beholds my sorrows in his courses;
And when from these my life itself divorces,
Let happen all that can or will!
I'll hear no more: 't is vain to ponder
If there we cherish love or hate,
Or, in the spheres we dream of yonder,
A High and Low our souls await.

MEPHISTOPHELES.

In this sense, even, canst thou venture.
Come, bind thyself by prompt indenture,
And thou mine arts with joy shalt see:
What no man ever saw, I'll give to thee.

FAUST.

Canst thou, poor Devil, give me whatsoever?
When was a human soul, in its supreme endeavor,
E'er understood by such as thou?
Yet, hast thou food which never satiates, now,—
The restless, ruddy gold hast thou,
That runs, quicksilver-like, one's fingers through,—
A game whose winnings no man ever knew,—
A maid, that, even from my breast,
Beckons my neighbor with her wanton glances,
And Honor's godlike zest,
The meteor that a moment dances,—
Show me the fruits that, ere they're gathered, rot,
And trees that daily with new leafage clothe them!

MEPHISTOPHELES.

Such a demand alarms me not:
Such treasures have I, and can show them.
But still the time may reach us, good my friend,
When peace we crave and more luxurious diet.

FAUST.

When on an idler's bed I stretch myself in quiet,

There let, at once, my record end!
Canst thou with lying flattery rule me,
Until, self-pleased, myself I see,—
Canst thou with rich enjoyment fool me,
Let that day be the last for me!
The bet I offer.

MEPHISTOPHELES.
Done!

FAUST.
And heartily!
When thus I hail the Moment flying:
"Ah, still delay—thou art so fair!"
Then bind me in thy bonds undying,
My final ruin then declare!
Then let the death-bell chime the token,
Then art thou from thy service free!
The clock may stop, the hand be broken,
Then Time be finished unto me!

MEPHISTOPHELES.
Consider well: my memory good is rated.

FAUST.
Thou hast a perfect right thereto.
My powers I have not rashly estimated:
A slave am I, whate'er I do—
If thine, or whose? 't is needless to debate it.

MEPHISTOPHELES.
Then at the Doctors'-banquet I, to-day,
Will as a servant wait behind thee.
But one thing more! Beyond all risk to bind thee,
Give me a line or two, I pray.

FAUST.
Demand'st thou, Pedant, too, a document?
Hast never known a man, nor proved his word's in-
        tent?
Is 't not enough, that what I speak to-day

Shall stand, with all my future days agreeing?
In all its tides sweeps not the world away,
And shall a promise bind my being?
Yet this delusion in our hearts we bear:
Who would himself therefrom deliver?
Blest he, whose bosom Truth makes pure and fair!
No sacrifice shall he repent of ever.
Nathless a parchment, writ and stamped with care,
A spectre is, which all to shun endeavor.
The word, alas! dies even in the pen,
And wax and leather keep the lordship then.
What wilt from me, Base Spirit, say?—
Brass, marble, parchment, paper, clay?
The terms with graver, quill, or chisel, stated?
I freely leave the choice to thee.

MEPHISTOPHELES.

Why heat thyself, thus instantly,
With eloquence exaggerated?
Each leaf for such a pact is good;
And to subscribe thy name thou 'lt take a drop of
      blood.

FAUST.

If thou therewith art fully satisfied,
So let us by the farce abide.

MEPHISTOPHELES.

Blood is a juice of rarest quality.

FAUST.

Fear not that I this pact shall seek to sever!
The promise that I make to thee
Is just the sum of my endeavor.
I have myself inflated all too high;
My proper place is thy estate:
The Mighty Spirit deigns me no reply,
And Nature shuts on me her gate.
The thread of Thought at last is broken,
And knowledge brings disgust unspoken.
Let us the sensual deeps explore,

To quench the fervors of glowing passion!
Let every marvel take form and fashion
Through the impervious veil it wore!
Plunge we in Time's tumultuous dance,
In the rush and roll of Circumstance!
Then may delight and distress,
And worry and success,
Alternately follow, as best they can:
Restless activity proves the man!

MEPHISTOPHELES.

For you no bound, no term is set.
Whether you everywhere be trying,
Or snatch a rapid bliss in flying,
May it agree with you, what you get!
Only fall to, and show no timid balking.

FAUST.

But thou hast heard, 't is not of joy we're talking.
I take the wildering whirl, enjoyment's keenest pain,
Enamored hate, exhilarant disdain.
My bosom, of its thirst for knowledge sated,
Shall not, henceforth, from any pang be wrested,
And all of life for all mankind created
Shall be within mine inmost being tested:
The highest, lowest forms my soul shall borrow,
Shall heap upon itself their bliss and sorrow,
And thus, my own sole self to all their selves expanded
I too, at last, shall with them all be stranded!

MEPHISTOPHELES.

Believe me, who for many a thousand year
The same tough meat have chewed and tested,
That from the cradle to the bier
No man the ancient leaven has digested!
Trust one of us, this Whole supernal
Is made but for a God's delight!
He dwells in splendor single and eternal,
But *us* he thrusts in darkness, out of sight,
And *you* he dowers with Day and Night.

FAUST.

Nay, but I will!

MEPHISTOPHELES.

A good reply!
One only fear still needs repeating:
The art is long, the time is fleeting.
Then let thyself be taught, say I!
Go, league thyself with a poet,
Give the rein to his imagination,
Then wear the crown, and show it,
Of the qualities of his creation,—
The courage of the lion's breed.
The wild stag's speed,
The Italian's fiery blood,
The North's firm fortitude!
Let him find for thee the secret tether
That binds the Noble and Mean together,
And teach thy pulses of youth and pleasure
To love by rule, and hate by measure!
I'd like, myself, such a one to see:
Sir Microcosm his name should be.

FAUST.

What am I, then, if 't is denied my part
The crown of all humanity to win me,
Whereto yearns every sense within me?

MEPHISTOPHELES.

Why, on the whole, thou 'rt—what thou art.
Set wigs of million curls upon thy head, to raise thee,
Wear shoes an ell in height,—the truth betrays thee,
And thou remainest—what thou art.

FAUST.

I feel, indeed, that I have made the treasure
Of human thought and knowledge mine, in vain;
And if I now sit down in restful leisure,
No fount of newer strength is in my brain:
I am no hair's-breadth more in height,
Nor nearer to the Infinite.

MEPHISTOPHELES.

Good Sir, you see the facts precisely
As they are seen by each and all.
We must arrange them now, more wisely,
Before the joys of life shall pall.
Why, Zounds! Both hands and feet are, truly—
And head and virile forces—thine:
Yet all that I indulge in newly,
Is 't thence less wholly mine?
If I've six stallions in my stall,
Are not their forces also lent me?
I speed along, completest man of all,
As though my legs were four-and-twenty.
Take hold, then! let reflection rest,
And plunge into the world with zest!
I say to thee, a speculative wight
Is like a beast on moorlands lean,
That round and round some fiend misleads to evil
      plight,
While all about lie pastures fresh and green.

FAUST.

Then how shall we begin?

MEPHISTOPHELES.

                    We'll try a wider sphere.
What place of martyrdom is here!
Is 't life, I ask, is 't even prudence,
To bore thyself and bore the students?
Let Neighbor Paunch to that attend!
Why plague thyself with threshing straw forever?
The best thou learnest, in the end
Thou dar'st not tell the youngsters—never!
I hear one's footsteps, hither steering.

FAUST.

To see him now I have no heart.

MEPHISTOPHELES.

So long the poor boy waits a hearing,
He must not unconsoled depart.

Thy cap and mantle straightway lend me!
I'll play the comedy with art.

(*He disguises himself.*)

My wits, be certain, will befriend me.
But fifteen minutes' time is all I need;
For our fine trip, meanwhile, prepare thyself with
     speed!

[*Exit* FAUST

MEPHISTOPHELES.

(*In* FAUST'S *long mantle.*)

Reason and Knowledge only thou despise,
The highest strength in man that lies!
Let but the Lying Spirit bind thee
With magic works and shows that blind thee,
And I shall have thee fast and sure!
Fate such a bold, untrammelled spirit gave him,
As forwards, onwards, ever must endure;
Whose over-hasty impulse drave him
Past earthly joys he might secure.
Dragged through the wildest life, will I enslave him,
Through flat and stale indifference;
With struggling, chilling, checking, so deprave him
That, to his hot, insatiate sense,
The dream of drink shall mock, but never lave him:
Refreshment shall his lips in vain implore—
Had he not made himself the Devil's, naught could
     save him,
Still were he lost forevermore!

(*A* STUDENT *enters.*)

STUDENT.

A short time, only, am I here,
And come, devoted and sincere,
To greet and know the man of fame,
Whom men to me with reverence name.

MEPHISTOPHELES.

Your courtesy doth flatter me:
You see a man, as others be.
Have you, perchance, elsewhere begun?

STUDENT.

Receive me now, I pray, as one
Who comes to you with courage good,
Somewhat of çash, and healthy blood:
My mother was hardly willing to let me;
But knowledge worth having I fain would get me.

MEPHISTOPHELES.

Then you have reached the right place now.

STUDENT.

I'd like to leave it, I must avow;
I find these walls, these vaulted spaces
Are anything but pleasant places.
'T is all so cramped and close and mean;
One sees no tree, no glimpse of green,
And when the lecture-halls receive me,
Seeing, hearing, and thinking leave me.

MEPHISTOPHELES.

All that depends on habitude.
So from its mother's breasts a child
At first, reluctant, takes its food,
But soon to seek them is beguiled.
Thus, at the breasts of Wisdom clinging,
Thou 'lt find each day a greater rapture bringing.

STUDENT.

I'll hang thereon with joy, and freely drain them;
But tell me, pray, the proper means to gain them.

MEPHISTOPHELES.

Explain, before you further speak,
The special faculty you seek.

STUDENT.

I crave the highest erudition;
And fain would make my acquisition
All that there is in Earth and Heaven,
In Nature and in Science too.

MEPHISTOPHELES.

Here is the genuine path for you;
Yet strict attention must be given.

STUDENT.

Body and soul thereon I'll wreak;
Yet, truly, I've some inclination
On summer holidays to seek
A little freedom and recreation.

MEPHISTOPHELES.

Use well your time! It flies so swiftly from us;
But time through order may be won, I promise.
So, Friend, (my views to briefly sum,)
First, the *collegium logicum*.
There will your mind be drilled and braced,
As if in Spanish boots 't were laced,
And thus, to graver paces brought,
'T will plod along the path of thought,
Instead of shooting here and there,
A will-o'-the-wisp in murky air.
Days will be spent to bid you know,
What once you did at a single blow,
Like eating and drinking, free and strong,—
That one, two, three! thereto belong.
Truly the fabric of mental fleece
Resembles a weaver's masterpiece,
Where a thousand threads one treadle throws,
Where fly the shuttles hither and thither,
Unseen the threads are knit together,
And an infinite combination grows.
Then, the philosopher steps in
And shows, no otherwise it could have been:
The first was so, the second so,

Therefore the third and fourth are so;
Were not the first and second, then
The third and fourth had never been.
The scholars are everywhere believers,
But never succeed in being weavers.
He who would study organic existence,
First drives out the soul with rigid persistence;
Then the parts in his hand he may hold and class,
But the spiritual link is lost, alas!
Encheiresin naturæ, this Chemistry names,
Nor knows how herself she banters and blames!

STUDENT.

I cannot understand you quite.

MEPHISTOPHELES.

Your mind will shortly be set aright,
When you have learned, all things reducing,
To classify them for your using.

STUDENT.

I feel as stupid, from all you've said,
As if a mill-wheel whirled in my head!

MEPHISTOPHELES.

And after—first and foremost duty—
Of Metaphysics learn the use and beauty!
See that you most profoundly gain
What does not suit the human brain!
A splendid word to serve, you'll find
For what goes in—or won't go in—your mind.
But first, at least this half a year,
To order rigidly adhere;
Five hours a day, you understand,
And when the clock strikes, be on hand!
Prepare beforehand for your part
With paragraphs all got by heart,
So you can better watch, and look
That naught is said but what is in the book:
Yet in thy writing as unwearied be,
As did the Holy Ghost dictate to thee!

STUDENT.

No need to tell me twice to do it!
I think, how useful 't is to write;
For what one has, in black and white,
One carries home and then goes through it.

MEPHISTOPHELES.

Yet choose thyself a faculty!

STUDENT.

I cannot reconcile myself to Jurisprudence.

MEPHISTOPHELES.

Nor can I therefore greatly blame you students:
I know what science this has come to be.
All rights and laws are still transmitted
Like an eternal sickness of the race,—
From generation unto generation fitted,
And shifted round from place to place.
Reason becomes a sham, Beneficence a worry:
Thou art a grandchild, therefore woe to thee!
The right born with us, ours in verity,
This to consider, there's, alas! no hurry.

STUDENT.

My own disgust is strengthened by your speech.
O lucky he, whom you shall teach!
I've almost for Theology decided.

MEPHISTOPHELES.

I should not wish to see you here misguided:
For, as regards this science, let me hint
'T is very hard to shun the false direction;
There's so much secret poison lurking in 't,
So like the medicine, it baffles your detection.
Hear, therefore, one alone, for that is best, in sooth,
And simply take your master's words for truth.
On *words* let your attention centre!
Then through the safest gate you'll enter
The temple-halls of Certainty.

STUDENT.

Yet in the word must some idea be.

MEPHISTOPHELES.

Of course! But only shun too over-sharp a tension,
For just where fails the comprehension,
A word steps promptly in as deputy.
With words 't is excellent disputing;
Systems to words 't is easy suiting;
On words 't is excellent believing;
No word can ever lose a jot from thieving.

STUDENT.

Pardon! With many questions I detain you,
Yet must I trouble you again.
Of Medicine I still would fain
Hear one strong word that might explain you.
Three years is but a little space,
And, God! who can the field embrace?
If one some index could be shown,
'T were easier groping forward, truly.

MEPHISTOPHELES (*aside*).

I'm tired enough of this dry tone,—
Must play the Devil again, and fully.
(*Aloud.*)
To grasp the spirit of Medicine is easy:
Learn of the great and little world your fill,
To let it go at last, so please ye,
Just as God will!
In vain that through the realms of science you may
    drift;
Each one learns only—just what learn he can:
Yet he who grasps the Moment's gift,
He is the proper man.
Well-made you are, 't is not to be denied,
The rest a bold address will win you;
If you but in yourself confide,
At once confide all others in you.
To lead the women, learn the special feeling!
Their everlasting aches and groans,

In thousand tones,
Have all one source, one mode of healing;
And if your acts are half discreet,
You'll always have them at your feet.
A title first must draw and interest them,
And show that yours all other arts exceeds;
Then, as a greeting, you are free to touch and test
    them,
While, thus to do, for years another pleads.
You press and count the pulse's dances,
And then, with burning sidelong glances,
You clasp the swelling hips, to see
If tightly laced her corsets be.

STUDENT.

That's better, now! The How and Where, one sees

MEPHISTOPHELES.

My worthy friend, gray are all theories,
And green alone Life's golden tree.

STUDENT.

I swear to you, 't is like a dream to me.
Might I again presume, with trust unbounded,
To hear your wisdom thoroughly expounded?

MEPHISTOPHELES.

Most willingly, to what extent I may.

STUDENT.

I cannot really go away:
Allow me that my album first I reach you,—
Grant me this favor, I beseech you!

MEPHISTOPHELES.

Assuredly.

    (*He writes, and returns the book.*)

STUDENT (*reads*).
Eritis sicut Deus, scientes bonum et malum.
(*Closes the book with reverence, and withdraws.*)

MEPHISTOPHELES.

Follow the ancient text, and the snake thou wast ordered to trample!
With all thy likeness to God, thou 'lt yet be a sorry
example!

(FAUST *enters.*)

FAUST.

Now, whither shall we go?

MEPHISTOPHELES.

As best it pleases thee.
The little world, and then the great, we'll see.
With what delight, what profit winning,
Shalt thou sponge through the term beginning!

FAUST.

Yet with the flowing beard I wear,
Both ease and grace will fail me there.
The attempt, indeed, were a futile strife;
I never could learn the ways of life.
I feel so small before others, and thence
Should always find embarrassments.

MEPHISTOPHELES.

My friend, thou soon shalt lose all such misgiving:
Be thou but self-possessed, thou hast the art of living!

FAUST.

How shall we leave the house, and start?
Where hast thou servant, coach and horses?

MEPHISTOPHELES.

We'll spread this cloak with proper art,
Then through the air direct our courses.
But only, on so bold a flight,
Be sure to have thy luggage light.
A little burning air, which I shall soon prepare us,
Above the earth will nimbly bear us,
And, if we're light, we'll travel swift and clear:
I gratulate thee on thy new career!

V.

AUERBACH'S CELLAR IN LEIPZIG.

Carousal of Jolly Companions.

FROSCH.

IS no one laughing? no one drinking?
   I'll teach you how to grin, I'm thinking.
To-day you're like wet straw, so tame;
And usually you're all aflame.

BRANDER.

Now that's your fault; from you we nothing see,
No beastliness and no stupidity.

FROSCH.

(*Pours a glass of wine over* BRANDER'S *head.*)

There's both together!

BRANDER.
            Twice a swine!

FROSCH.

You wanted them: I've given you mine.

SIEBEL.

Turn out who quarrels—out the door!
With open throat sing chorus, drink and roar!
Up! holla! ho!

ALTMAYER.
            Woe's me, the fearful bellow!
Bring cotton, quick! He's split my ears, that fellow.

SIEBEL.

When the vault echoes to the song,
One first perceives the bass is deep and strong.

FROSCH.

Well said! and out with him that takes the least offence!

> *Ah, tara, lara, da!*

ALTMAYER.

> *Ah, tara, lara, da!*

FROSCH.

The throats are tuned, commence!

> (*Sings.*)
> *The dear old holy Roman realm,*
> *How does it hold together?*

BRANDER.

A nasty song! Fie! a political song—
A most offensive song! Thank God, each morning, therefore,
That you have not the Roman realm to care for!
At least, I hold it so much gain for me,
That I nor Chancellor nor Kaiser be.
Yet also we must have a ruling head, I hope,
And so we'll choose ourselves a Pope.
You know the quality that can
Decide the choice, and elevate the man.

FROSCH (*sings*).

> *Soar up, soar up, Dame Nightingale!*
> *Ten thousand times my sweetheart hail!*

SIEBEL.

No, greet my sweetheart not! I tell you, I'll resent it.

FROSCH.

My sweetheart greet and kiss! I dare you to prevent it!

> (*Sings.*)
> *Draw the latch! the darkness makes:*
> *Draw the latch! the lover wakes.*
> *Shut the latch! the morning breaks.*

SIEBEL.

Yes, sing away, sing on, and praise, and brag of her!
I'll wait my proper time for laughter:
Me by the nose she led, and now she'll lead you after.
Her paramour should be an ugly gnome,
Where four roads cross, in wanton play to meet her:
An old he-goat, from Blocksberg coming home,
Should his good-night in lustful gallop bleat her!
A fellow made of genuine flesh and blood
Is for the wench a deal too good.
Greet her? Not I: unless, when meeting,
To smash her windows be a greeting!

BRANDER (*pounding on the table*).

Attention! Hearken now to me!
Confess, Sirs, I know how to live.
Enamored persons here have we,
And I, as suits their quality,
Must something fresh for their advantage give.
Take heed! 'T is of the latest cut, my strain,
And all strike in at each refrain!

(*He sings.*)

There was a rat in the cellar-nest,
Whom fat and butter made smoother:
He had a paunch beneath his vest
Like that of Doctor Luther.
The cook laid poison cunningly,
And then as sore oppressed was he
As if he had love in his bosom.

CHORUS (*shouting*).

As if he had love in his bosom!

BRANDER.

He ran around, he ran about,
His thirst in puddles laving;
He gnawed and scratched the house throughout,
But nothing cured his raving.
He whirled and jumped, with torment mad,

And soon enough the poor beast had,
As if he had love in his bosom.

CHORUS.
As if he had love in his bosom!

BRANDER.
And driven at last, in open day,
He ran into the kitchen,
Fell on the hearth, and squirming lay,
In the last convulsion twitching.
Then laughed the murderess in her glee:
"Ha! ha! he's at his last gasp," said she.
"As if he had love in his bosom!"

CHORUS.
As if he had love in his bosom!

SIEBEL.
How the dull fools enjoy the matter!
To me it is a proper art
Poison for such poor rats to scatter.

BRANDER.
Perhaps you'll warmly take their part?

ALTMAYER.
The bald-pate pot-belly I have noted:
Misfortune tames him by degrees;
For in the rat by poison bloated
His own most natural form he sees.

FAUST AND MEPHISTOPHELES.

MEPHISTOPHELES.
Before all else, I bring thee hither
Where boon companions meet together,
To let thee see how smooth life runs away.
Here, for the folk, each day's a holiday:
With little wit, and ease to suit them,
They whirl in narrow, circling trails,

Like kittens playing with their tails;
And if no headache persecute them,
So long the host may credit give,
They merrily and careless live.

BRANDER.

The fact is easy to unravel,
Their air's so odd, they've just returned from travel:
A single hour they've not been here.

FROSCH.

You've verily hit the truth! Leipzig to me is dear:
Paris in miniature, how it refines its people!

SIEBEL.

Who are the strangers, should you guess?

FROSCH.

Let me alone! I'll set them first to drinking,
And then, as one a child's tooth draws, with cleverness,
I'll worm their secret out, I'm thinking.
They're of a noble house, that's very clear:
Haughty and discontented they appear.

BRANDER.

They're mountebanks, upon a revel.

ALTMAYER.

Perhaps.

FROSCH.

Look out, I'll smoke them now!

MEPHISTOPHELES (*to* FAUST).

Not if he had them by the neck, I vow,
Would e'er these people scent the Devil!

FAUST.

Fair greeting, gentlemen!

SIEBEL.

Our thanks: we give the same.

(*Murmurs, inspecting* MEPHISTOPHELES *from the side.*)

In one foot is the fellow lame?

MEPHISTOPHELES.

Is it permitted that we share your leisure?
In place of cheering drink, which one seeks vainly here,
Your company shall give us pleasure.

ALTMAYER.

A most fastidious person you appear.

FROSCH.

No doubt 't was late when you from Rippach started?
And supping there with Hans occasioned your delay?

MEPHISTOPHELES.

We passed, without a call, to-day.
At our last interview, before we parted
Much of his cousins did he speak, entreating
That we should give to each his kindly greeting

(*He bows to* FROSCH.)

ALTMAYER (*aside*).

You have it now! he understands.

SIEBEL.

　　　　　　　　A knave sharp-set!

FROSCH.

Just wait awhile: I'll have him yet.

MEPHISTOPHELES.

If I am right, we heard the sound
Of well-trained voices, singing chorus;
And truly, song must here rebound
Superbly from the arches o'er us.

FROSCH.

Are you, perhaps, a virtuoso?

MEPHISTOPHELES.

O no! my wish is great, my power is only so-so.

ALTMAYER.

Give us a song!

MEPHISTOPHELES.
If you desire, a number.

SIEBEL.

So that it be a bran-new strain!

MEPHISTOPHELES.

We've just retraced our way from Spain,
The lovely land of wine, and song, and slumber.

(*Sings.*)

There was a king once reigning,
Who had a big black flea—

FROSCH.

Hear, hear! A flea! D' ye rightly take the jest?
I call a flea a tidy guest.

MEPHISTOPHELES (*sings*).
There was a king once reigning,
Who had a big black flea,
And loved him past explaining,
As his own son were he.
He called his man of stitches;
The tailor came straightway:
Here, measure the lad for breeches,
And measure his coat, I say!

BRANDER.

But mind, allow the tailor no caprices:
Enjoin upon him, as his head is dear,
To most exactly measure, sew and shear,
So that the breeches have no creases!

MEPHISTOPHELES.

In silk and velvet gleaming
He now was wholly drest—
Had a coat with ribbons streaming,
A cross upon his breast.
He had the first of stations,
A minister's star and name;
And also all his relations
Great lords at court became.

And the lords and ladies of honor
Were plagued, awake and in bed;
The queen she got them upon her,
The maids were bitten and bled.
And they did not dare to brush them,
Or scratch them, day or night:
We crack them and we crush them,
At once, whene'er they bite.

CHORUS (*shouting*).

We crack them and we crush them,
At once, whene'er they bite!

FROSCH.

Bravo! bravo! that was fine.

SIEBEL.

Every flea may it so befall!

BRANDER.

Point your fingers and nip them all!

ALTMAYER.

Hurrah for Freedom! Hurrah for wine!

MEPHISTOPHELES.

I fain would drink with you, my glass to Freedom
    clinking,
If 't were a better wine that here I see you drinking.

SIEBEL.

Don't let us hear that speech again!

MEPHISTOPHELES.

Did I not fear the landlord might complain,
I'd treat these worthy guests, with pleasure,
To some from out our cellar's treasure.

SIEBEL.

Just treat, and let the landlord me arraign!

FROSCH.

And if the wine be good, our praises shall be ample,
But do not give too very small a sample;
For, if its quality I decide,
With a good mouthful I must be supplied.

ALTMAYER (*aside*).

They 're from the Rhine! I guessed as much, before.

MEPHISTOPHELES.

Bring me a gimlet here!

BRANDER.

What shall therewith be done?
You 've not the casks already at the door?

ALTMAYER.

Yonder, within the landlord's box of tools, there 's
one!

MEPHISTOPHELES (*takes the gimlet*).

(*To* FROSCH.)

Now, give me of your taste some intimation.

FROSCH.

How do you mean? Have you so many kinds?

MEPHISTOPHELES.

The choice is free: make up your minds.

ALTMAYER (*to* FROSCH.)

Aha! you lick your chops, from sheer anticipation.

FROSCH.

Good! if I have the choice, so let the wine be
    Rhenish!
Our Fatherland can best the sparkling cup replenish.

MEPHISTOPHELES
(*boring a hole in the edge of the table, at the place
where* FROSCH *sits*).

Get me a little wax, to make the stoppers, quick!

ALTMAYER.

Ah! I perceive a juggler's trick.

MEPHISTOPHELES (*to* BRANDER).
And you?

BRANDER.

Champagne shall be my wine.
And let it sparkle fresh and fine!

MEPHISTOPHELES
(*bores: in the mean time one has made the wax stoppers, and plugged the holes with them*).

BRANDER.

What 's foreign one can't always keep quite clear of,
For good things, oft, are not so near;
A German can't endure the French to see or hear of,
Yet drinks their wines with hearty cheer.

SIEBEL
(*as* MEPHISTOPHELES *approaches his seat*).
For me, I grant, sour wine is out of place;
Fill up my glass with sweetest, will you?

MEPHISTOPHELES (*boring*).
Tokay shall flow at once, to fill you!

ALTMAYER.

No—look me, Sirs, straight in the face!
I see you have your fun at our expense.

MEPHISTOPHELES.

O no! with gentlemen of such pretence,
That were to venture far, indeed.
Speak out, and make your choice with speed!
With what a vintage can I serve you?

ALTMAYER.

With any—only satisfy our need.

(*After the holes have been bored and plugged.*)

MEPHISTOPHELES
(*with singular gestures*).

Grapes the vine-stem bears,
Horns the he-goat wears!
The grapes are juicy, the vines are wood,
The wooden table gives wine as good!
Into the depths of Nature peer,—
Only believe, there's a miracle here!

Now draw the stoppers, and drink your fill!

ALL

(*as they draw out the stoppers, and the wine which
has been desired flows into the glass of each*).

O beautiful fountain, that flows at will!

MEPHISTOPHELES.

But have a care, that you nothing spill!

(*They drink repeatedly.*)

ALL (*sing*).

As 't were five hundred hogs, we feel
So cannibalic jolly!

MEPHISTOPHELES.

See, now, the race is happy—it is free!

FAUST.

To leave them is my inclination.

MEPHISTOPHELES.
Take notice, first! their bestiality
Will make a brilliant demonstration.

SIEBEL
(*drinks carelessly: the wine spills upon the earth, and turns to flame*).

Help! Fire! Help! Hell-fire is sent!

MEPHISTOPHELES
(*charming away the flame*).

Be quiet, friendly element!

(*To the revellers.*)

A bit of purgatory 't was for this time, merely.

SIEBEL.
What mean you? Wait!—you 'll pay for 't dearly!
You 'll know us, to your detriment.

FROSCH.
Don't try that game a second time upon us!

ALTMAYER.
I think we 'd better send him packing quietly.

SIEBEL.
What, Sir! you dare to make so free,
And play your hocus-pocus on us!

MEPHISTOPHELES.
Be still, old wine-tub.

SIEBEL.
Broomstick, you!
You face it out, impertinent and heady?

BRANDER.
Just wait! a shower of blows is ready.

ALTMAYER
(*draws a stopper out of the table: fire flies in
his face*).

I burn! I burn!

SIEBEL.
'T is magic! Strike—
The knave is outlawed! Cut him as you like!

(*They draw their knives, and rush upon
MEPHISTOPHELES.*)

MEPHISTOPHELES
(*with solemn gestures*).
False word and form of air,
Change place, and sense ensnare!
Be here—and there!
(*They stand amazed and look at each other.*)

ALTMAYER.
Where am I? What a lovely land!

FROSCH.
Vines? Can I trust my eyes?

SIEBEL.
And purple grapes at hand!

BRANDER.
Here, over this green arbor bending,
See, what a vine! what grapes depending!
(*He takes SIEBEL by the nose: the others do the same
reciprocally, and raise their knives.*)

MEPHISTOPHELES (*as above*).
Loose, Error, from their eyes the band,
And how the Devil jests, be now enlightened!
(*He disappears with FAUST: the revellers start and
separate.*)

SIEBEL.
What happened?

ALTMAYER.

How?

FROSCH.

Was that your nose I tightened?

BRANDER (*to* SIEBEL).

And yours that still I have in hand?

ALTMAYER.

It was a blow that went through every limb!
Give me a chair! I sink! my senses swim.

FROSCH.

But what has happened, tell me now?

SIEBEL.

Where is he? If I catch the scoundrel hiding,
He shall not leave alive, I vow.

ALTMAYER.

I saw him with these eyes upon a wine-cask riding
Out of the cellar-door, just now.
Still in my feet the fright like lead is weighing.

(*He turns towards the table.*)

Why! If the fount of wine should still be playing?

SIEBEL.

'T was all deceit, and lying, false design!

FROSCH.

And yet it seemed as I were drinking wine.

BRANDER.

But with the grapes how was it, pray?

ALTMAYER.

Shall one believe no miracles, just say!

VI.

WITCHES' KITCHEN.

Upon a low hearth stands a great caldron, under which a fire is burning. Various figures appear in the vapors which rise from the caldron. An ape sits beside it, skims it, and watches lest it boil over. The he-ape, with the young ones, sits near and warms himself. Ceiling and walls are covered with the most fantastic witch-implements.

FAUST. MEPHISTOPHELES.

FAUST.

These crazy signs of witches' craft repel me!
I shall recover, dost thou tell me,
Through this insane, chaotic play?
From an old hag shall I demand assistance?
And will her foul mess take away
Full thirty years from my existence?
Woe 's me, canst thou naught better find!
Another baffled hope must be lamented:
Has Nature, then, and has a noble mind
Not any potent balsam yet invented?

MEPHISTOPHELES.

Once more, my friend, thou talkest sensibly.
There is, to make thee young, a simpler mode and
      apter;
But in another book 't is writ for thee,
And is a most eccentric chapter.

FAUST.

Yet will I know it.

MEPHISTOPHELES.

            Good! the method is revealed
Without or gold or magic or physician.
Betake thyself to yonder field,
There hoe and dig, as thy condition;

Restrain thyself, thy sense and will
Within a narrow sphere to flourish;
With unmixed food thy body nourish;
Live with the ox as ox, and think it not a theft
That thou manur'st the acre which thou reapest;—
That, trust me, is the best mode left,
Whereby for eighty years thy youth thou keepest!

FAUST.

I am not used to that; I cannot stoop to try it—
To take the spade in hand, and ply it.
The narrow being suits me not at all.

MEPHISTOPHELES.

Then to thine aid the witch must call.

FAUST.

Wherefore the hag, and her alone?
Canst thou thyself not brew the potion?

MEPHISTOPHELES.

That were a charming sport, I own:
I 'd build a thousand bridges meanwhile, I 've a
    notion,
Not Art and Science serve, alone;
Patience must in the work be shown.
Long is the calm brain active in creation;
Time, only, strengthens the fine fermentation.
And all, belonging thereunto,
Is rare and strange, howe'er you take it:
The Devil taught the thing, 't is true,
And yet the Devil cannot make it.

(*Perceiving the Animals.*)

See, what a delicate race they be!
That is the maid! the man is he!

(*To the Animals.*)

It seems the mistress has gone away?

THE ANIMALS.

Carousing, to-day!
Off and about,
By the chimney out!

MEPHISTOPHELES.
What time takes she for dissipating?

THE ANIMALS.
While we to warm our paws are waiting.

MEPHISTOPHELES (*to* FAUST).
How findest thou the tender creatures?

FAUST.
Absurder than I ever yet did see.

MEPHISTOPHELES.
Why, just such talk as this, for me,
Is that which has the most attractive features!

(*To the Animals.*)

But tell me now, ye curséd puppets,
Why do ye stir the porridge so?

THE ANIMALS.
We 're cooking watery soup for beggars.

MEPHISTOPHELES.
Then a great public you can show.

THE HE-APE
(*comes up and fawns on* MEPHISTOPHELES).
O cast thou the dice!
Make me rich in a trice,
Let me win in good season!
Things are badly controlled,
And had I but gold,
So had I my reason.

MEPHISTOPHELES.
How would the ape be sure his luck enhances,
Could he but try the lottery's chances!

(*In the mean time the young apes have been playing
with a large ball, which they now roll forward.*)

THE HE-APE.
The world 's the ball:
Doth rise and fall,
And roll incessant:
Like glass doth ring,
A hollow thing,—
How soon will 't spring,
And drop, quiescent?
Here bright it gleams,
Here brighter seems:
I live at present!
Dear son, I say,
Keep thou away!
Thy doom is spoken!
'T is made of clay,
And will be broken.

MEPHISTOPHELES.
What means the sieve?

THE HE-APE (*taking it down*).
Wert thou the thief,
I'd know him and shame.

(*He runs to the* SHE-APE, *and lets her look through it.*)

Look through the sieve!
Know'st thou the thief,
And darest not name him?

MEPHISTOPHELES (*approaching the fire*).
And what's this pot?

HE-APE AND SHE-APE.
The fool knows it not!
He knows not the pot,
He knows not the kettle!

MEPHISTOPHELES.
Impertinent beast!

THE HE-APE.

Take the brush here, at least,
And sit down on the settle!

(*He invites* MEPHISTOPHELES *to sit down.*)

FAUST

(*who during all this time has been standing before a*
mirror, now approaching and now retreating from it).

What do I see? What heavenly form revealed
Shows through the glass from Magic's fair dominions!
O lend me, Love, the swiftest of thy pinions,
And bear me to her beauteous field!
Ah, if I leave this spot with fond designing,
If I attempt to venture near,
Dim, as through gathering mist, her charms appear!—
A woman's form, in beauty shining!
Can woman, then, so lovely be?
And must I find her body, there reclining,
Of all the heavens the bright epitome?
Can Earth with such a thing be mated?

MEPHISTOPHELES.

Why, surely, if a God first plagues Himself six days.
Then, self-contented, *Bravo!* says,
Must something clever be created.
This time, thine eyes be satiate!
I 'll yet detect thy sweetheart and ensnare her,
And blest is he, who has the lucky fate,
Some day, as bridegroom, home to bear her.

(FAUST *gazes continually in the mirror.* MEPHISTOPH-
ELES *stretching himself out on the settle, and playing*
with the brush, continues to speak.)

So sit I, like the King upon his throne:
I hold the sceptre, here,—and lack the crown alone.

THE ANIMALS

(*who up to this time have been making all kinds of
fantastic movements together, bring a crown to
MEPHISTOPHELES with great noise*).

> O be thou so good
> With sweat and with blood
> The crown to belime!

(*They handle the crown awkwardly and break it into
two pieces, with which they spring around.*)

> 'T is done, let it be!
> We speak and we see,
> We hear and we rhyme!

FAUST (*before the mirror*).
Woe 's me! I fear to lose my wits.

MEPHISTOPHELES (*pointing to the Animals*).
My own head, now, is really nigh to sinking.

THE ANIMALS.

> If lucky our hits,
> And everything fits,
> 'T is thoughts, and we 're thinking!

FAUST (*as above*).
My bosom burns with that sweet vision;
Let us, with speed, away from here!

MEPHISTOPHELES (*in the same attitude*).
One must, at least, make this admission—
They 're poets, genuine and sincere.

(*The caldron, which the SHE-APE has up to this time
neglected to watch, begins to boil over: there ensues
a great flame, which blazes out the chimney. The
WITCH comes careering down through the flame,
with terrible cries.*)

THE WITCH.

Ow! ow! ow! ow!
The damnéd beast—the curséd sow!
To leave the kettle, and singe the Frau!
Accurséd fere!

(*Perceiving* FAUST *and* MEPHISTOPHELES.)

What is that here?
Who are you here?
What want you thus?
Who sneaks to us?
The fire-pain
Burn bone and brain!

(*She plunges the skimming-ladle into the caldron, and
scatters flames towards* FAUST, MEPHISTOPHELES,
and the Animals. The Animals whimper.)

MEPHISTOPHELES
(*reversing the brush, which he has been holding in his
hand, and striking among the jars and glasses*).

In two! in two!
There lies the brew!
There lies the glass!
The joke will pass,
As time, foul ass!
To the singing of thy crew.

(*As the* WITCH *starts back, full of wrath and
horror* :)

Ha! know'st thou me? Abomination, thou!
Know'st thou, at last, thy Lord and Master?
What hinders me from smiting now
Thee and thy monkey-sprites with fell disaster?
Hast for the scarlet coat no reverence?
Dost recognize no more the tall cock's-feather?
Have I concealed this countenance?—
Must tell my name, old face of leather?

THE WITCH.

O pardon, Sir, the rough salute!
Yet I perceive no cloven foot;
And both your ravens, where are *they* now?

MEPHISTOPHELES.

This time, I 'll let thee 'scape the debt;
For since we two together met,
'T is verily full many a day now.
Culture, which smooth the whole world licks,
Also unto the Devil sticks.
The days of that old Northern phantom now are over:
Where canst thou horns and tail and claws discover?
And, as regards the foot, which I can't spare, in truth,
'T would only make the people shun me;
Therefore I 've worn, like many a spindly youth,
False calves these many years upon me.

THE WITCH (*dancing*).

Reason and sense forsake my brain,
Since I behold Squire Satan here again!

MEPHISTOPHELES.

Woman, from such a name refrain!

THE WITCH.

Why so? What has it done to thee?

MEPHISTOPHELES.

It 's long been written in the Book of Fable;
Yet, therefore, no whit better men we see:
The Evil One has left, the evil ones are stable.
Sir Baron call me thou, then is the matter good;
A cavalier am I, like others in my bearing.
Thou hast no doubt about my noble blood:
See, here 's the coat-of-arms that I am wearing!

(*He makes an indecent gesture.*)

THE WITCH (*laughs immoderately*).

Ha! ha! That 's just your way, I know:
A rogue you are, and you were always so.

MEPHISTOPHELES (*to* FAUST).
My friend, take proper heed, I pray!
To manage witches, this is just the way.

THE WITCH.
Wherein, Sirs, can I be of use?

MEPHISTOPHELES.
Give us a goblet of the well-known juice!
But, I must beg you, of the oldest brewage;
The years a double strength produce.

THE WITCH.
With all my heart! Now, here 's a bottle,
Wherefrom, sometimes, I wet my throttle,
Which, also, not the slightest, stinks;
And willingly a glass I'll fill him.

(*Whispering.*)

Yet, if this man without due preparation drinks,
As well thou know'st, within an hour 't will kill him.

MEPHISTOPHELES.
He is a friend of mine, with whom it will agree,
And he deserves thy kitchen's best potation:
Come, draw thy circle, speak thine adjuration,
And fill thy goblet full and free!

THE WITCH
(*with fantastic gestures draws a circle and places
mysterious articles therein; meanwhile the glasses
begin to ring, the caldron to sound, and make a
musical accompaniment. Finally she brings a great
book, and stations in the circle the Apes, who are
obliged to serve as reading-desk, and to hold the
torches. She then beckons* FAUST *to approach*).

FAUST (*to* MEPHISTOPHELES).
Now, what shall come of this? the creatures antic,
The crazy stuff, the gestures frantic,—

All the repulsive cheats I view,—
Are known to me, and hated, too.

MEPHISTOPHELES.

O, nonsense! That 's a thing for laughter;
Don't be so terribly severe!
She juggles you as doctor now, that, after,
The beverage may work the proper cheer.

(*He persuades* FAUST *to step into the circle.*)

THE WITCH
(*begins to declaim, with much emphasis, from the book*).

See, thus it 's done!
Make ten of one,
And two let be,
Make even three,
And rich thou 'lt be.
Cast o'er the four!
From five and six
(The witch's tricks)
Make seven and eight,
'T is finished straight!
And nine is one,
And ten is none.
This is the witch's once-one's-one!

FAUST.
She talks like one who raves in fever.

MEPHISTOPHELES.
Thou 'lt hear much more before we leave her.
'T is all the same: the book I can repeat,
Such time I 've squandered o'er the history:
A contradiction thus complete
Is always for the wise, no less than fools, a mystery.
The art is old and new, for verily
All ages have been taught the matter,—
By Three and One, and One and Three,
Error instead of Truth to scatter.

They prate and teach, and no one interferes;
All from the fellowship of fools are shrinking.
Man usually believes, if only words he hears,
That also with them goes material for thinking!

THE WITCH (*continues*).
The lofty skill
Of Science, still
From all men deeply hidden!
Who takes no thought,
To him 't is brought,
'T is given unsought, unbidden!

FAUST.
What nonsense she declaims before us!
My head is nigh to split, I fear:
It seems to me as if I hear
A hundred thousand fools in chorus.

MEPHISTOPHELES.
O Sibyl excellent, enough of adjuration!
But hither bring us thy potation,
And quickly fill the beaker to the brim!
This drink will bring my friend no injuries:
He is a man of manifold degrees,
And many draughts are known to him.

(*The* WITCH, *with many ceremonies, pours the drink
into a cup; as* FAUST *sets it to his lips, a light flame
arises.*)

Down with it quickly! Drain it off!
'T will warm thy heart with new desire:
Art with the Devil hand and glove,
And wilt thou be afraid of fire?

(*The* WITCH *breaks the circle*: FAUST *steps forth.*)

MEPHISTOPHELES.
And now, away! Thou dar'st not rest.

THE WITCH.
And much good may the liquor do thee!

MEPHISTOPHELES (*to the* WITCH).

Thy wish be on Walpurgis Night expressed;
What boon I have, shall then be given unto thee.

THE WITCH.

Here is a song, which, if you sometimes sing,
You 'll find it of peculiar operation.

MEPHISTOPHELES (*to* FAUST).

Come, walk at once! A rapid occupation
Must start the needful perspiration,
And through thy frame the liquor's potence fling.
The noble indolence I 'll teach thee then to treasure,
And soon thou 'lt be aware, with keenest thrills of
     pleasure,
How Cupid stirs and leaps, on light and restless wing.

FAUST.

One rapid glance within the mirror give me,
How beautiful that woman-form!

MEPHISTOPHELES.

No, no! The paragon of all, believe me,
Thou soon shalt see, alive and warm.

(*Aside.*)

Thou 'lt find, this drink thy blood compelling,
Each woman beautiful as Helen!

VII.

A STREET.

FAUST. MARGARET (*passing by*).

FAUST.

Fair lady, let it not offend you,
That arm and escort I would lend you!

MARGARET.

I 'm neither lady, neither fair,

And home I can go without your care.
                    [*She releases herself, and exit.*

FAUST.

By Heaven, the girl is wondrous fair!
Of all I 've seen, beyond compare;
So sweetly virtuous and pure,
And yet a little pert, be sure!
The lip so red, the cheek's clear dawn,
I 'll not forget while the world rolls on!
How she cast down her timid eyes,
Deep in my heart imprinted lies:
How short and sharp of speech was she,
Why, 't was a real ecstasy!

(MEPHISTOPHELES *enters.*)

FAUST.

Hear, of that girl I 'd have possession!

MEPHISTOPHELES.

Which, then?

FAUST.

The one who just went by.

MEPHISTOPHELES.

She, there? She 's coming from confession,
Of every sin absolved; for I,
Behind her chair, was listening nigh.
So innocent is she, indeed,
That to confess she had no need.
I have no power o'er souls so green.

FAUST.

And yet, she 's older than fourteen.

MEPHISTOPHELES.

How now! You 're talking like Jack Rake,
Who every flower for himself would take,
And fancies there are no favors more,
Nor honors, save for him in store;
Yet always does n't the thing succeed.

FAUST.

Most Worthy Pedagogue, take heed!
Let not a word of moral law be spoken!
I claim, I tell thee, all my right;
And if that image of delight
Rest not within mine arms to-night,
At midnight is our compact broken.

MEPHISTOPHELES.

But think, the chances of the case!
I need, at least, a fortnight's space,
To find an opportune occasion.

FAUST.

Had I but seven hours for all,
I should not on the Devil call,
But win her by my own persuasion.

MEPHISTOPHELES.

You almost like a Frenchman prate;
Yet, pray, don't take it as annoyance!
Why, all at once, exhaust the joyance?
Your bliss is by no means so great
As if you 'd use, to get control,
All sorts of tender rigmarole,
And knead and shape her to your thought,
As in Italian tales 't is taught.

FAUST.

Without that, I have appetite.

MEPHISTOPHELES.

But now, leave jesting out of sight!
I tell you, once for all, that speed
With this fair girl will not succeed;
By storm she cannot captured be;
We must make use of strategy.

FAUST.

Get me something the angel keeps!
Lead me thither where she sleeps!
Get me a kerchief from her breast,—
A garter that her knee has pressed!

MEPHISTOPHELES.

That you may see how much I 'd fain
Further and satisfy your pain,
We will no longer lose a minute;
I 'll find her room to-day, and take you in it.

FAUST.

And shall I see—possess her?

MEPHISTOPHELES.

No!

Unto a neighbor she must go,
And meanwhile thou, alone, mayst glow
With every hope of future pleasure,
Breathing her atmosphere in fullest measure.

FAUST.

Can we go thither?

MEPHISTOPHELES.

'T is too early yet.

FAUST.

A gift for her I bid thee get!   [*Exit.*

MEPHISTOPHELES.

Present's at once? That 's good: he 's certain to get
    at her!
Full many a pleasant place I know,
And treasures, buried long ago:
I must, perforce, look up the matter.

                                        [*Exit.*

VIII.

EVENING.

A SMALL, NEATLY KEPT CHAMBER.

MARGARET.
(*plaiting and binding up the braids of her hair*).

I 'd something give, could I but say
Who was that gentleman, to-day.

Surely a gallant man was he,
And of a noble family;
So much could I in his face behold,—
And he would n't, else, have been so bold!

[*Exit.*

MEPHISTOPHELES. FAUST.

MEPHISTOPHELES.
Come in, but gently: follow me!

FAUST (*after a moment's silence*).
Leave me alone, I beg of thee!

MEPHISTOPHELES (*prying about*).
Not every girl keeps things so neat.

FAUST (*looking around*).
O welcome, twilight soft and sweet,
That breathes throughout this hallowed shrine!
Sweet pain of love, bind thou with fetters fleet
The heart that on the dew of hope must pine!
How all around a sense impresses
Of quiet, order, and content
This poverty what bounty blesses!
What bliss within this narrow den is pent!

(*He throws himself into a leather arm-chair
near the bed.*)
Receive me, thou, that in thine open arms
Departed joy and pain wert wont to gather!
How oft the children, with their ruddy charms,
Hung here, around this throne, where sat the father!
Perchance my love, amid the childish band,
Grateful for gifts the Holy Christmas gave her,
Here meekly kissed the grandsire's withered hand.
I feel, O maid! thy very soul
Of order and content around me whisper,—
Which leads thee with its motherly control,
The cloth upon thy board bids smoothly thee unroll,
The sand beneath thy feet makes whiter, crisper.
O dearest hand, to thee 't is given

To change this hut into a lower heaven!
And here!

      (*He lifts one of the bed-curtains.*)

      What sweetest thrill is in my blood!
Here could I spend whole hours, delaying:
Here Nature shaped, as if in sportive playing,
The angel blossom from the bud.

Here lay the child, with Life's warm essence
The tender bosom filled and fair,
And here was wrought, through holier, purer pres-
    ence.
The form diviner beings wear!

And I? What drew me here with power?
How deeply am I moved, this hour!
What seek I? Why so full my heart, and sore?
Miserable Faust! I know thee now no more.

Is there a magic vapor here?
I came, with lust of instant pleasure,
And lie dissolved in dreams of love's sweet leisure!
Are we the sport of every changeful atmosphere?

And if, this moment, came she in to me,
How would I for the fault atonement render!
How small the giant lout would be,
Prone at her feet, relaxed and tender!

        MEPHISTOPHELES.
Be quick! I see her there, returning.

        FAUST.
Go! go! I never will retreat.

        MEPHISTOPHELES.
Here is a casket, not unmeet,
Which elsewhere I have just been earning.
Here, set it in the press, with haste!

I swear, 't will turn her head, to spy it:
Some baubles I therein had placed,
That you might win another by it.
True, child is child, and play is play.

FAUST.
I know not, should I do it?

MEPHISTOPHELES.
Ask you, pray?
Yourself, perhaps, would keep the bubble?
Then I suggest, 't were fair and just
To spare the lovely day your lust,
And spare to me the further trouble.
You are not miserly, I trust?
I rub my hands, in expectation tender—

(*He places the casket in the press, and locks it
again.*)

Now quick, away!
The sweet young maiden to betray,
So that by wish and will you bend her;
And you look as though
To the lecture-hall you were forced to go,—
As if stood before you, gray and loath,
Physics and Metaphysics both!
But away!

[*Exeunt.*

MARGARET (*with a lamp*).
It is so close, so sultry, here!

(*She opens the window.*)

And yet 't is not so warm outside.
I feel, I know not why, such fear!—
Would mother came!—where can she bide?
My body 's chill and shuddering,—
I 'm but a silly, fearsome thing!

(*She begins to sing, while undressing.*)

There was a King in Thule,
Was faithful till the grave,—
To whom his mistress, dying,
A golden goblet gave.

Naught was to him more precious;
He drained it at every bout:
His eyes with tears ran over.
As oft as he drank thereout.

When came his time of dying,
The towns in his land he told,
Naught else to his heir denying
Except the goblet of gold.

He sat at the royal banquet
With his knights of high degree,
In the lofty hall of his fathers
In the Castle by the Sea.

There stood the old carouser,
And drank the last life-glow;
And hurled the hallowed goblet
Into the tide below.

He saw it plunging and filling,
And sinking deep in the sea:
Then fell his eyelids forever,
And never more drank he!

(*She opens the press in order to arrange her clothes,
and perceives the casket of jewels.*)

How comes that lovely casket here to me?
I locked the press, most certainly.
'T is truly wonderful! What can within it be?
Perhaps 't was brought by some one as a pawn,
And mother gave a loan thereon?
And here there hangs a key to fit:
I have a mind to open it.
What is that? God in Heaven! Whence came

Such things? Never beheld I aught so fair!
Rich ornaments, such as a noble dame
On highest holidays might wear!
How would the pearl-chain suit my hair?
Ah, who may all this splendor own?

(*She adorns herself with the jewelry, and steps before
the mirror.*)

Were but the ear-rings mine, alone!
One has at once another air.
What helps one's beauty, youthful blood?
One may possess them, well and good;
But none the more do others care.
They praise us half in pity, sure:
To gold still tends,
On gold depends
All, all! Alas, we poor!

IX.

PROMENADE.

(FAUST, *walking thoughtfully up and down. To him*
MEPHISTOPHELES.)

MEPHISTOPHELES.

By all love ever rejected! By hell-fire hot and unsparing!
I wish I knew something worse, that I might use it
for swearing!

FAUST.

What ails thee? What is 't gripes thee, elf?
A face like thine beheld I never.

MEPHISTOPHELES.

I would myself unto the Devil deliver,
If I were not a Devil myself!

FAUST.

Thy head is out of order, sadly:
It much becomes thee to be raving madly.

MEPHISTOPHELES.

Just think, the pocket of a priest should get
The trinkets left for Margaret!
The mother saw them, and, instanter,
A secret dread began to haunt her.
Keen scent has she for tainted air;
She snuffs within her book of prayer,
And smells each article, to see
If sacred or profane it be;
So here she guessed, from every gem,
That not much blessing came with them.
"My child," she said, "ill-gotten good
Ensnares the soul, consumes the blood.
Before the Mother of God we 'll lay it;
With heavenly manna she 'll repay it!"
But Margaret thought, with sour grimace,
"A gift-horse is not out of place,
And, truly! godless cannot be
The one who brought such things to me."
A parson came, by the mother bidden:
He saw, at once, where the game was hidden,
And viewed it with a favor stealthy.
He spake: "That is the proper view,—
Who overcometh, winneth too.
The Holy Church has a stomach healthy:
Hath eaten many a land as forfeit,
And never yet complained of surfeit:
The Church alone, beyond all question,
Has for ill-gotten goods the right digestion."

FAUST.

A general practice is the same,
Which Jew and King may also claim.

MEPHISTOPHELES.

Then bagged the spangles, chains, and rings,
As if but toadstools were the things,

And thanked no less, and thanked no more
Than if a sack of nuts he bore,—
Promised them fullest heavenly pay,
And deeply edified were they.

FAUST.

And Margaret?

MEPHISTOPHELES.

Sits unrestful still,
And knows not what she should, or will;
Thinks on the jewels, day and night,
But more on him who gave her such delight.

FAUST.

The darling's sorrow gives me pain.
Get thou a set for her again!
The first was not a great display.

MEPHISTOPHELES.

O yes, the gentleman finds it all child's-play!

FAUST.

Fix and arrange it to my will;
And on her neighbor try thy skill!
Don't be a Devil stiff as paste,
But get fresh jewels to her taste!

MEPHISTOPHELES.

Yes, gracious Sir, in all obedience!

[*Exit* FAUST

Such an enamored fool in air would blow
Sun, moon, and all the starry legions,
To give his sweetheart a diverting show.

[*Exit.*

X.

THE NEIGHBOR'S HOUSE.

MARTHA (*solus*).

God forgive my husband, yet he

Has n't done his duty by me!
Off in the world he went straightway,—
Left me lie in the straw where I lay,
And, truly, I did naught to fret him:
God knows I loved, and can't forget him!

(*She weeps.*)

Perhaps he 's even dead! Ah, woe!—
Had I a certificate to show!

MARGARET (*comes*).
Dame Martha!

MARTHA
Margaret! what 's happened thee?

MARGARET.
I scarce can stand, my knees are trembling!
I find a box, the first resembling,
Within my press! Of ebony,—
And things, all splendid to behold,
And richer far than were the old.

MARTHA.
You must n't tell it to your mother!
'T would go to the priest, as did the other.

MARGARET.
Ah, look and see—just look and see!

MARTHA (*adorning her*).
O, what a blessed luck for thee!

MARGARET.
But, ah! in the streets I dare not bear them,
Nor in the church be seen to wear them.

MARTHA.
Yet thou canst often this way wander,
And secretly the jewels don,

Walk up and down an hour, before the mirror yon-
          der,—
We'll have our private joy thereon.
And then a chance will come, a holiday,
When, piece by piece, can one the things abroad dis-
          play,
A chain at first, then other ornament:
Thy mother will not see, and stories we'll invent.

MARGARET.

Whoever could have brought me things so precious?
That something's wrong, I feel suspicious.

(*A knock.*)

Good Heaven! My mother can that have been?

MARTHA (*peeping through the blind*).

'T is some strange gentleman.—Come in!

(MEPHISTOPHELES *enters.*)

MEPHISTOPHELES.

That I so boldly introduce me,
I beg you, ladies, to excuse me.

(*Steps back reverently, on seeing* MARGARET.)

For Martha Schwerdtlein I'd inquire!

MARTHA.

I'm she: what does the gentleman desire?

MEPHISTOPHELES (*aside to her*).

It is enough that you are she:
You 've a visitor of high degree.
Pardon the freedom I have ta'en,—
Will after noon return again.

MARTHA (*aloud*).

Of all things in the world! Just hear—
He takes thee for a lady, dear!

MARGARET.

I am a creature young and poor:
The gentleman's too kind, I'm sure.
The jewels don't belong to me.

MEPHISTOPHELES.

Ah, not alone the jewelry!
The look, the manner, both betray—
Rejoiced am I that I may stay!

MARTHA.

What is your business? I would fain—

MEPHISTOPHELES.

I would I had a more cheerful strain!
Take not unkindly its repeating:
Your husband's dead, and sends a greeting.

MARTHA.

Is dead? Alas, that heart so true!
My husband dead! Let me die, too!

MARGARET.

Ah, dearest dame, let not your courage fail!

MEPHISTOPHELES.

Hear me relate the mournful tale!

MARGARET.

Therefore I'd never love, believe me!
A loss like this to death would grieve me.

MEPHISTOPHELES.

Joy follows woe. woe after joy comes flying.

MARTHA.

Relate his life's sad close to me!

MEPHISTOPHELES.

In Padua buried, he is lying
Beside the good Saint Antony,

Within a grave well consecrated,
For cool, eternal rest created.

MARTHA.

He gave you, further, no commission?

MEPHISTOPHELES.

Yes, one of weight, with many sighs:
Three hundred masses buy, to save him from perdition!
My hands are empty, otherwise.

MARTHA.

What! Not a pocket-piece? no jewelry?
What every journeyman within his wallet spares,
And as a token with him bears,
And rather starves or begs, than loses?

MEPHISTOPHELES.

Madam, it is a grief to me;
Yet, on my word, his cash was put to proper uses.
Besides, his penitence was very sore,
And he lamented his ill fortune all the more.

MARGARET.

Alack, that men are so unfortunate!
Surely for his soul's sake full many a prayer I'll
         proffer.

MEPHISTOPHELES.

You well deserve a speedy marriage-offer:
You are so kind, compassionate.

MARGARET.

O, no! As yet, it would not do.

MEPHISTOPHELES.

If not a husband, then a beau for you!
It is the greatest heavenly blessing,
To have a dear thing for one's caressing.

MARGARET.

The country's custom is not so.

MEPHISTOPHELES.

Custom, or not! It happens, though.

MARTHA.

Continue, pray!

MEPHISTOPHELES.
      I stood beside his bed of dying.
'T was something better than manure,—
Half-rotten straw: and yet, he died a Christian, sure,
And found that heavier scores to his account were
    lying.
He cried: "I find my conduct wholly hateful!
To leave my wife, my trade, in manner so ungrateful!
Ah, the remembrance makes me die!
Would of my wrong to her I might be shriven!"

MARTHA (*weeping*).
The dear, good man! Long since was he forgiven.

MEPHISTOPHELES.
"Yet she, God knows! was more to blame than I."

MARTHA.
He lied! What! On the brink of death he slandered?

MEPHISTOPHELES.
In the last throes his senses wandered,
If I such things but half can judge.
He said: "I had no time for play, for gaping freedom:
First children, and then work for bread to feed 'em,—
For bread, in the widest sense, to drudge,
And could not even eat my share in peace and quiet!"

MARTHA.
Had he all love, all faith forgotten in his riot?
My work and worry, day and night?

MEPHISTOPHELES.
Not so: the memory of it touched him quite.
Said he: "When I from Malta went away

My prayers for wife and little ones were zealous,
And such a luck from Heaven befell us,
We made a Turkish merchantman our prey,
That to the Soldan bore a mighty treasure.
Then I received, as was most fit,
Since bravery was paid in fullest measure,
My well-apportioned share of it."

MARTHA.

Say, how? Say, where? If buried, did he own it?

MEPHISTOPHELES.

Who knows, now, whither the four winds have blown
    it?
A fair young damsel took him in her care,
As he in Naples wandered round, unfriended;
And she much love, much faith to him did bear,
So that he felt it till his days were ended.

MARTHA.

The villain! From his children thieving!
Even all the misery on him cast
Could not prevent his shameful way of living!

MEPHISTOPHELES.

But see! He's dead therefrom, at last.
Were I in *your* place, do not doubt me,
I'd mourn him decently a year,
And for another keep, meanwhile, my eyes about me.

MARTHA.

Ah, God! another one so dear
As was my first, this world will hardly give me.
There never was a sweeter fool than mine,
Only he loved to roam and leave me,
And foreign wenches and foreign wine,
And the damned throw of dice, indeed.

MEPHISTOPHELES.

Well, well! That might have done, however,
If he had only been as clever,

And treated *your* slips with as little heed.
I swear, with this condition, too,
I would, myself, change rings with you.

MARTHA.
The gentleman is pleased to jest.

MEPHISTOPHELES (*aside*).
I'll cut away, betimes, from here:
She 'd take the Devil at his word, I fear.

(*To* MARGARET.)
How fares the heart within your breast?

MARGARET.
What means the gentleman?

MEPHISTOPHELES (*aside*).
Sweet innocent, thou art!

(*Aloud.*)
Ladies, farewell!

MARGARET.
Farewell!

MARTHA.
A moment, ere we part!
I'd like to have a legal witness,
Where, how, and when he died, to certify with fitness.
Irregular ways I've always hated;
I want his death in the weekly paper stated.

MEPHISTOPHELES.
Yes, my good dame, a pair of witnesses
Always the truth establishes.
I have a friend of high condition,
Who'll also add his deposition.
I'll bring him here.

MARTHA.
Good Sir, pray do!

MEPHISTOPHELES.
And this young lady will be present, too?
A gallant youth! has travelled far:
Ladies with him delighted are.

MARGARET.
Before him I should blush, ashamed.

MEPHISTOPHELES.
Before no king that could be named!

MARTHA.
Behind the house, in my garden, then,
This eve we'll expect the gentlemen.

XI.

STREET.

FAUST. MEPHISTOPHELES.

FAUST.

Ｈow is it? under way? and soon complete?

MEPHISTOPHELES.
Ah, bravo! Do I find you burning?
Well, Margaret soon will still your yearning:
At Neighbor Martha's you'll this evening meet.
A fitter woman ne'er was made
To ply the pimp and gypsy trade!

FAUST.
'T is well.

MEPHISTOPHELES.
Yet something is required from us.

FAUST.
One service pays the other thus.

MEPHISTOPHELES.

We've but to make a deposition valid
That now her husband's limbs, outstretched and pallid,
At Padua rest, in consecrated soil.

FAUST.

Most wise! And first, of course, we'll make the journey thither?

MEPHISTOPHELES.

Sancta simplicitas! no need of such a toil;
Depose, with knowledge or without it, either!

FAUST.

If you've naught better, then, I'll tear your pretty
plan!

MEPHISTOPHELES.

Now, there you are! O holy man!
Is it the first time in your life you're driven
To bear false witness in a case?
Of God, the world and all that in it has a place,
Of Man, and all that moves the being of his race,
Have you not terms and definitions given
With brazen forehead, daring breast?
And, if you'll probe the thing profoundly,
Knew you so much—and you'll confess it roundly!—
As here of Schwerdtlein's death and place of rest?

FAUST.

Thou art, and thou remain'st, a sophist, liar.

MEPHISTOPHELES.

Yes, knew I not more deeply thy desire.
For wilt thou not, no lover fairer,
Poor Margaret flatter, and ensnare her,
And all thy soul's devotion swear her?

FAUST.

And from my heart.

MEPHISTOPHELES.
'T is very fine!
Thine endless love, thy faith assuring,
The one almighty force enduring,—
Will that, too, prompt this heart of thine?

FAUST.
Hold! hold! It will!—If such my flame,
And for the sense and power intense
I seek, and cannot find, a name;
Then range with all my senses through creation,
Craving the speech of inspiration,
And call this ardor, so supernal,
Endless, eternal and eternal,—
Is that a devilish lying game?

MEPHISTOPHELES.
And yet I'm right!

FAUST.
Mark this, I beg of thee!
And spare my lungs henceforth: whoever
Intends to have the right, if but his tongue be clever
Will have it, certainly.
But come: the further talking brings disgust,
For thou art right, especially since I must.

XII.

GARDEN.

(MARGARET *on* FAUST'S *arm.* MARTHA *and* MEPHIS-
TOPHELES *walking up and down.*)

MARGARET.
I FEEL, the gentleman allows for me,
Demeans himself, and shames me by it;
A traveller is so used to be
Kindly content with any diet.
I know too well that my poor gossip can
Ne'er entertain such an experienced man.

FAUST.

A look from thee, a word, more entertains
Than all the lore of wisest brains.

(*He kisses her hand.*)

MARGARET.

Don't incommode yourself! How could you ever kiss
     it!
It is so ugly, rough to see!
What work I do,—how hard and steady is it!
Mother is much too close with me.

                              [*They pass.*

MARTHA.

And you, Sir, travel always, do you not?

MEPHISTOPHELES.

Alas, that trade and duty us so harry!
With what a pang one leaves so many a spot,
And dares not even now and then to tarry!

MARTHA.

In young, wild years it suits your ways,
This round and round the world in freedom sweeping;
But then come on the evil days,
And so, as bachelor, into his grave a-creeping,
None ever found a thing to praise.

MEPHISTOPHELES.

I dread to see how such a fate advances.

MARTHA.

Then, worthy Sir, improve betimes your chances!

                              [*They pass.*

MARGARET.

Yes, out of sight is out of mind!
Your courtesy an easy grace is;
But you have friends in other places,
And sensibler than I, you'll find.

FAUST.

Trust me, dear heart! what men call sensible
Is oft mere vanity and narrowness.

MARGARET.

How so?

FAUST.

Ah, that simplicity and innocence ne'er know
Themselves, their holy value, and their spell!
That meekness, lowliness, the highest graces
Which Nature portions out so lovingly—

MARGARET.

So you but think a moment's space on me,
All times I'll have to think on you, all places!

FAUST.

No doubt you're much alone?

MARGARET.

Yes, for our household small has grown,
Yet must be cared for, you will own.
We have no maid: I do the knitting, sewing, sweeping,
The cooking, early work and late, in fact;
And mother, in her notions of housekeeping,
Is so exact!
Not that she needs so much to keep expenses down:
We, more than others, might take comfort, rather:
A nice estate was left us by my father,
A house, a little garden near the town.
But now my days have less of noise and hurry;
My brother is a soldier,
My little sister's dead.
True, with the child a troubled life I led,
Yet I would take again, and willing, all the worry,
So very dear was she.

FAUST.

An angel, if like thee!

MARGARET.

I brought it up, and it was fond of me.

Father had died before it saw the light,
And mother's case seemed hopeless quite,
So weak and miserable she lay;
And she recovered, then, so slowly, day by day.
She could not think, herself, of giving
The poor wee thing its natural living;
And so I nursed it all alone
With milk and water: 't was my own.
Lulled in my lap with many a song,
It smiled, and tumbled, and grew strong.

FAUST.

The purest bliss was surely then thy dower.

MARGARET.

But surely, also, many a weary hour.
I kept the baby's cradle near
My bed at night: if 't even stirred, I'd guess it,
And waking, hear.
And I must nurse it, warm beside me press it,
And oft, to quiet it, my bed forsake,
And dandling back and forth the restless creature take,
Then at the wash-tub stand, at morning's break;
And then the marketing and kitchen-tending,
Day after day, the same thing, never-ending.
One's spirits, Sir, are thus not always good,
But then one learns to relish rest and food.

[*They pass.*

MARTHA.

Yes, the poor women are bad off, 't is true:
And stubborn bachelor there's no converting.

MEPHISTOPHELES.

It but depends upon the like of you,
And I should turn to better ways than flirting.

MARTHA.

Speak plainly, Sir, have you no one detected?
Has not your heart been anywhere subjected?

MEPHISTOPHELES.

The proverb says: One's own warm hearth
And a good wife, are gold and jewels worth.

MARTHA.

I mean, have you not felt desire, though ne'er so
  slightly?

MEPHISTOPHELES.

I've everywhere, in fact, been entertained politely.

MARTHA.

I meant to say, were you not touched in earnest, ever?

MEPHISTOPHELES.

One should allow one's self to jest with ladies never.

MARTHA.

Ah, you don't understand!

MEPHISTOPHELES.

                    I'm sorry I'm so blind:
But I am sure—that you are very kind.

                                        [*They pass.*

FAUST.

And me, thou angel! didst thou recognize,
As through the garden-gate I came?

MARGARET.

Did you not see it? I cast down my eyes.

FAUST.

And thou forgiv'st my freedom, and the blame
To my impertinence befitting,
As the Cathedral thou wert quitting?

MARGARET.

I was confused, the like ne'er happened me;
No one could ever speak to my discredit.
Ah, thought I, in my conduct has he read it—
Something immodest or unseemly free?
He seemed to have the sudden feeling
That with this wench 't were very easy dealing.
I will confess, I knew not what appeal
On your behalf, here, in my bosom grew;
But I was angry with myself, to feel
That I could not be angrier with you.

FAUST.

Sweet darling!

MARGARET.
Wait a while!

(*She plucks a star-flower, and pulls off the leaves, one after the other.*)

FAUST.
Shall that a nosegay be?

MARGARET.

No, it is just in play.

FAUST.
How?

MARGARET.
Go! you'll laugh at me.

(*She pulls off the leaves and murmurs.*)

FAUST.

What murmurest thou?

MARGARET (*half aloud*).
He loves me—loves me not.

FAUST.

Thou sweet, angelic soul!

MARGARET (*continues*).
Loves me—not—loves me—not—

(*plucking the last leaf, she cries with frank delight:*)

He loves me!

FAUST.
Yes, child! and let this blossom-word
For thee be speech divine! He loves thee!
Ah, know'st thou what it means? He loves thee!

(*He grasps both her hands.*)

MARGARET.

I'm all a-tremble!

FAUST.

   O tremble not! but let this look,
Let this warm clasp of hands declare thee
What is unspeakable!
To yield one wholly, and to feel a rapture
In yielding, that must be eternal!
Eternal!—for the end would be despair.
No, no,—no ending! no ending!

MARTHA (*coming forward*).
The night is falling.

MEPHISTOPHELES.
   Ay! we must away.

MARTHA.

I'd ask you, longer here to tarry,
But evil tongues in this town have full play.
It's as if nobody had nothing to fetch and carry,
Nor other labor,
But spying all the doings of one's neighbor:
And one becomes the talk, do whatsoe'er one may.
Where is our couple now?

MEPHISTOPHELES.
    Flown up the alley yonder,
The wilful summer-birds!

MARTHA.
   He seems of her still fonder.

MEPHISTOPHELES.
And she of him. So runs the world away!

XIII.

A GARDEN-ARBOR.

(MARGARET *comes in, conceals herself behind the door,
puts her finger to her lips, and peeps through the
crack.*)

MARGARET.

HE comes!

FAUST (*entering*).
Ah, rogue! a tease thou **art**:
I have thee!

(*He kisses her.*)

MARGARET
(*clasping him, and returning the kiss.*)
Dearest man! I love thee from my heart.

(MEPHISTOPHELES *knocks.*)

FAUST (*stamping his foot*).
Who's there?

MEPHISTOPHELES.
A friend!

FAUST.
A beast!

MEPHISTOPHELES.
'T is time to separate

MARTHA (*coming*).
Yes, Sir, 't is late.

FAUST.
May I not, then, upon you wait?

MARGARET.
My mother would—farewell!

FAUST.
Ah, can I not remain?
Farewell!

MARTHA.
Adieu!

MARGARET.

And soon to meet again!

[*Exeunt* FAUST *and* MEPHISTOPHELES.

MARGARET.

Dear God! However is it, such
A man can think and know so much?
I stand ashamed and in amaze,
And answer "Yes" to all he says,
A poor, unknowing child! and he—
I can't think what he finds in me!

[*Exit.*

XIV.

FOREST AND CAVERN.

FAUST (*solus*).

SPIRIT sublime, thou gav'st me, gav'st me all
   For which I prayed. Not unto me in vain
Hast thou thy countenance revealed in fire.
Thou gav'st me Nature as a kingdom grand,
With power to feel and to enjoy it. Thou
Not only cold, amazed acquaintance yield'st,
But grantest, that in her profoundest breast
I gaze, as in the bosom of a friend.
The ranks of living creatures thou dost lead
Before me, teaching me to know my brothers
In air and water and the silent wood.
And when the storm in forests roars and grinds,
The giant firs, in falling, neighbor boughs
And neighbor trunks with crushing weight bear down,
And falling, fill the hills with hollow thunders,—
Then to the cave secure thou leadest me,
Then show'st me mine own self, and in my breast
The deep, mysterious miracles unfold.
And when the perfect moon before my gaze
Comes up with soothing light, around me float
From every precipice and thicket damp
The silvery phantoms of the ages past,
And temper the austere delight of thought.

That nothing can be perfect unto Man
I now am conscious. With this ecstasy,
Which brings me near and nearer to the Gods,
Thou gav'st the comrade, whom I now no more
Can do without, though, cold and scornful, he
Demeans me to myself, and with a breath,
A word, transforms thy gifts to nothingness.
Within my breast he fans a lawless fire,
Unwearied, for that fair and lovely form:
Thus in desire I hasten to enjoyment,
And in enjoyment pine to feel desire.

(MEPHISTOPHELES *enters.*)

MEPHISTOPHELES.

Have you not led this life quite long enough?
How can a further test delight you?
'T is very well, that once one tries the stuff,
But something new must then requite you.

FAUST.

Would there were other work for thee!
To plague my day auspicious thou returnest.

MEPHISTOPHELES.

Well! I'll engage to let thee be:
Thou darest not tell me so in earnest.
The loss of thee were truly very slight,—
A comrade crazy, rude, repelling:
One has one's hands full all the day and night;
If what one does, or leaves undone, is right,
From such a face as thine there is no telling.

FAUST.

There is, again, thy proper tone!—
That thou hast bored me, I must thankful be!

MEPHISTOPHELES.

Poor Son of Earth, how couldst thou thus alone
Have led thy life, bereft of me?
I, for a time, at least, have worked thy cure;

Thy fancy's rickets plague thee not at all:
Had I not been, so hadst thou, sure,
Walked thyself off this earthly ball.
Why here to caverns, rocky hollows slinking,
Sit'st thou, as 't were an owl a-blinking?
Why suck'st, from sodden moss and dripping stone,
Toad-like, thy nourishment alone?
A fine way, this, thy time to fill!
The Doctor's in thy body still.

FAUST.

What fresh and vital forces, canst thou guess,
Spring from my commerce with the wilderness?
But, if thou hadst the power of guessing,
Thou wouldst be devil enough to grudge my soul the
    blessing.

MEPHISTOPHELES.

A blessing drawn from supernatural fountains!
In night and dew to lie upon the mountains;
All Heaven and Earth in rapture penetrating;
Thyself to Godhood haughtily inflating;
To grub with yearning force through Earth's dark
    marrow,
Compress the six days' work within thy bosom nar-
    row,—
To taste, I know not what, in haughty power,
Thine own ecstatic life on all things shower,
Thine earthly self behind thee cast,
And then the lofty instinct, thus—

(*With a gesture*:)

                at last,—
I dare n't say how—to pluck the final flower!

FAUST.

Shame on thee!

MEPHISTOPHELES.

          Yes, thou findest that unpleasant!
Thou hast the moral right to cry me "shame!" at
    present.
One dares not that before chaste ears declare,

Which chaste hearts, notwithstanding, cannot spare;
And, once for all, I grudge thee not the pleasure
Of lying to thyself in moderate measure.
But such a course thou wilt not long endure;
Already art thou o'er-excited,
And, if at last, wilt soon be plighted
To madness and to horror, sure.
Enough of that! Thy love sits lonely yonder,
By all things saddened and oppressed;
Her thoughts and yearnings seek thee, tenderer,
         fonder,—
A mighty love is in her breast.
First came thy passion's flood and poured around her
As when from melted snow a streamlet overflows;
Thou hast therewith so filled and drowned her,
That now *thy* stream all shallow shows.
Methinks, instead of in the forests lording,
The noble Sir should find it good,
The love of this young silly blood
At once to set about rewarding.
Her time is miserably long;
She haunts her window, watching clouds that stray
O'er the old city-wall, and far away.
"Were I a little bird!" so runs her song,
Day long, and half night long.
Now she is lively, mostly sad,
Now, wept beyond her tears;
Then again quiet she appears,—
Always love-mad.

FAUST.

Serpent! serpent!

MEPHISTOPHELES (*aside*).

Ha! do I trap thee!

FAUST.

Get thee away with thine offences,
Reprobate! Name not that fairest thing,
Nor the desire for her sweet body bring
Again before my half-distracted senses!

MEPHISTOPHELES.

What wouldst thou, then? She thinks that thou art
     flown;
And half and half thou art, I own.

FAUST.

Yet am I near, and love keeps watch and ward;
Though I were ne'er so far, it cannot falter:
I envy even the Body of the Lord
The touching of her lips, before the altar.

MEPHISTOPHELES.

'T is very well! *My* envy oft reposes
On your twin-pair, that feed among the roses.

FAUST.

Away, thou pimp!

MEPHISTOPHELES.

         You rail, and it is fun to me.
The God, who fashioned youth and maid,
Perceived the noblest purpose of His trade,
And also made their opportunity.
Go on! It is a woe profound!
'T is for your sweetheart's room you're bound,
And not for death, indeed.

FAUST.

What are, within her arms, the heavenly blisses?
Though I be glowing with her kisses,
Do I not always share her need?
I am the fugitive, all houseless roaming,
The monster without aim or rest,
That like a cataract, down rocks and gorges foaming,
Leaps, maddened, into the abyss's breast!
And side-wards she, with young unwakened senses,
Within her cabin on the Alpine field
Her simple, homely life commences,
Her little world therein concealed.
And I, God's hate flung o'er me,
Had not enough, to thrust

The stubborn rocks before me
And strike them into dust!
She and her peace I yet must undermine:
Thou, Hell, hast claimed this sacrifice as thine!
Help, Devil! through the coming pangs to push me;
What must be, let it quickly be!
Let fall on me her fate, and also crush me,—
One ruin whelm both her and me!

MEPHISTOPHELES.

Again it seethes, again it glows!
Thou fool, go in and comfort her!
When such a head as thine no outlet knows,
It thinks the end must soon occur.
Hail him, who keeps a steadfast mind!
Thou, else, dost well the devil-nature wear:
Naught so insipid in the world I find
As is a devil in despair.

XV.

MARGARET'S ROOM.

MARGARET
(*at the spinning-wheel, alone*).

MY peace is gone,
    My heart is sore:
I never shall find it,
Ah, nevermore!

Save I have him near,
The grave is here;
The world is gall
And bitterness all.

My poor weak head
Is racked and crazed;
My thought is lost,
My senses mazed.

My peace is gone,
My heart is sore:
I never shall find it,
Ah, nevermore!

To see him, him only,
At the pane I sit;
To meet him, him only,
The house I quit.

His lofty gait,
His noble size,
The smile of his mouth,
The power of his eyes,

And the magic flow
Of his talk, the bliss
In the clasp of his hand,
And, ah! his kiss!

My peace is gone,
My heart is sore:
I never shall find it,
Ah, nevermore!

My bosom yearns
For him alone;
Ah, dared I clasp him,
And hold, and own!

And kiss his mouth,
To heart's desire,
And on his kisses
At last expire!

XVI.

MARTHA'S GARDEN.

MARGARET. FAUST.

MARGARET.

PROMISE me, Henry!—

FAUST.
What I can!

MARGARET.
How is 't with thy religion, pray?
Thou art a dear, good-hearted man,
And yet, I think, dost not incline that way.

FAUST.
Leave tnat, my child! Thou know'st my love is tender;
For love, my blood and life would I surrender,
And as for Faith and Church, I grant to each his own

MARGARET.
That's not enough: we must believe thereon.

FAUST.
Must we?

MARGARET.
Would that I had some influence!
Then, too, thou honorest not the Holy Sacraments.

FAUST.
I honor them.

MARGARET.
Desiring no possession.
'T is long since thou hast been to mass or to confession.
Believest thou in God?

FAUST.
My darling, who shall dare
"I believe in God!" to say?
Ask priest or sage the answer to declare,
And it will seem a mocking play,
A sarcasm on the asker.

MARGARET.
Then thou believest not!

FAUST.
Hear me not falsely, sweetest countenance!

Who dare express Him?
And who profess Him,
Saying: I believe in Him!
Who, feeling, seeing,
Deny His being,
Saying: I believe Him not!
The All-enfolding,
The All-upholding,
Folds and upholds he not
Thee, me, Himself?
Arches not there the sky above us?
Lies not beneath us, firm, the earth?
And rise not, on us shining,
Friendly, the everlasting stars?
Look I not, eye to eye, on thee,
And feel'st not, thronging
To head and heart, the force,
Still weaving its eternal secret,
Invisible, visible, round thy life?
Vast as it is, fill with that force thy heart,
And when thou in the feeling wholly blessed art,
Call it, then, what thou wilt,—
Call it Bliss! Heart! Love! God!
I have no name to give it!
Feeling is all in all:
The Name is sound and smoke,
Obscuring Heaven's clear glow.

MARGARET.

All that is fine and good, to hear it so:
Much the same way the preacher spoke,
Only with slightly different phrases.

FAUST.

The same thing, in all places,
All hearts that beat beneath the heavenly day—
Each in its language—say;
Then why not I, in mine, as well?

MARGARET.

To hear it thus, it may seem passable;

And yet, some hitch in 't there must be
For thou hast no Christianity.

FAUST.

Dear love!

MARGARET.

  I've long been grieved to see
That thou art in such company.

FAUST.

How so?

MARGARET.

   The man who with thee goes, thy mate,
Within my deepest, inmost soul I hate.
In all my life there's nothing
Has given my heart so keen a pang of loathing,
As his repulsive face has done.

FAUST.

Nay, fear him not, my sweetest one!

MARGARET.

I feel his presence like something ill.
I've else, for all, a kindly will,
But, much as my heart to see thee yearneth,
The secret horror of him returneth;
And I think the man a knave, as I live!
If I do him wrong, may God forgive!

FAUST.

There must be such queer birds, however.

MARGARET.

Live with the like of him, may I never!
When once inside the door comes he,
He looks around so sneeringly,
And half in wrath:
One sees that in nothing no interest he hath:
'T is written on his very forehead
That love, to him, is a thing abhorréd.
I am so happy on thine arm,

So free, so yielding, and so warm,
And in his presence stifled seems my heart.

FAUST.

Foreboding angel that thou art!

MARGARET.

It overcomes me in such degree,
That wheresoe'er he meets us, even,
I feel as though I'd lost my love for thee.
When he is by, I could not pray to Heaven.
That burns within me like a flame,
And surely, Henry, 't is with thee the same.

FAUST.

There, now, is thine antipathy!

MARGARET.

But I must go.

FAUST.

       Ah, shall there never be
A quiet hour, to see us fondly plighted,
With breast to breast, and soul to soul united?

MARGARET.

Ah, if I only slept alone!
I'd draw the bolts to-night, for thy desire;
But mother's sleep so light has grown,
And if we were discovered by her,
'T would be my death upon the spot!

FAUST.

Thou angel, fear it not!
Here is a phial: in her drink
But three drops of it measure,
And deepest sleep will on her senses sink.

MARGARET.

What would I not, to give thee pleasure?
It will not harm her, when one tries it?

FAUST.

If 't would, my love, would I advise it?

MARGARET.

Ah, dearest man, if but thy face I see,
I know not what compels me to thy will:
So much have I already done for thee,
That scarcely more is left me to fulfil.

[*Exit.*

(*Enter* MEPHISTOPHELES.)

MEPHISTOPHELES.

The monkey! Is she gone?

FAUST.

Hast played the spy again?

MEPHISTOPHELES.

I've heard, most fully, how she drew thee.
The Doctor has been catechised, 't is plain;
Great good, I hope, the thing will do thee.
The girls have much desire to ascertain
If one is prim and good, as ancient rules compel:
If there he's led, they think, he'll follow them as well.

FAUST.

Thou, monster, wilt nor see nor own
How this pure soul, of faith so lowly,
So loving and ineffable,—
The faith alone
That her salvation is,—with scruples holy
Pines, lest she hold as lost the man she loves so well!

MEPHISTOPHELES.

Thou, full of sensual, super-sensual desire,
A girl by the nose is leading thee.

FAUST.

Abortion, thou, of filth and fire!

MEPHISTOPHELES.

And then, how masterly she reads physiognomy!

When I am present she's impressed, she knows not
    how;
She in my mask a hidden sense would read:
She feels that surely I'm a genius now,—
Perhaps the very Devil, indeed!
Well, well,—to-night—?

FAUST.

             What's that to thee?

MEPHISTOPHELES.

Yet my delight 't will also be!

XVII.

AT THE FOUNTAIN.

MARGARET *and* LISBETH *with pitchers.*

LISBETH.

HAST nothing heard of Barbara?

MARGARET.

No, not a word. I go so little out.

LISBETH.

It's true, Sibylla said, to-day.
She's played the fool at last, there's not a doubt.
Such taking on of airs!

MARGARET.

          How so?

LISBETH.

                    It stinks!
She's feeding two, whene'er she eats and drinks.

MARGARET.

Ah!

LISBETH.

And so, at last, it serves her rightly.

She clung to the fellow so long and tightly!
That was a promenading!
At village and dance parading!
As the first they must everywhere shine,
And he treated her always to pies and wine,
And she made a to-do with her face so fine;
So mean and shameless was her behavior,
She took all the presents the fellow gave her.
'T was kissing and coddling, on and on!
So now, at the end, the flower is gone.

MARGARET.

The poor, poor thing!

LISBETH.

Dost pity her, at that?
When one of us at spinning sat,
And mother, nights, ne'er let us out the door
She sported with her paramour.
On the door-bench, in the passage dark,
The length of the time they'd never mark.
So now her head no more she'll lift,
But do church-penance in her sinner's shift!

MARGARET.

He'll surely take her for his wife.

LISBETH.

He'd be a fool! A brisk young blade
Has room, elsewhere, to ply his trade.
Besides, he's gone.

MARGARET.

That is not fair!

LISBETH.

If him she gets, why let her beware!
The boys shall dash her wreath on the floor,
And we'll scatter chaff before her door!

[*Exit.*

MARGARET (*returning home*).

How scornfully I once reviled,
When some poor maiden was beguiled!
More speech than any tongue suffices
I craved, to censure others' vices.
Black as it seemed, I blackened still,
And blacker yet was in my will;
And blessed myself, and boasted high,—
And now—a living sin am I!
Yet—all that drove my heart thereto,
God! was so good, so dear, so true!

XVIII.

DONJON.

(*In a niche of the wall a shrine, with an image of the
Mater Dolorosa. Pots of flowers before it.*)

MARGARET
(*putting fresh flowers in the pots*).

INCLINE, O Maiden,
  Thou sorrow-laden,
Thy gracious countenance upon my pain!

The sword Thy heart in,
With anguish smarting,
Thou lookest up to where Thy Son is slain!

Thou seest the Father;
Thy sad sighs gather,
And bear aloft Thy sorrow and His pain!

Ah, past guessing,
Beyond expressing,
The pangs that wring my flesh and bone!
Why this anxious heart so burneth,
Why it trembleth, why it yearneth,
Knowest Thou, and Thou alone!

Where'er I go, what sorrow,
What woe, what woe and sorrow
Within my bosom aches!
Alone, and ah! unsleeping,
I'm weeping, weeping, weeping,
The heart within me breaks.

The pots before my window,
Alas! my tears did wet,
As in the early morning
For thee these flowers I set.

Within my lonely chamber
The morning sun shone red:
I sat, in utter sorrow,
Already on my bed.

Help! rescue me from death and stain!
O Maiden!
Thou sorrow-laden,
Incline Thy countenance upon my pain!

XIX.

NIGHT.

STREET BEFORE MARGARET'S DOOR.

VALENTINE
(*a soldier*, MARGARET'S *brother*).

WHEN I have sat some carouse,
   Where each to each his brag allows,
And many a comrade praised to me
His pink of girls right lustily,
With brimming glass that spilled the toast,
And elbows planted as in boast:
I sat in unconcerned repose,
And heard the swagger as it rose.
And stroking then my beard, I'd say,
Smiling, the bumper in my hand:
"Each well enough in her own way,
But is there one in all the land

Like sister Margaret, good as gold,—
One that to her can a candle hold?"
Cling! clang! "Here 's to her!" went around
The board: "He speaks the truth!" cried some;
"In her the flower o' the sex is found!"
And all the swaggerers were dumb.
And now!—I could tear my hair with vexation,
And dash out my brains in desperation!
With turned-up nose each scamp may face me,
With sneers and stinging taunts disgrace me,
And, like a bankrupt debtor sitting,
A chance-dropped word may set me sweating!
Yet, though I thresh them all together,
I cannot call them liars, either.

But what comes sneaking, there, to view?
If I mistake not, there are two.
If *he's* one, let me at him drive!
He shall not leave the spot alive.

FAUST. MEPHISTOPHELES.

FAUST.

How from the window of the sacristy
Upward th' eternal lamp sends forth a glimmer,
That, lessening side-wards, fainter grows and dimmer,
Till darkness closes from the sky!
The shadows thus within my bosom gather.

MEPHISTOPHELES.

I'm like a sentimental tom-cat, rather,
That round the tall fire-ladders sweeps,
And stealthy, then, along the coping creeps:
Quite virtuous, withal, I come,
A little thievish and a little frolicsome.
I feel in every limb the presage
Forerunning the grand Walpurgis-Night:
Day after to-morrow brings its message,
And one keeps watch then with delight.

FAUST.

Meanwhile, may not the treasure risen be,
Which there, behind, I glimmering see?

MEPHISTOPHELES.

Shalt soon experience the pleasure,
To lift the kettle with its treasure.
I lately gave therein a squint—
Saw splendid lion-dollars in 't.

FAUST.

Not even a jewel, not a ring,
To deck therewith my darling girl?

MEPHISTOPHELES.

I saw, among the rest, a thing
That seemed to be a chain of pearl.

FAUST.

That's well, indeed! For painful is it
To bring no gift when her I visit.

MEPHISTOPHELES.

Thou shouldst not find it so annoying,
Without return to be enjoying.
Now, while the sky leads forth its starry throng,
Thou 'lt hear a masterpiece, no work completer:
I'll sing her, first, a moral song,
The surer, afterwards, to cheat her.
    (*Sings to the cither.*)
        What dost thou here
        In daybreak clear,
        Kathrina dear,
        Before thy lover's door?
        Beware! the blade
        Lets in a maid,
        That out a maid
        Departeth nevermore!

        The coaxing shun
        Of such an one!

When once 't is done
Good-night to thee, poor **thing!**
Love's time is brief:
Unto no thief
Be warm and lief,
But with the wedding-ring!

VALENTINE (*comes forward*).
Whom wilt thou lure? God's-element!
Rat-catching piper, thou!—perdition!
To the Devil, first, the instrument!
To the Devil, then, the curst musician!

MEPHISTOPHELES.
The cither's smashed! For nothing more 't is fitting.

VALENTINE.
There's yet a skull I must be splitting!

MEPHISTOPHELES (*to* FAUST).
Sir Doctor, don't retreat, I pray!
Stand by: I'll lead, if you'll but tarry:
Out with your spit, without delay!
You've but to lunge, and I will parry.

VALENTINE.
Then parry that!

MEPHISTOPHELES.
Why not? 't is light.

VALENTINE.
That too!

MEPHISTOPHELES.
Of course.

VALENTINE.
I think the Devil must fight!
How is it, then? my hand's already lame.

MEPHISTOPHELES (to FAUST).
Thrust home!

VALENTINE (*falls*).
O God!

MEPHISTOPHELES.
       Now is the lubber tame!
But come, away! 'T is time for us to fly;
For there arises now a murderous cry.
With the police 't were easy to compound it,
But here the penal court will sift and sound it.
         [*Exit with* FAUST.

MARTHA (*at the window*).
Come out! come out!

MARGARET (*at the window*).
       Quick, bring a light!

MARTHA (*as above*).
They swear and storm, they yell and fight!

PEOPLE.
Here lies one dead already—see!

MARTHA (*coming from the house*).
The murderers, whither have they run?

MARGARET (*coming out*).
Who lies here?

PEOPLE.
'T is thy mother's son!

MARGARET.
Almighty God! what misery!

VALENTINE.
I'm dying! That is quickly said,
And quicker yet 't is done.
Why howl, you women there? Instead,

Come here and listen, every one!
           (*All gather around him.*)
My Margaret, see! still young thou art,
But not the least bit shrewd or smart,
Thy business thus to slight:
So this advice I bid thee heed—
Now that thou art a whore indeed,
Why, be one then, outright!

MARGARET.

My brother! God! such words to me!

VALENTINE.

In this game let our Lord God be!
What's done's already done, alas!
What follows it, must come to pass.
With one begin'st thou secretly,
Then soon will others come to thee,
And when a dozen thee have known,
Thou 'rt also free to all the town.

When Shame is born and first appears,
She is in secret brought to light,
And then they draw the veil of night
Over her head and ears;
Her life, in fact, they 're loath to spare her.
But let her growth and strength display,
She walks abroad unveiled by day,
Yet is not grown a whit the fairer.
The uglier she is to sight,
The more she seeks the day's broad light.
The time I verily can discern
When all the honest folk will turn
From thee, thou jade! and seek protection
As from a corpse that breeds infection.
Thy guilty heart shall then dismay thee,
When they but look thee in the face:—
Shalt not in a golden chain array thee,
Nor at the altar take thy place!
Shalt not, in lace and ribbons flowing,
Make merry when the dance is going!

But in some corner, woe betide thee!
Among the beggars and cripples hide thee;
And so, though even God forgive,
On earth a damned existence live!

MARTHA.

Commend your soul to God for pardon,
That you your heart with slander harden!

VALENTINE.

Thou pimp most infamous, be still!
Could I thy withered body kill,
'T would bring, for all my sinful pleasure,
Forgiveness in the richest measure.

MARGARET.

My brother! This is Hell's own pain!

VALENTINE.

I tell thee, from thy tears refrain!
When thou from honor didst depart
It stabbed me to the very heart.
Now through the slumber of the grave
I go to God as a soldier brave.

           (*Dies.*)

XX.

CATHEDRAL.

SERVICE, ORGAN AND ANTHEM.

(MARGARET *among much people*: *the* EVIL SPIRIT
behind MARGARET.)

EVIL SPIRIT.

HOW otherwise was it, Margaret,
   When thou, still innocent,
Here to the altar cam'st,
And from the worn and fingered book

Thy prayers didst prattle,
Half sport of childhood,
Half God within thee!
Margaret!
Where tends thy thought?
Within thy bosom
What hidden crime?
Pray'st thou for mercy on thy mother's soul,
That fell asleep to long, long torment, and through
    thee?
Upon thy threshold whose the blood?
And stirreth not and quickens
Something beneath thy heart,
Thy life disquieting
With most foreboding presence?

MARGARET.

Woe! woe!
Would I were free from the thoughts
That cross me, drawing hither and thither,
Despite me!

CHORUS.

Dies iræ, dies illa,
Solvet sæclum in favilla!
(Sound of the organ.)

EVIL SPIRIT.

Wrath takes thee!
The trumpet peals!
The graves tremble!
And thy heart
From ashy rest
To fiery torments
Now again requickened,
Throbs to life!

MARGARET.

Would I were forth!
I feel as if the organ here
My breath takes from me,
My very heart
Dissolved by the anthem!

CHORUS.

Judex ergo cum sedebit,
Quidquid latet, adparebit,
Nil inultum remanebit.

MARGARET.

I cannot breathe!
The massy pillars
Imprison me!
The vaulted arches
Crush me!—Air!

EVIL SPIRIT.

Hide thyself! Sin and shame
Stay never hidden.
Air? Light?
Woe to thee!

CHORUS.

Quid sum miser tunc dicturus,
Quem patronum rogaturus,
Cum vix justus sit securus?

EVIL SPIRIT.

They turn their faces,
The glorified, from thee:
The pure, their hands to offer,
Shuddering, refuse thee!
Woe!

CHORUS.

Quid sum miser tunc dicturus?

MARGARET.

Neighbor! your cordial!
(*She falls in a swoon.*)

XXI.

WALPURGIS-NIGHT.

THE HARTZ MOUNTAINS.

District of Schierke and Elend.

Faust. Mephistopheles.

Mephistopheles.

Dost thou not wish a broomstick-steed's assistance?
The sturdiest he-goat I would gladly see:
The way we take, our goal is yet some distance.

Faust.

So long as in my legs I feel the fresh existence,
This knotted staff suffices me.
What need to shorten so the way?
Along this labyrinth of vales to wander,
Then climb the rocky ramparts yonder,
Wherefrom the fountain flings eternal spray,
Is such delight, my steps would fain delay.
The spring-time stirs within the fragrant birches,
And even the fir-tree feels it now:
Should then our limbs escape its gentle searches?

Mephistopheles

I notice no such thing, I vow!
'T is winter still within my body:
Upon my path I wish for frost and snow.
How sadly rises, incomplete and ruddy,
The moon's lone disk, with its belated glow,
And lights so dimly, that, as one advances,
At every step one strikes a rock or tree!
Let us, then, use a Jack-o'-lantern's glances:
I see one yonder, burning merrily.
Ho, there! my friend! I'll levy thine attendance:
Why waste so vainly thy resplendence?
Be kind enough to light us up the steep!

Will-o'-the-wisp.

My reverence, I hope, will me enable
To curb my temperament unstable;
For zigzag courses we are wont to keep.

Mephistopheles

Indeed? he'd like mankind to imitate!
Now, in the Devil's name, go straight,
Or I'll blow out his being's flickering spark!

WILL-O'-THE-WISP.

You are the master of the house, I mark,
And I shall try to serve you nicely.
But then, reflect: the mountain's magic-mad to-day,
And if a will-o'-the-wisp must guide you on the way,
You must n't take things too precisely.

FAUST, MEPHISTOPHELES, WILL-O'-THE-WISP
(*in alternating song*).

We, it seems, have entered newly
In the sphere of dreams enchanted.
Do thy bidding, guide us truly,
That our feet be forwards planted
In the vast, the desert spaces!

See them swiftly changing places,
Trees on trees beside us trooping,
And the crags above us stooping,
And the rocky snouts, outgrowing,—
Hear I noises? songs that follow?
O'er the stones, the grasses, flowing
Stream and streamlet seek the hollow.
Hear I noises? songs that follow?
Hear I tender love-petitions?
Voices of those heavenly visions?
Sounds of hope, of love undying!
And the echoes, like traditions
Of old days, come faint and hollow.

Hoo-hoo! Shoo-hoo! Nearer hover
Jay and screech-owl, and the plover,—
Are they all awake and crying?
Is 't the salamander pushes,
Bloated-bellied, through the bushes?
And the roots, like serpents twisted,
Through the sand and boulders toiling,
Fright us, weirdest links uncoiling
To entrap us, unresisted:
Living knots and gnarls uncanny
Feel with polypus-antennæ

For the wanderer. Mice are flying,
Thousand-colored, herd-wise hieing
Through the moss and through the heather!
And the fire-flies wink and darkle,
Crowded swarms that soar and sparkle,
And in wildering escort gather!

Tell me, if we still are standing
Or if further we're ascending?
All is turning, whirling, blending,
Trees and rocks with grinning faces,
Wandering lights that spin in mazes,
Still increasing and expanding!

MEPHISTOPHELES.

Grasp my skirt with heart undaunted!
Here a middle-peak is planted,
Whence one seëth, with amaze,
Mammon in the mountain blaze.

FAUST.

How strangely glimmers through the hollows
A dreary light, like that of dawn!
Its exhalation tracks and follows
The deepest gorges, faint and wan.
Here steam, there rolling vapor sweepeth;
Here burns the glow through film and haze:
Now like a tender thread it creepeth,
Now like a fountain leaps and plays.
Here winds away, and in a hundred
Divided veins the valley braids:
There, in a corner pressed and sundered,
Itself detaches, spreads and fades.
Here gush the sparkles incandescent
Like scattered showers of golden sand;—
But, see! in all their height, at present,
The rocky ramparts blazing stand.

MEPHISTOPHELES.

Has not Sir Mammon grandly lighted
His palace for this festal night?

'T is lucky thou hast seen the sight;
The boisterous guests approach that were invited.

FAUST.

How raves the tempest through the air!
With what fierce blows upon my neck 't is beating!

MEPHISTOPHELES.

Under the old ribs of the rock retreating,
Hold fast, lest thou be hurled down the abysses there!
The night with the mist is black;
Hark! how the forests grind and crack!
Frightened, the owlets are scattered:
Hearken! the pillars are shattered,
The evergreen palaces shaking!
Boughs are groaning and breaking,
The tree-trunks terribly thunder,
The roots are twisting asunder!
In frightfully intricate crashing
Each on the other is dashing,
And over the wreck-strewn gorges
The tempest whistles and surges!
Hear'st thou voices higher ringing?
Far away, or nearer singing?
Yes, the mountain's side along,
Sweeps an infuriate glamouring song!

WITCHES (*in chorus*).

The witches ride to the Brocken's top,
The stubble is yellow, and green the crop.
There gathers the crowd for carnival:
Sir Urian sits over all.
And so they go over stone and stock;
The witch she ——s, and ——s the buck.

A VOICE.

Alone, old Baubo's coming now;
She rides upon a farrow-sow.

CHORUS.

Then honor to whom the honor is due!

Dame Baubo first, to lead the crew!
A tough old sow and the mother thereon,
Then follow the witches, every one.

A VOICE.

Which way com'st thou hither?

VOICE.

O'er the Ilsen-stone.
I peeped at the owl in her nest alone:
How she stared and glared!

VOICE.

Betake thee to Hell!
Why so fast and so fell?

VOICE.

She has scored and has flayed me:
See the wounds she has made me!

WITCHES (*chorus*).

The way is wide, the way is long:
See, what a wild and crazy throng!
The broom it scratches, the fork it thrusts,
The child is stifled, the mother bursts.

WIZARDS (*semichorus*).

As doth the snail in shell, we crawl:
Before us go the women all.
When towards the Devil's House we tread,
Woman's a thousand steps ahead.

OTHER SEMICHORUS.

We do not measure with such care:
Woman in thousand steps is there,
But howsoe'er she hasten may,
Man in one leap has cleared the way.

VOICE (*from above*).

Come on, come on, from Rocky Lake!

VOICE (*from below*).

Aloft we'd fain ourselves betake.
We've washed, and are bright as ever you will,
Yet we're eternally sterile still.

BOTH CHORUSES.

The wind is hushed, the star shoots by,
The deary moon forsakes the sky;
The magic notes, like spark on spark,
Drizzle, whistling through the dark.

VOICE (*from below*).

Halt, there! Ho, there!

VOICE (*from above*).

Who calls from the rocky cleft below there?

VOICE (*below*).

Take me, too! take me, too!
I'm climbing now three hundred years,
And yet the summit cannot see:
Among my equals I would be.

BOTH CHORUSES.

Bears the broom and bears the stock,
Bears the fork and bears the buck:
Who cannot raise himself to-night
Is evermore a ruined wight.

HALF-WITCH (*below*).

So long I stumble, ill bestead,
And the others are now so far ahead!
At home I've neither rest nor cheer,
And yet I cannot gain them here.

CHORUS OF WITCHES.

To cheer the witch will salve avail;
A rag will answer for a sail;
Each trough a goodly ship supplies;
He ne'er will fly, who now not flies.

BOTH CHORUSES.

When round the summit whirls our flight
Then lower, and on the ground alight;
And far and wide the heather press
With witchhood's swarms of wantonness!
(*They settle down.*)

MEPHISTOPHELES.

They crowd and push, they roar and clatter!
They whirl and whistle, pull and chatter!
They shine, and spirt, and stink, and burn!
The true witch-element we learn.
Keep close! or we are parted, in our turn.
Where art thou?

FAUST (*in the distance*).
Here!

MEPHISTOPHELES.

What! whirled so far astray!
Then house-right I must use and clear the way.
Make room! Squire Voland comes! Room, gentle
    rabble, room!
Here, Doctor, hold to me: in one jump we'll resume
An easier space, and from the crowd be free:
It's too much, even for the like of me.
Yonder, with special light, there's something shining
    clearer
Within those bushes; I've a mind to see
Come on! we'll slip a little nearer.

FAUST.

Spirit of Contradiction! On! I'll follow straight.
'T is planned most wisely, if I judge aright:
We climb the Brocken's top in the Walpurgis-Night,
That arbitrarily, here, ourselves we isolate.

MEPHISTOPHELES.

But see, what motley flames among the heather!
There is a lively club together:
In smaller circles one is not alone.

FAUST.

Better the summit, I must own:
There fire and whirling smoke I see.
They seek the Evil One in wild confusion:
Many enigmas there might find solution.

MEPHISTOPHELES.

But there enigmas also knotted be.
Leave to the multitude their riot!
Here will we house ourselves in quiet.
It is an old, transmitted trade,
That in the greater world the little worlds are made.
I see stark-nude young witches congregate,
And old ones, veiled and hidden shrewdly:
On my account be kind, nor treat them rudely!
The trouble's small, the fun is great.
I hear the noise of instruments attuning,—
Vile din! yet one must learn to bear the crooning.
Come, come along! It *must* be, I declare!
I'll go ahead and introduce thee there,
Thine obligation newly earning.
That is no little space: what say'st thou, friend?
Look yonder! thou canst scarcely see the end:
A hundred fires along the ranks are burning.
They dance, they chat, they cook, they drink, they
    court:
Now where, just tell me, is there better sport?

FAUST.

Wilt thou, to introduce us to the revel,
Assume the part of wizard or of devil?

MEPHISTOPHELES.

I'm mostly used, 't is true, to go incognito,
But on a gala-day one may his orders show.
The Garter does not deck my suit,
But honored and at home is here the cloven foot.
Perceiv'st thou yonder snail? It cometh, slow and
    steady;
So delicately its feelers pry,
That it hath scented me already:

I cannot here disguise me, if I try.
But come! we'll go from this fire to a newer:
I am the go-between, and thou the wooer.

(*To some, who are sitting around dying embers*:)
Old gentlemen, why at the outskirts? Enter!
I'd praise you if I found you snugly in the centre,
With youth and revel round you like a zone:
You each, at home, are quite enough alone.

GENERAL.

Say, who would put his trust in nations,
Howe'er for them one may have worked and planned?
For with the people, as with women,
Youth always has the upper hand.

MINISTER.

They're now too far from what is just and sage.
I praise the old ones, not unduly:
When we were all-in-all, then, truly,
Then was the real golden age.

PARVENU.

We also were not stupid, either,
And what we should not, often did;
But now all things have from their bases slid,
Just as we meant to hold them fast together.

AUTHOR.

Who, now, a work of moderate sense will read?
Such works are held as antiquate and mossy;
And as regards the younger folk, indeed,
They never yet have been so pert and saucy.

MEPHISTOPHELES
(*who all at once appears very old*).

I feel that men are ripe for Judgment-Day,
Now for the last time I've the witches'-hill ascended:
Since to the lees *my* cask is drained away,
The world's, as well, must soon be ended.

HUCKSTER-WITCH.

Ye gentlemen, don't pass me thus!
Let not the chance neglected be!
Behold my wares attentively:
The stock is rare and various.
And yet, there's nothing I've collected—
No shop, on earth, like this you'll find!—
Which has not, once, sore hurt inflicted
Upon the world, and on mankind.
No dagger's here, that set not blood to flowing;
No cup, that hath not once, within a healthy frame
Poured speedy death, in poison glowing:
No gems, that have not brought a maid to shame;
No sword, but severed ties for the unwary,
Or from behind struck down the adversary.

MEPHISTOPHELES.

Gossip! the times thou badly comprehendest:
What's done has happened—what haps, is done!
'T were better if for novelties thou sendest:
By such alone can we be won.

FAUST.

Let me not lose myself in all this pother!
This is a fair as never was another!

MEPHISTOPHELES.

The whirlpool swirls to get above:
Thou 'rt shoved thyself imagining to shove.

FAUST.

But who is that?

MEPHISTOPHELES.

                Note her especially,
'T is Lilith.

FAUST.

        Who?

MEPHISTOPHELES.

                Adam's first wife is she.
Beware the lure within her lovely tresses,
The splendid sole adornment of her hair!

'When she succeeds therewith a youth to snare,
Not soon again she frees him from her jesses.

FAUST.
Those two, the old one with the young one sitting,
They've danced already more than fitting.

MEPHISTOPHELES.
No rest to-night for young or old!
They start another dance: come now, let us take hold!

FAUST (*dancing with the young witch*).
A lovely dream once came to me;
I then beheld an apple-tree,
And there two fairest apples shone:
They lured me so, I climbed thereon.

THE FAIR ONE.
Apples have been desired by you,
Since first in Paradise they grew;
And I am moved with joy, to know
That such within my garden grow.

MEPHISTOPHELES (*dancing with the old one*).
A dissolute dream once came to me:
Therein I saw a cloven tree,
Which had a —— —— ——;
Yet, —— as 't was, I fancied it.

THE OLD ONE.
I offer here my best salute
Unto the knight with cloven foot!
Let him a —— —— prepare,
If him —— —— —— does not scare.

PROKTOPHANTASMIST.
Accurséd folk! How dare you venture thus?
Had you not, long since, demonstration
That hosts can't stand on ordinary foundation?
And now you even dance, like one of us!

THE FAIR ONE (*dancing*).
Why does he come, then, to our ball?

FAUST (*dancing*).

O, everywhere on him you fall!
When others dance, he weighs the matter:
If he can't every step bechatter,
Then 't is the same as were the step not made;
But if you forwards go, his ire is most displayed.
If you would whirl in regular gyration
As he does in his dull old mill,
He'd show, at any rate, good-will,—
Especially if you heard and heeded his hortation.

PROKTOPHANTASMIST.

You still are here? Nay, 't is a thing unheard!
Vanish, at once! We've said the enlightening word.
The pack of devils by no rules is daunted:
We are so wise, and yet is Tegel haunted.
To clear the folly out, how have I swept and stirred!
'T will ne'er be clean: why, 't is a thing unheard!

THE FAIR ONE.

Then cease to bore us at our ball!

PROKTOPHANTASMIST.

I tell you, spirits, to your face,
I give to spirit-despotism no place;
My spirit cannot practise it at all.

FAUST.
(*The dance continues.*)

Naught will succeed, I see, amid such revels;
Yet something from a tour I always save,
And hope, before my last step to the grave,
To overcome the poets and the devils.

MEPHISTOPHELES.

He now will seat him in the nearest puddle;
The solace this, whereof he's most assured:
And when upon his rump the leeches hang and fuddle,
He'll be of spirits and of Spirit cured.
(*To* FAUST, *who has left the dance*:)

Wherefore forsaketh thou the lovely maiden,
That in the dance so sweetly sang?

FAUST.

Ah! in the midst of it there sprang
A red mouse from her mouth—sufficient reason!

MEPHISTOPHELES.

That's nothing! One must not so squeamish be;
So the mouse was not gray, enough for thee.
Who'd think of that in love's selected season?

FAUST.

Then saw I—

MEPHISTOPHELES.

What?

FAUST.

Mephisto, seest thou there,
Alone and far, a girl most pale and fair?
She falters on, her way scarce knowing,
As if with fettered feet that stay her going.
I must confess, it seems to me
As if my kindly Margaret were she.

MEPHISTOPHELES.

Let the thing be! All thence have evil drawn:
It is a magic shape, a lifeless eidolon.
Such to encounter is not good:
Their blank, set stare benumbs the human blood,
And one is almost turned to stone.
Medusa's tale to thee is known.

FAUST.

Forsooth, the eyes they are of one whom, dying,
No hand with loving pressure closed;
That is the breast whereon I once was lying,—
The body sweet, beside which I reposed!

MEPHISTOPHELES.

'T is magic all, thou fool, seduced so easily!
Unto each man his love she seems to be.

FAUST.

The woe, the rapture, so ensnare me,
That from her gaze I cannot tear me!
And, strange! around her fairest throat
A single scarlet band is gleaming,
No broader than a knife-blade seeming!

MEPHISTOPHELES.

Quite right! The mark I also note.
Her head beneath her arm she'll sometimes carry;
'T was Perseus lopped it, her old adversary.
Thou crav'st the same illusion still!
Come, let us mount this little hill;
The Prater shows no livelier stir,
And, if they've not bewitched my sense,
I verily see a theatre.
What's going on?

SERVIBILIS.

       'T will shortly recommence:
A new performance—'t is the last of seven.
To give that number is the custom here:
'T was by a Dilettante written,
And Dilettanti in the parts appear.
That now I vanish, pardon, I entreat you!
As Dilettante I the curtain raise.

MEPHISTOPHELES.

When I upon the Blocksberg meet you,
I find it good: for that's your proper place.

XXII.

WALPURGIS-NIGHT'S DREAM.

OBERON AND TITANIA'S GOLDEN WEDDING.

INTERMEZZO.

MANAGER.

SONS of Mieding, rest to-day!
Needless your machinery:

Misty vale and mountain gray,
That is all the scenery.

HERALD.

That the wedding golden be,
Must fifty years be rounded:
But *the Golden* give to me,
When the strife's compounded.

OBERON.

Spirits, if you're here, be seen—
Show yourselves, delighted!
Fairy king and fairy queen,
They are newly plighted.

PUCK.

Cometh Puck, and, light of limb,
Whisks and whirls in measure:
Come a hundred after him,
To share with him the pleasure.

ARIEL.

Ariel's song is heavenly-pure,
His tones are sweet and rare ones:
Though ugly faces he allure,
Yet he allures the fair ones.

OBERON.

Spouses, who would fain agree,
Learn how we were mated!
If your pairs would loving be,
First be separated!

TITANIA.

If her whims the wife control,
And the man berate her,
Take him to the Northern Pole,
And her to the Equator!

ORCHESTRA. TUTTI.
Fortissimo.
Snout of fly, mosquito-bill,

And kin of all conditions,
Frog in grass, and cricket-trill,—
These are the musicians!

SOLO.
See the bagpipe on our track!
'T is the soap-blown bubble:
Hear the *schnecke-schnicke-schnack*
Through his nostrils double!

SPIRIT, JUST GROWING INTO FORM.
Spider's foot and paunch of toad,
And little wings—we know 'em!
A little creature 't will not be,
But yet, a little poem.

A LITTLE COUPLE.
Little step and lofty leap
Through honey-dew and fragrance:
You'll never mount the airy steep
With all your tripping vagrance.

INQUISITIVE TRAVELLER.
Is 't but masquerading play?
See I with precision?
Oberon, the beauteous fay,
Meets, to-night, my vision!

ORTHODOX.
Not a claw, no tail I see!
And yet, beyond a cavil,
Like "the Gods of Greece," must he
Also be a devil.

NORTHERN ARTIST.
I only seize, with sketchy air,
Some outlines of the tourney;
Yet I betimes myself prepare
For my Italian journey.

PURIST.
My bad luck brings me here, alas!
How roars the orgy louder!

And of the witches in the mass,
But only two wear powder.

YOUNG WITCH.

Powder becomes, like petticoat,
A gray and wrinkled noddy;
So I sit naked on my goat,
And show a strapping body.

MATRON.

We've too much tact and policy
To rate with gibes a scolder;
Yet, young and tender though you be,
I hope to see you moulder.

LEADER OF THE BAND.

Fly-snout and mosquito-bill,
Don't swarm so round the Naked!
Frog in grass and cricket-trill,
Observe the time, and make it!

WEATHERCOCK (*towards one side*).

Society to one's desire!
Brides only, and the sweetest!
And bachelors of youth and fire,
And prospects the completest!

WEATHERCOCK (*towards the other side*).

And if the Earth don't open now
To swallow up each ranter,
Why, then will I myself, I vow,
Jump into hell instanter!

XENIES.

Us as little insects see!
With sharpest nippers flitting,
That our Papa Satan we
May honor as is fitting.

HENNINGS.

How, in crowds together massed,

They are jesting, shameless!
They will even say, at last,
That their hearts are blameless.

MUSAGETES.

Among this witches' revelry
His way one gladly loses;
And, truly, it would easier be
Than to command the Muses.

CI-DEVANT GENIUS OF THE AGE.

The proper folks one's talents laud:
Come on, and none shall pass us!
The Blocksberg has a summit broad,
Like Germany's Parnassus.

INQUISITIVE TRAVELLER.

Say, who's the stiff and pompous **man?**
He walks with haughty paces:
He snuffles all he snuffle can:
"He scents the Jesuits' traces."

CRANE.

Both clear and muddy streams, **for me**
Are good to fish and sport in:
And thus the pious man you see
With even devils consorting.

WORLDLING.

Yes, for the pious, I suspect,
All instruments are fitting;
And on the Blocksberg they **erect**
Full many a place of meeting.

DANCER.

A newer chorus now succeeds!
I hear the distant drumming.
"Don't be disturbed! 't is, in the **reeds,**
The bittern's changeless booming."

DANCING-MASTER.

How each his legs in nimble trip

Lifts up, and makes a clearance!
The crooked jump, the heavy skip,
Nor care for the appearance.

GOOD FELLOW.

The rabble by such hate are held,
To maim and slay delights them:
As Orpheus' lyre the brutes compelled,
The bagpipe here unites them.

DOGMATIST.

I'll not be led by any lure
Of doubts or critic-cavils:
The Devil must be something, sure,—
Or how should there be devils?

IDEALIST.

This once, the fancy wrought in me
Is really too despotic:
Forsooth, if I am all I see,
I must be idiotic!

REALIST.

This racking fuss on every hand,
It gives me great vexation;
And, for the first time, here I stand
On insecure foundation.

SUPERNATURALIST.

With much delight I see the play,
And rant to these their merits,
Since from the devils I also may
Infer the better spirits.

SCEPTIC.

The flame they follow, on and on,
And think they're near the treasure:
But *Devil* rhymes with *Doubt* alone,
So I am here with pleasure.

LEADER OF THE BAND.

Frog in green, and cricket-trill,

Such dilettants!—perdition!
Fly-snout and mosquito-bill,—
Each one's a fine musician!

THE ADROIT.

Sanssouci, we call the clan
Of merry creatures so, then;
Go a-foot no more we can
And on our heads we go, then.

THE AWKWARD.

Once many a bit we sponged; but now,
God help us! that is done with:
Our shoes are all danced out, we trow,
We've but naked soles to run with.

WILL-O'-THE-WISPS.

From the marshes we appear,
Where we originated;
Yet in the ranks, at once, we're here
As glittering gallants rated.

SHOOTING-STAR.

Darting hither from the sky,
In star and fire light shooting,
Cross-wise now in grass I lie:
Who'll help me to my footing?

THE HEAVY FELLOWS.

Room! and round about us, room!
Trodden are the grasses:
Spirits also, spirits come,
And they are bulky masses.

PUCK.

Enter not so stall-fed quite,
Like elephant-calves about one!
And the heaviest weight to-night
Be Puck, himself, the stout one!

ARIEL.

If loving Nature at your back,

Or Mind, the wing uncloses,
Follow up my airy track
To the mount of roses!

ORCHESTRA.
Pianissimo.

Cloud and trailing mist o'erhead
Are now illuminated:
Air in leaves, and wind in reed,
And all is dissipated.

XXIII.

DREARY DAY.

A FIELD.

FAUST. MEPHISTOPHELES.

FAUST.

IN misery! In despair! Long wretchedly astray on the face of the earth, and now imprisoned! That gracious, ill-starred creature shut in a dungeon as a criminal, and given up to fearful torments! To this has it come! to this!—Treacherous, contemptible spirit, and thou hast concealed it from me!—Stand, then—stand! Roll the devilish eyes wrathfully in thy head! Stand and defy me with thine intolerable presence! Imprisoned! In irretrievable misery! Delivered up to evil spirits, and to condemning, unfeeling Man! And thou hast lulled me, meanwhile, with the most insipid dissipations, hast concealed from me her increasing wretchedness, and suffered her to go helplessly to ruin!

MEPHISTOPHELES.
She is not the first.

FAUST.
Dog! Abominable monster! Transform him, thou Infinite Spirit! transform the reptile again into his dog-shape, in which it pleased him often at night to

scamper on before me, to roll himself at the feet of the unsuspecting wanderer, and hang upon his shoulders when he fell! Transform him again into his favorite likeness, that he may crawl upon his belly in the dust before me,—that I may trample him, the outlawed, under foot! Not the first! O woe! woe which no human soul can grasp, that more than one being should sink into the depths of this misery,—that the first, in its writhing death-agony under the eyes of the Eternal Forgiver, did not expiate the guilt of all others! The misery of this single one pierces to the very marrow of my life; and thou art calmly grinning at the fate of thousands!

MEPHISTOPHELES.

Now we are already again at the end of our wits, where the understanding of you men runs wild. Why didst thou enter into fellowship with us, if thou canst not carry it out? Wilt fly, and art not secure against dizziness? Did we thrust ourselves upon thee, or thou thyself upon us?

FAUST.

Gnash not thus thy devouring teeth at me! It fills me with horrible disgust. Mighty, glorious Spirit, who hast vouchsafed to me Thine apparition, who knowest my heart and my soul, why fetter me to the felon-comrade, who feeds on mischief and gluts himself with ruin?

MEPHISTOPHELES.

Hast thou done?

FAUST.

Rescue her, or woe to thee! The fearfullest curse be upon thee for thousands of ages!

MEPHISTOPHELES.

I cannot loosen the bonds of the Avenger, nor undo his bolts. Rescue her? Who was it that plunged her into ruin? I, or thou?

(FAUST *looks around wildly*.)

Wilt thou grasp the thunder? Well, that it has not

been given to you, miserable mortals! To crush to pieces the innocent respondent—that is the tyrant-fashion of relieving one's self in embarrassments.

FAUST.

Take me thither! She shall be free!

MEPHISTOPHELES.

And the danger to which thou wilt expose thyself? Know that the guilt of blood, from thy hand, still lies upon the town! Avenging spirits hover over the spot where the victim fell, and lie in wait for the returning murderer.

FAUST.

That, too, from thee? Murder and death of a world upon thee, monster! Take me thither, I say, and liberate her!

MEPHISTOPHELES.

I will convey thee there; and hear, what I can do! Have I all the power in Heaven and on Earth? I will becloud the jailer's senses: get possession of the key, and lead her forth with human hand! I will keep watch: the magic steeds are ready, I will carry you off. So much is in my power.

FAUST.

Up and away!

XXIV.

NIGHT.

OPEN FIELD.

(FAUST *and* MEPHISTOPHELES *speeding onward on black horses.*)

FAUST.

W HAT weave they there round the raven-stone?

MEPHISTOPHELES.

I know not what they are brewing and doing.

FAUST.

Soaring up, sweeping down, bowing and bending!

MEPHISTOPHELES.

A witches'-guild.

FAUST.

They scatter, devote and doom!

MEPHISTOPHELES.

On! on!

XXV.

DUNGEON.

FAUST

(*with a bunch of keys and a lamp, before an iron door*).

A SHUDDER, long unfelt, comes o'er me;
Mankind's collected woe o'erwhelms me, here.
She dwells within the dark, damp walls before me,
And all her crime was a delusion dear!
What! I delay to free her?
I dread, once again to see her?
On! my shrinking but lingers Death more near.
(*He grasps the lock: the sound of singing is heard
inside.*)

> *My mother, the harlot,*
> *Who put me to death;*
> *My father, the varlet,*
> *Who eaten me hath!*
> *Little sister, so good,*
> *Laid my bones in the wood,*
> *In the damp moss and clay:*
> *Then was I a beautiful bird o' the wood;*
> *Fly away! Fly away!*

FAUST (*unlocking*).

She does not dream her lover listens near;
That he the rattling chain, the rustling straw, can hear.

(*He enters.*)

MARGARET *(hiding herself on the pallet).*
Woe! woe!
They come. O death of bitterness!

FAUST *(whispering).*
Hush! hush! The hour is come that frees thee.

MARGARET *(throwing herself before him).*
Art thou a man, then pity my distress!

FAUST.
Thy cries will wake the guards, and they will seize
    thee!
    (He takes hold of the fetters to unlock them.)

MARGARET *(on her knees).*
Who, headsman! unto thee such power
Over me could give?
Thou 'rt come for me at midnight-hour:
Have mercy on me, let me live!
Is 't not soon enough when morning chime has rung?
    (She rises.)
And I am yet so young, so young!
And now Death comes, and ruin!
I, too, was fair, and that was my undoing.
My love was near, but now he's far;
Torn lies the wreath, scattered the blossoms are.
Seize me not thus so violently!
Spare me! What have I done to thee?
Let me not vainly entreat thee!
I never chanced, in all my days, to meet thee!

FAUST.
Shall I outlive this misery?

MARGARET.
Now am I wholly in thy might.
But let me suckle, first, my baby!
I blissed it all this livelong night;
They took 't away, to vex me, maybe,
And now they say I killed the child outright.

And never shall I be glad again.
They sing songs about me! 't is bad of the folk to do it!
There's an old story has the same refrain;
Who bade them so construe it?

FAUST (*falling upon his knees*).
Here lieth one who loves thee ever,
The thraldom of thy woe to sever.

MARGARET (*flinging herself beside him*).
O let us kneel, and call the Saints to hide us!
Under the steps beside us,
The threshold under,
Hell heaves in thunder!
The Evil One
With terrible wrath
Seeketh a path
His prey to discover!

FAUST (*aloud*).
Margaret! Margaret!

MARGARET (*attentively listening*).
That was the voice of my lover!
(*She springs to her feet: the fetters fall off.*)
Where is he? I heard him call me.
I am free! No one shall enthrall me.
To his neck will I fly,
On his bosom lie!
On the threshold he stood, and *Margaret!* calling.
Midst of Hell's howling and noises appalling,
Midst of the wrathful, infernal derision,
I knew the sweet sound of the voice of the vision!

FAUST.
'T is I!

MARGARET.
'T is thou! O, say it once again!
(*Clasping him.*)
'T is he! 't is he! Where now is all my pain?
The anguish of the dungeon, and the chain?

'T is thou! Thou comest to save me,
And I am saved!—
Again the street I see
Where first I looked on thee;
And the garden, brightly blooming,
Where I and Martha wait thy coming.

FAUST (*struggling to leave*).
Come! Come with me!

MARGARET.
Delay, now!
So fain I stay, when thou delayest!
(*Caressing him.*)

FAUST.
Away, now!
If longer here thou stayest,
We shall be made to dearly rue it.

MARGARET.
Kiss me!—canst no longer do it?
My friend, so short a time thou 'rt missing,
And hast unlearned thy kissing?
Why is my heart so anxious, on thy breast?
Where once a heaven thy glances did create me,
A heaven thy loving words expressed,
And thou didst kiss, as thou wouldst suffocate me—
Kiss me!
Or I'll kiss thee!
(*She embraces him.*)
Ah, woe! thy lips are chill,
And still.
How changed in fashion
Thy passion!
Who has done me this ill?
(*She turns away from him.*)

FAUST.
Come, follow me! My darling, be more bold:
I'll clasp thee, soon, with warmth a thousand-fold;
But follow now! 'T is all I beg of thee.

MARGARET (*turning to him*).
And is it thou? Thou, surely, certainly?

FAUST.

'T is I! Come on!

MARGARET.

Thou wilt unloose my chain,
And in thy lap wilt take me once again.
How comes it that thou dost not shrink from me?—
Say, dost thou know, my friend, whom thou mak'st
 free?

FAUST.

Come! come! The night already vanisheth.

MARGARET.

My mother have I put to death;
I've drowned the baby born to thee.
Was it not given to thee and me?
Thee, too!—'T is thou! It scarcely true doth seem—
Give me thy hand! 'T is not a dream!
Thy dear, dear hand!—But, ah, 't is wet!
Why, wipe it off! Methinks that yet
There's blood thereon.
Ah, God! what hast thou done?
Nay, sheathe thy sword at last!
Do not affray me!

FAUST.

O, let the past be past!
Thy words will slay me!

MARGARET.

No, no! Thou must outlive us.
Now I'll tell thee the graves to give us:
Thou must begin to-morrow
The work of sorrow!
The best place give to my mother,
Then close at her side my brother,
And me a little away,

But not too very far, I pray!
And here, on my right breast, my baby lay!
Nobody else will lie beside me!—
Ah, within thine arms to hide me,
That was a sweet and a gracious bliss,
But no more, no more can I attain it!
I would force myself on thee and constrain it,
And it seems thou repellest my kiss:
And yet 't is thou, so good, so kind to see!

FAUST.

If thou feel'st it is I, then come with me!

MARGARET.

Out yonder?

FAUST.

To freedom.

MARGARET.

If the grave is there,
Death lying in wait, then come!
From here to eternal rest:
No further step—no, no!
Thou goest away! O Henry, if I could go!

FAUST.

Thou canst! Just will it! Open stands the door.

MARGARET.

I dare not go: there's no hope any more.
Why should I fly? They'll still my steps waylay!
It is so wretched, forced to beg my living,
And a bad conscience sharper misery giving!
It is so wretched, to be strange, forsaken,
And I'd still be followed and taken!

FAUST.

I'll stay with thee.

MARGARET.

Be quick! Be quick!
Save thy perishing child!
Away! Follow the ridge

Up by the brook,
Over the bridge,
Into the wood,
To the left, where the plank is placed
In the pool!
Seize it in haste!
'T is trying to rise,
'T is struggling still!
Save it!   Save it!

FAUST.

Recall thy wandering will!
One step, and thou art free at last!

MARGARET.

If the mountain we had only passed!
There sits my mother upon a stone,—
I feel an icy shiver!
There sits my mother upon a stone,
And her head is wagging ever.
She beckons, she nods not, her heavy head falls o'er;
She slept so long that she wakes no more.
She slept, while we were caressing:
Ah, those were the days of blessing!

FAUST.

Here words and prayers are nothing worth;
I'll venture, then, to bear thee forth.

MARGARET.

No—let me go!   I'll suffer no force!
Grasp me not so murderously!
I've done, else, all things for the love of thee.

FAUST.

The day dawns: Dearest!   Dearest!

MARGARET.

Day? Yes, the day comes,—the last day breaks for me!
My wedding-day it was to be!
Tell no one thou hast been with Margaret!

Woe for my garland! The chances
Are over—'t is all in vain!
We shall meet once again,
But not at the dances!
The crowd is thronging, no word is spoken:
The square below
And the streets overflow:
The death-bell tolls, the wand is broken.
I am seized, and bound, and delivered—
Shoved to the block—they give the sign!
Now over each neck has quivered
The blade that is quivering over mine.
Dumb lies the world like the grave!

FAUST.

O had I ne'er been born!

MEPHISTOPHELES (*appears outside*).

Off! or you're lost ere morn.
Useless talking, delaying and praying!
My horses are neighing:
The morning twilight is near.

MARGARET.

What rises up from the threshold here?
He! he! suffer him not!
What does he want in this holy spot?
He seeks me!

FAUST.

Thou shalt live.

MARGARET.

Judgment of God! myself to thee I give.

MEPHISTOPHELES (*to* FAUST).

Come! or I'll leave her in the lurch, and thee!

MARGARET.

Thine am I, Father! rescue me!
Ye angels, holy cohorts, guard me,

Camp around, and from evil ward me!
Henry! I shudder to think of thee.

MEPHISTOPHELES.

She is judged!

VOICE (*from above*).
She is saved!

MEPHISTOPHELES (*to* FAUST).
Hither to me!

(*He disappears with* FAUST.)

VOICE (*from within, dying away*).
Henry! Henry!

CONTENTS OF THE
SECOND PART OF THE TRAGEDY

FAUST.

ACT IV.

ACT V.

SECOND PART OF THE TRAGEDY

IN FIVE ACTS.

ACT I.

I.

A PLEASANT LANDSCAPE.

TWILIGHT.

FAUST, *bedded on flowery turf, fatigued, restless, endeavoring to sleep. Circle of hovering spirits in motion: graceful, diminutive figures.*

ARIEL.
(Chant, accompanied by Æolian harps.)

WHEN the Spring returns serener
　　Raining blossoms over all;
When the fields with blessing greener
On the earth-born children call;
Then the craft of elves propitious
Hastes to help where help it can:
Be he holy, be he vicious,
Pity they the luckless man.

Who round this head in airy circles hover,
Yourselves in guise of noble Elves discover!
The fierce convulsions of his heart compose;
Remove the burning barbs of his remorses,
And cleanse his being from the suffered woes!
Four pauses makes the Night upon her courses,
And now, delay not, let them kindly close!
First on the coolest pillow let him slumber,
Then sprinkle him with Lethe's drowsy spray!
His limbs no more shall cramps and chills encumber,
When sleep has made him strong to meet the day.
Perform, ye Elves, your fairest rite:
Restore him to the holy Light!

CHORUS

CHORUS

(*singly, by two or more, alternately and collectively*).

When around the green-girt meadow
Balm the tepid winds exhale,
Then in fragrance and in shadow
Twilight spreads her misty veil:
Whispers peace in accepts cheery,
Rocks the heart in childhood's play,
And upon these eyelids weary
Shuts the golden gates of Day.

Now the Night already darkles,
Holy star succeeds to star;
Dazzling lights and fainter sparkles
Glimmer near and gleam afar:
Glimmer here, the lake reflecting,
Gleam in cloudless dark aboon;
While, the bliss of rest protecting,
Reigns in pomp the perfect moon.

Now the Hours are cancelled for thee,
Pain and bliss have fled away:
Thou art whole: let faith restore thee!
Trust the new, the rising Day!
Vales grow green, and hills are lifting
Through the shadow-rest of morn;
And in waves of silver, drifting
On to harvest, rolls the corn.

Wouldst thou win desires unbounded,
Yonder see the glory burn!
Lightly is thy life surrounded—
Sleep's a shell, to break and spurn!
When the crowd sways, unbelieving,
Show the daring will that warms!
He is crowned with all achieving,
Who perceives and then performs.

(*A tremendous tumult announces the approach of the
Sun.*)

ARIEL.

Hearken! Hark!—the Hours careering!
Sounding loud to spirit-hearing,
See the new-born Day appearing!
Rocky portals jarring shatter,
Phœbus' wheels in rolling clatter,
With a crash the Light draws near!
Pealing rays and trumpet-blazes,—
Eye is blinded, ear amazes:
The Unheard can no one hear!
Slip within each blossom-bell,
Deeper, deeper, there to dwell,—
In the rocks, beneath the leaf!
If it strikes you, you are deaf.

FAUST.

Life's pulses now with fresher force awaken
To greet the mild ethereal twilight o'er me;
This night, thou, Earth! hast also stood unshaken,
And now thou breathest new-refreshed before me,
And now beginnest, all thy gladness granting,
A vigorous resolution to restore me,
To seek that highest life for which I'm panting.—
The world unfolded lies in twilight glimmer,
A thousand voices in the grove are chanting;
Vale in, vale out, the misty streaks grow dimmer;
The deeps with heavenly light are penetrated;
The boughs, refreshed, lift up their leafy shimmer
From gulfs of air where sleepily they waited;
Color on color from the background cleareth,
Where flower and leaf with trembling pearls are
      freighted
And all around a Paradise appeareth.
Look up!—The mountain summits, grand, supernal,
Herald, e'en now, the solemn hour that neareth;
They earliest enjoy the light eternal
That later sinks, till here below we find it.
Now to the Alpine meadows, sloping vernal,
A newer beam descends ere we divined it,
And step by step unto the base hath bounded:
The sun comes forth! Alas, already blinded,
I turn away, with eyesight pierced and wounded!

'T is thus, when, unto yearning hope's endeavor,
Its highest wish on sweet attainment grounded,
The portals of fulfilment widely sever:
But if there burst from those eternal spaces
A flood of flame, we stand confounded ever;
For Life's pure torch we sought the shining traces,
And seas of fire—and what a fire!—surprise us.
Is 't Love? Is 't Hate? that burningly embraces,
And that with pain and joy alternate tries us?
So that, our glances once more earthward throwing,
We seek in youthful drapery to disguise us.

Behind me, therefore, let the sun be glowing!
The cataract between the crags deep-riven,
I thus behold with rapture ever-growing.
From plunge to plunge in thousand streams 't is given,
And yet a thousand, to the valleys shaded,
While foam and spray in air are whirled and driven.
Yet how superb, across the tumult braided,
The painted rainbow's changeful life is bending,
Now clearly drawn, dissolving now and faded,
And evermore the showers of dew descending!
Of human striving there's no symbol fuller:
Consider, and 't is easy comprehending—
Life is not light, but the refracted color.

II.

THE EMPEROR'S CASTLE.

HALL OF THE THRONE.

Council of State Awaiting the Emperor.

Trumpets.

Enter Court Retainers *of all kinds, splendidly
dressed. The* Emperor *advances to the throne: the*
Astrologer *on his right hand.*

EMPEROR.

I GREET you, Well-beloved and Trusty,
Assembled here from far and wide!
I see the Wise Man at my side;
But where's the Fool, his rival lusty?

SQUIRE.

Behind thy mantle's flowing swell
Suddenly on the stairs he fell:
They bore away the weight of fat;
If dead, or drunk? none knoweth that.

SECOND SQUIRE.

As quick as thought, through all the pother
Him to replace there came another,
Adorned and prinked with wondrous art,
Yet so grotesque that all men start.
The guards their halberds cross-wise hold
To bar him—them he thrusts apart:
Lo! here he comes, the Fool so bold!

MEPHISTOPHELES (*kneeling before the throne*).

What's cursed and welcomely expected?
What is desired, yet always chased?
What evermore with care protected?
What is accused, condemned, disgraced?
To whom dar'st thou not give a hearing?
Whose name hears each man willingly?
What is 't, before thy throne appearing?
What keeps itself away from thee?

EMPEROR.

Spare us thy words! the time is pressing;
This is no place for riddle-guessing:
These gentlemen such things explain.
Solve it thyself!—to hear I'm fain.
My old Fool went, I fear, an endless distance;
Take thou his place, come here and lend assistance!

(MEPHISTOPHELES *goes up and stations himself on the*
EMPEROR'S *left hand.*)

MURMURS OF THE CROWD.

Another fool—for worries new!—
Whence came he?—how did he get through?
The old one fell—he's walked his path.—
He was a barrel—this, a lath!

EMPEROR.

So now, my Well-beloved and Loyal,
Be welcome all, from near and far!
You meet beneath a fortunate star;
Welfare and luck are now the aspects royal.
But tell me why, in days so fair,
When we've withdrawn ourselves from care,
And beards of beauty masquerading wear,—
When gay delights for us are waiting,
Why should we plague ourselves, deliberating?
Yet, since the task you think we cannot shun,
'T is settled then, so be it done!

CHANCELLOR.

The highest virtue, like a halo-zone
Circles the Emporer's head; and he alone
Is worthy validly to exercise it.
'T is Justice!—all men love and prize it,
None can forego, but all require and want it:
The people look to him, that he should grant it.
But, ah! what help can human wit impart,
Or readiness of hand, or kindly heart,
When lies the State, as if in fever fretting,
And brooded Evil evil is begetting?
Who looks abroad from off this height supreme
Throughout the realm, 't is like a weary dream,
Where one deformity another mouldeth,
Where lawlessness itself by law upholdeth,
And 't is an age of Error that unfoldeth!

One plunders flocks, a woman one,
Cup, cross, and candlestick from altar,
And then to boast it does not palter,
Of limb or life nowise undone.
To Court behold the plaintiffs urging,
Where puffs the judge on cushions warm,
And swells, meanwhile, with fury surging,
Rebellion's fast-increasing storm!
His easy way through crime is broken,
Who his accomplices selects;
And "Guilty!" hears one only spoken

Where Innocence itself protects.
They all pull down what they should care for,—
Destroy their weal, in self-despite:
How can the sense develop, therefore,
Which, only, leads us to the Right?
At last, the man of good intent
To flatterer and briber bendeth;
The judge, debarred from punishment,
Mates with the felon, ere he endeth.
I've painted black, but denser screen
I'd rather draw before the scene.

                (Pause.)

Here measures cannot be evaded;
When all offend, and none are aided,
His Majesty a victim stands.

          GENERAL-IN-CHIEF.

In these wild days, how discords thicken!
Each strikes and in return is stricken,
And they are deaf to all commands.
The burgher in his fortifications,
The knight upon his rocky nest,
Have sworn to worry out our patience
And keep their strength with stubborn crest.
The mercenaries, no whit better,
Impatiently demand their pay,
And, if we were not still their debtor,
They'd start forthwith and march away.
Let one forbid what all would practise
And in a hornet's nest he stands:
The realm which they should guard, the fact is,
'T is devastated by their hands.
They give the reign to wild disorder,
And half the world is wasted now;
There still are kings beyond our border,
But none thinks it concerns him anyhow.

          TREASURER.

Trust allies, and we soon shall rue us!
The subsidies they promised to us—
Like water in leaky pipes—don't come.

Then, Sire, in all thy states extended
To whom hath now the rule descended?
Where'er one goes, a new lord is at home,
And hopes to live in independence;
He takes his course and we look on:
Such rights we've given to our attendants
That all *our* right to anything is gone.
On parties, too, whate'er the name be,
Our trust, to-day, is far from great;
Though loud their praise or fierce their blame be,
Indifferent is their love and hate.
The Ghibellines and Guelfs from labor
Are resting—both laid on the shelf.
Who, therefore, now will help his neighbor?
Each has enough, to help himself.
The gate of gold no more unlatches,
And each one gathers, digs, and scratches,
While our strong-box is void indeed.

LORD HIGH STEWARD.

What evil I, as well, am having!
We're always trying to be saving,
And ever greater is our need:
Thus daily grows this task of mine.
The cooks have all they want at present,—
Wild-boar and deer, and hare and pheasant,
Duck, peacock, turkey, goose, and chicken:
These, paid in kind, are certain picking,
And do not seriously decline;
Yet, after all, we're short of wine.
Where casks on casks were once our cellars filling,
Rare vintages of flavors finely thrilling,
The noble lords' eternal swilling
Has drained them off, till not a drop appears.
The City Council, too, must tap their liquor;
They drink from mug, and jug, and beaker,
Till no one longer sees or hears.
'T is I must pay for all the dances;
The Jew will have me, past all chances;
His notes of hand and his advances
Will soon eat up the coming years.

Before they're fat the swine are taken;
Pawned is the pillow, ere one waken,
The bread is eaten ere the board it sees.

EMPEROR
(*after some reflection, to* MEPHISTOPHELES).
Say, Fool, canst thou not add a want to these?

MEPHISTOPHELES.
I? Not at all! I see the circling splendor—
Thyself, and thine! Should one his trust surrender,
Where Majesty thus unopposed commands,
Where ready power the hostile force disbands,
Where loyal wills, through understanding strong,
And mixed activities, around thee throng?
What powers for evil could one see combining,—
For darkness, where such brilliant stars are shining?

MURMURS.
He is a scamp—who comprehends.—
He lies his way—until it ends.—
I know it now—what's in his mind.—
What then?—A project lurks behind!

MEPHISTOPHELES.
Where, in this world, doth not some lack appear?
Here this, there that,—but money's lacking here.
True, from the floor you can't at once collect it,
But, deepliest hidden, wisdom may detect it.
In veins of mountains, under building-bases,
Coined and uncoined, there's gold in many places:
And ask you who shall bring it to the light?
A man endowed with Mind's and Nature's might.

CHANCELLOR.
Nature and Mind—to Christians we don't speak so,
Thence to burn Atheists we seek so,
For such discourses very dangerous be.
Nature is Sin, and Mind is Devil:
Doubt they beget in shameless revel,
Their hybrid in deformity.

Not so with us!—Two only races
Have in the Empire kept their places,
And prop the throne with worthy weight.
The Saints and Knights are they: together
They breast each spell of thunder-weather,
And take for pay the Church and State.
The vulgar minds that breed confusion
Are met with an opposing hand:
They're wizards!—heretics! Delusion
Through them will ruin town and land.
And these will you, with brazen juggle,
Within this high assembly smuggle?
For hearts corrupt you scheme and struggle;
The Fool's rear kin are all the band.

MEPHISTOPHELES.

By that, I know the learned lord you are!
What you don't touch, is lying leagues afar;
What you don't grasp, is wholly lost to you;
What you don't reckon, think you, can't be true;
What you don't weigh, it has no weight, alas!
What you don't coin, you're sure it will not pass.

EMPEROR.

Therewith to help our needs you naught determine.
What wilt thou, here, with such a Lenten sermon?
I'm tired of the eternal If and How:
Money we want: good, then, procure it now!

MEPHISTOPHELES.

I'll furnish what you wish, and more: 't is, true,
A light task, but light things are hard to do.
The gold's on hand,—yet, skilfully to win it,
That is the art: who knows how to begin it?
Consider only, in those days of blood
When o'er the Empire poured a human flood,
How many men, such deadly terror steeled them,
Took their best goods, and here and there concealed
    them!
'T was so beneath the mighty Roman sway,
And ever so repeated, till our day.

All that was buried in the earth, to save it:
The Emperor owns the earth, and he should have it.

TREASURER.

Now, for a Fool, his words are rather bright:
That is indeed the old Imperial right.

CHANCELLOR.

Satan has laid his golden snares, to try us;
Such things as these are neither right nor pious.

LORD HIGH STEWARD.

Let him but bring his gifts to Court, and share them,
And if things were a little wrong, I'd bear them!

GENERAL-IN-CHIEF.

The Fool is shrewd, to promise each his needs;
Whence it may come the soldier never heeds.

MEPHISTOPHELES.

And should you think, perchance, I overreach you,
Here's the Astrologer—ask him to teach you!
The spheres of Hour and House are in his ken:
What are the heavenly aspects?—tell us, then!

MURMURS.

Two rogues are they,—in league they've grown,
Dreamer and Fool—so near the throne!
The song is old—and flatly sung.—
The Fool he prompts—the Wise Man's tongue!

ASTROLOGER

(*speaks*: MEPHISTOPHELES *prompts*).

The Sun himself is gold of purest ray;
The herald, Mercury, serve for love and pay;
Dame Venus has bewitched you all, for she,
Early and late, looks on you lovingly;
Chaste Luna has her whims, no two alike;
Mars threatens you, although he may not strike,
And Jupiter is still the splendid star.
Saturn is great, though seeming small and far:

As metal, him we don't much venerate,
Of value slight, though heavy in his weight.
Now, when of Sol and Luna union's born
Silver with gold,—then is the world made glad:
All else, with them, is easy to attain,—
Palaces, gardens, cheeks of rosy stain;
And these procures this highly learned man,
Who that can do which none of us e'er can.

EMPEROR.
Two meanings in his words I find,
And yet they don't convince my mind.

MURMURS.
Why tell us that?—stuff stale and flat!
'T is quackery!—'t is chemistry!
I've heard the strain—and hoped in vain,—
And though it come—'t is all a hum.

MEPHISTOPHELES.
They stand around, amazed, unknowing;
They do not trust the treasure-spell;
One dreams of mandrake, nightly growing,
The other of the dog of Hell.
Why, then, should one suspect bewitching,
And why the other jest and prate,
When in their feet, they, too, shall feel the itching,
When they shall walk with tottering gait?

All feel the secret operation
Of Nature's ever-ruling might,
And from the bases of Creation
A living track winds up to light.
In every limb when something twitches
In any place uncanny, old,—
Decide at once, and dig for riches!
There lies the fiddler, there the gold!

MURMURS.
It hangs like lead my feet about.—
I've cramp i' the arm—but that is gout.—

I've tickling in the greater toe.—
Down all my back it pains me so.—
From signs like these 't is very clear
The richest treasure-ground is here.

EMPEROR.

Haste, then! Thou 'lt not again make off!
Test now thy frothy, lying graces,
And show at once the golden places!
My sword and sceptre I will doff,
Mine own imperial hands I'll lend thee,
If thou liest not, therein befriend thee,
But, if thou liest, to Hell will send thee!

MEPHISTOPHELES.

I'd find, in any case, the pathway there!—
Yet I cannot enough declare
What, ownerless, waits everywhere.
The farmer, following his share,
Turns out a gold-crock with the mould:
He seeks saltpetre where the clay-walls stand,
And findest rolls of goldenest gold,
With joyful fright, in his impoverished hand.
What vaults there are to be exploded,
Along what shafts and mines corroded,
The gold-diviner's steps are goaded,
Until the Under-world is night!
In cellars vast he sees the precious
Cups, beakers, vases, plates, and dishes,
Row after row, resplendent lie:
Rich goblets, cut from rubies, stand there,
And, would he use them, lo! at hand there
Is ancient juice of strength divine.
Yet, trust to him who's knowledge gotten,
The wood o' the staves has long been rotten,
A cask of tartar holds the wine.
Not only gold and gems are hiding,
But of proud wines the heart abiding,
In terror and in night profound:
Herein assiduously explore the wise;
It is a farce, by day to recognize,
But mysteries are with darkness circled round.

EMPEROR.

See thou to them! What profits the Obscure?
Whate'er has value comes to daylight, sure.
At dead of night who can the rogue betray?
Then all the cows are black, the cats are gray.
If pots are down there, full of heavy gold,
Drive on thy plough and turn them from the mould!

MEPHISTOPHELES.

Take hoe and spade thyself, I pray thee,—
Thou shalt be great through peasant-toil!
A herd of golden calves, to pay thee,
Will loose their bodies from the soil.
And then at once canst thou, with rapture,
Gems for thyself and for thy mistress capture:
Their tints and sparkles heighten the degree
Of Beauty as of Majesty.

EMPEROR.

Then quick! at once! how long will it require?

ASTROLOGER

(*prompted by* MEPHISTOPHELES).

Sire, moderate such urgence of desire!
Let first the gay, the motley pastime end!
Not to the goal doth such distraction tend.
First self-command must quiet and assure us;
The upper things the lower will procure us.
Who seeks for Good, must first be good;
Who seeks for joy, must moderate his blood;
Who wine desires, let him the ripe grapes tread;
Who miracles, by stronger faith be led!

EMPEROR.

Let us the time in merriment efface!
And, to our wish, Ash-Wednesday comes apace,
Meanwhile, we'll surely celebrate withal
More jovially the maddening Carnival.

[*Trumpets. Exeunt.*

MEPHISTOPHELES.

How closely linked are Luck and Merit,

Doth never to these fools occur:
Had they the Philosopher's Stone, I swear it,
The Stone would lack the Philosopher!

III.

SPACIOUS HALL.

WITH ADJOINING APARTMENTS.

Arranged and Decorated for the Carnival Masquerade.

HERALD.

THINK not, as in our German bounds, your
chance is
Of Death's or Fools' or Devils' dances:
Here cheerful revels you await.
Our Ruler, on his Roman expedition,
Hath for his profit, your fruition,
Crossed o'er the Alpine high partition,
And won himself a gayer State.
He to the holy slipper bowed him
And first the right of power besought;
Then, as he went to get the Crown allowed him,
For us the Fool's-cap he has also brought.
Now are we all new-born, to wear it:
Each tactful and experienced man,
Drawn cosily o'er head and ears, doth bear it;
A fool he seems, yet he must share it,
And be, thereby, as sober as he can.
They crowding come, I see already,
Close coupling, or withdrawn unsteady,—
The choruses, like youth from school.
Come in or out, bring on your ranks!
Before or after—'t is the rule—
With all its hundred thousand pranks,
The World is one enormous Fool!

GARDEN-GIRLS.
(*Song, accompanied with mandolines.*)
That we win your praises tender

We are decked in festal gear;
At the German Court of splendor,
Girls of Florence, we appear.

On our locks of chestnut glosses
Wear we many a flowery bell;
Silken threads and silken flosses
Here must play their parts, as well.

Our desert, not over-rated,
Seems to us assured and clear,
For by art we've fabricated
Flowers that blossom all the year.

Every sort of colored snipping
Won its own symmetric right:
Though your wit on each be tripping,
In the whole you take delight.

We are fair to see and blooming,
Garden-girls, and gay of heart;
For the natural way of woman
Is so near akin to art.

HERALD.

Let us see the wealth of blossoms
Basket-crowning heads that bear them,
Garlanding your arms and bosoms!
Each select, and lightly wear them.
Haste! and bosky arbors dressing,
Let a garden here enring us!
Worthy they of closer pressing,
Hucksters and the wares they bring us.

GARDEN-GIRLS.

Now in cheerful places chaffer,
But no marketing be ours!
Briefly, clearly, let each laugher
Know the meaning of his flowers.

OLIVE BRANCH, WITH FRUIT.

Flowery sprays I do not covet;

The charcoal-burners,
To you we turn us:
For all such plodding,
Affirmative nodding,
Tortuous phrases,
Blowing both ways—is
Warming or chilling,
Just as you're feeling:
What profit from it?
There might fall fire,
Enormous, dire,
From heaven's summit,
Were there not billets
And coal in wagons,
To boil your skillets
And warm your flagons.
It roasts and frizzles;
It boils and sizzles!
The taster and picker,
The platter-licker,
He sniffs the roasting,
Suspects the fishes,
And clears, with boasting,
His patron's dishes.

DRUNKEN MAN (*unconsciously*).
Naught, to-day, bring melancholy!
Since I feel so frank and free:
Fresh delight and songs so jolly,
And I brought them both with me!
Thus I'm drinking, drinking, drinking!
Clink your glasses, clinking, clinking!
You behind there, join the rout!
Clink them stout, and then it's out!

Though my wife assailed me loudly,
Rumpled me through thin and thick;
And, howe'er I swaggered proudly,
Called me "masquerading stick":
Yet I'm drinking, drinking, drinking!
Clink your glasses! clinking, clinking!

Masking sticks, another bout!
When you've clinked them, drink them out!

Say not mine a silly boast is!
I am here in clover laid:
Trusts the host not, trusts the hostess,—
She refusing, trusts the maid.
Still I'm drinking, drinking, drinking!
Come, ye others, clinking, clinking!
Each to each! keep up the rout!
We, I'm thinking, drink them out.

How and where my fun I'm spying.
Let me have it as I planned!
Let me lie where I am lying,
For I cannot longer stand.

CHORUS.
Every chum be drinking, drinking!
Toast afresh, with clinking, clinking!
Bravely keep your seats, and shout!
Under the table *he's* drunk out.

[*The* HERALD *announces various Poets—Poets of
Nature, Courtly and Knightly Minstrels, Senti-
mentalists as well as Enthusiasts. In the crowd of
competitors of all kinds, no one allows another to
commence his declamation. One slips past with a
few words*:]

SATIRIST.
Know ye what myself, the Poet,
Would the most rejoice and cheer?
If I dared to sing, and utter,
That which no one wants to hear.

[*The Night and Churchyard Poets excuse themselves,
because they have just become engaged in a most
interesting conversation with a newly-arisen vam-
pire, and therefrom a new school of poetry may
possibly be developed. The* HERALD *is obliged to*

*accept their excuses, and meanwhile calls forth the
Grecian Mythology, which, even in modern masks,
loses neither its character nor its power to charm.*]

The Graces.

AGLAIA.

Life we bless with graces living;
So be graceful in your giving!

HEGEMONE.

Graceful be in your receival;
Wish attained is sweet retrieval.

EUPHROSYNE.

And in days serene and spacious,
In your thanks be chiefly gracious!

The Parcæ.

ATROPOS.

I, the eldest, to the spinning
Have received the invitation;
When the thread of Life's beginning
There is need of meditation.

Finest flax I winnow featly
That your thread be softly given;
Draw it through my fingers neatly,
Make it thin, and smooth, and even.

If too wanton your endeavor,
Grasping here of joy each token,
Think, the thread won't stretch forever!
Have a care! it might be broken.

CLOTHO.

Know that, given to me for wearing,
Lately were the shears supplied;
Since men were not by the bearing
Of our eldest edified.

Useless webs she long untangled,
Dragging them to air and light;
Dreams of fortunes, hope-bespangled,
Clipped and buried out of sight.

Also I, in ignorance idle,
Made mistakes in younger years,
But to-day, myself to bridle,
In their sheath I stick the shears.

Thus restrained in proper measure,
Favor I this cheerful place:
You these hours of liberal pleasure
Use at will, and run your race!

LACHESIS.

In my hands, the only skilful,
Was the ordered twisting placed;
Active are my ways, not wilful,
Erring not through over-haste.

Threads are coming, threads are reeling;
In its course I each restrain:
None, from off the circle wheeling,
Fails to fit within the skein.

If I once regardless gadded,
For the world my hopes were vain:
Hours are counted, years are added,
And the weaver takes the chain.

HERALD.

You would not recognize who now appear,
Though ne'er so learned you were in ancient writing;
To look at them, in evil so delighting,
You'd call them worthy guests, and welcome here.

They are THE FURIES, no one will believe us,—
Fair, well-proportioned, friendly, young in years:
But make acquaintance, and straightway appears
How snake-like are such doves to wound, deceive us.

Though they are spiteful, yet on this occasion,
When every fool exults in all his blame,
They also do not crave angelic fame,
But own themselves the torments of the nation.

ALECTO.

What good of that, for you will trust us still!—
Each of us young and fair, a wheedling kitten.
Hath one of you a girl with whom he's smitten,
We'll rub and softly stroke his ears, until

'T is safe to tell him, spite of all his loathing,
That she has also this and the other flame,—
A blockhead he, or humpbacked, squint and lame,
And if betrothed to him, she's good-for-nothing!

We're skilled, as well, the bride to vex and sever:
Why scarce a week ago, her very lover
Contemptuous things *to her* was saying of her!
Though they make up, there's something rankles ever.

MEGÆRA.

That's a mere jest! For, let them once be married,
I go to work, and can, in every case,
The fairest bliss by wilful whims displace.
Man has his various moods, the hours are varied,

And, holding the Desired that once did charm him,
Each for the More-desired, a yearning fool,
Leaves the best fortune, use has rendered cool:
He flies the sun, and seeks the frost to warm him.

Of ills for all I understand the brewing,
And here Asmodi as my follower lead,
To scatter mischief at the proper need,
And send the human race, in pairs, to ruin.

TISIPHONE.

Steel and poison I, not malice,
Mix and sharpen for the traitor:
Lov'st thou others, soon or later,
Ruin pours for thee the chalice.

Through the moment's sweet libation
See the gall and wormwood stealing!
Here no bargaining, no dealing!
Like the act and retaliation.

No one babble of forgiving!
To the rocks I cry: *Revenge!* is
Echo's anwser: he who changes
Shall be missed among the living.

HERALD.

Do me the favor, now, to stand aside,
For that which comes is not to you allied.
You see a mountain pressing through the throng,
The flanks with brilliant housings grandly hung,
A head with tusks, a snaky trunk below,—
A mystery, yet I the key will show.
A delicate woman sits upon his neck,
And with a wand persuades him to her beck;
The other, throned aloft, superb to see,
Stands in a glory, dazzling, blinding me.
Beside him walk two dames in chains; one fearful
And sore depressed, the other glad and cheerful.
One longs for freedom and one feels she's free:
Let each declare us who she be!

FEAR.

Smoky torches, lamps are gleaming
Through the festal's wildering train;
Ah! amid these faces scheming
I am fastened by my chain.

Off, ridiculously merry!
I mistrust your grinning spite:
Each relentless adversary
Presses nearer in the night.

Friend would here as foe waylay me,
But I know the masking shapes;
Yonder's one that wished to slay me,—
Now, discovered, he escapes.

From the world I fain would wander
Through whatever gate I find;
But perdition threatens yonder,
And the horror holds my mind.

HOPE.

Good my sisters, I salute you!
Though to-day already suit you,
Masquerading thus demurely,
Yet I know your purpose surely
To reveal yourselves to-morrow.
And if we, by torches lighted,
Fail to feel a special pleasure,
Yet in days of cheerful leisure,
At our will, delight we'll borrow,
Or alone or disunited
Free through fairest pastures ranging
Rest and action interchanging,
And in life no cares that fetter
Naught forego, but strive for better.
Welcome guests are all around us,
Let us mingle with the rest!
Surely, what is best hath found us,
Or we'll somewhere find the best.

PRUDENCE.

Two of human foes, the greatest,
Fear and Hope, I bind the faster,
Thus to save you at the latest:
Clear the way for me, their master.

I conduct the live colossus,
Turret-crowned with weighty masses;
And unweariedly he crosses,
Step by step, the steepest passes.

But aloft the goddess planted,
With her broad and ready pinions,
Turns to spy where gain is granted
Everywhere in Man's dominions.

Round her all is bright and glorious;
Splendor streams on all her courses;
Victory is she—the victorious
Goddess of all active forces.

ZOÏLO-THERSITES.

Ho! ho! I've hit the time of day.
You're all together bad, I say!
But what appeared my goal to me
Is she up there, Dame Victory.
She, with her snowy wings spread out,
Thinks she's an eagle, past a doubt;
And, wheresoever she may stir,
That land and folk belong to her;
But when a famous thing is done
I straightway put my harness on,
To lift the low, the high upset,
The bent to straighten, bend the straight,—
That, only, gives my heart a glow,
And on this earth I'll have it so.

HERALD.

Then take, thou beggar-cur, the blow,
This magic baton's stroke of skill!—
So, twist and wriggle at thy will!
See how the double dwarfish ape
Rolls to a hideous ball in shape!—
A marvel! 'T is an egg we view;
It puffs itself and cracks in two:
A pair of twins come forth to-day,
The Adder and the Bat are they.
Forth in the dust one winds and creeps;
One darkly round the ceiling sweeps.
They haste to join in company:
The third therein I would not be!

MURMURS.

Come! the dance is yonder gay.—
No! I would I were away.—
Feel'st thou how the phantom race
Flits about us in this place?—

Something whizzes past my hair.—
Round my feet I saw it fare.—
None of us are injured, though.—
But we all are frightened so.—
Wholly spoiled is now the fun.—
Which the vermin wanted done.

HERALD.

Since, as Herald, I am aiding
At your merry masquerading,
At the gate I'm watching, fearful
Lest within your revels cheerful
Something slips of evil savor;
And I neither shrink nor waver.
Yet, I fear, the airy spectres
Enter, baffling all detectors,
And from goblins that deceive you
I'm unable to relieve you.
First, the dwarf became suspicious;
Now a mightier pageant issues
Yonder, and it is my duty
To explain those forms of beauty:
But the thing I comprehend not,
How can I its meaning mention?
Help me to its comprehension!
Through the crowd you see it wend not?
Lo! a four-horse chariot wondrous,
Hither drawn, the tumult sunders;
Yet the crowd seems not to share in 't—
Nowhere is a crush apparent.
Colored lights, in distance dimmer,
Motley stars around it shimmer;
Magic lantern-like they glimmer.
On it storms, as to assault.
Clear the way! I shudder!

BOY CHARIOTEER.
                              Halt!
Steeds, restrain the eager pinion,
Own the bridle's old dominion,
Check yourselves, as I desire you,

Sweep away, when I inspire you!—
Honor we these festal spaces!
See, the fast increasing faces,
Circles, full of admiration!
Herald, come! and in thy fashion,
Ere we take from here our glories,
Name us, and describe and show us!
For we're naught but allegories,
Therefore 't is thy place to know us.

HERALD.

No, thy name from me is hidden,—
Could describe thee, were I bidden.

BOY CHARIOTEER.

Try it!

HERALD.

Granted, at the start,
Young and beautiful thou art,—
A half-grown boy; and yet the woman-nature
Would rather see thee in completed stature.
To me thou seem'st a future fickle wooer,
Changing the old betrayed love for a newer.

BOY CHARIOTEER.

Go on! So far, 't is very fine:
Make the enigma's gay solution thine!

HERALD.

Black lightning of the eyes, the dark locks glowing,
Yet bright with jewelled anadem,
And light thy robe as flower on stem,
From shoulder unto buskin flowing
With tinsel-braid and purple hem!
One for a maiden might surmise thee,
Yet, good or ill, as it might be,
The maids, e'en now, would take and prize **thee:**
They'd teach thee soon thy A B C.

BOY CHARIOTEER.

And he, who like a splendid vision,
Sits proudly on the chariot's throne?

HERALD.

He seems a king, of mien Elysian;
Blest those, who may his favor own!
No more has he to earn or capture;
His glance detects where aught's amiss,
And to bestow his perfect rapture
Is more than ownership and bliss.

BOY CHARIOTEER.

Thou darest not at this point desist:
Describe him fully, I insist!

HERALD.

But undescribed is Dignity.
The healthy, full-moon face I see,
The ample mouth, the cheeks that fresher
Shine out beneath his turban's pressure,
Rich comfort in the robe he's wearing,—
What shall I say of such a bearing?
He seems, as ruler, known to me.

BOY CHARIOTEER.

Plutus, the God of Wealth, is he.
He hither comes in proud attire;
Much doth the Emperor him desire.

HERALD.

Of thee the *What* and *How* declare to me!

BOY CHARIOTEER.

I am Profusion, I am Poesy.
The Poet I, whose perfect crown is sent
When he his own best goods hath freely spent.
Yet, rich in mine unmeasured pelf,
Like Plutus I esteem myself:
I prank and cheer his festal show
And whatsoe'er he lacks bestow.

HERALD.

Fresh charm to thee thy brag imparts,
But let us now behold thine arts!

BOY CHARIOTEER.

Just see me fillip with my fingers!
What brilliance round the chariot lingers,
And there a string of pearls appear!

(*Continuing to fillip and snap his fingers in all
directions*:)

Take golden spangles for neck and ears,
Combs, and diadems free of flaw,
And jewelled rings as ne'er ye saw!
I also scatter flamelets bright,
Awaiting where they may ignite.

HERALD.

How strives the crowd with eager longing,
Almost upon the giver thronging!
As in a dream he snaps the toys;
All catch and snatch with crush and noise.
But now new tricks have I detected:
What each has zealously collected
His trouble doth but poorly pay;
The gifts take wings and fly away.
The pearls are loosened from their band
And beetles crawl within his hand;
He shakes them off, and then instead,
Poor dolt, they hum around his head!
The others find their solid things
Are butterflies with gaudy wings.
How much the scamp to promise seems,
And only gives what golden gleams!

BOY CHARIOTEER.

Masks to announce, I grant, thou 'rt worthy;
But 'neath the shell of Being to bestir thee
Is not a herald's courtly task:
A sharper sight for that we ask.
Yet every quarrel I evade;
To thee, my Chief, be speech and question made!

(*Turning to* PLUTUS.)

Didst thou not unto me confide
The tempest of the steeds I guide?
Canst thou not on my guidance reckon?

Am I not there, where thou dost beckon?
And have I not, on pinions boldest,
Conquered for thee the palm thou holdest?
When in thy battles I have aided,
I ever have been fortunate;
Thy brow when laurels decorate,
Have I not them with hand and fancy braided?

PLUTUS.

If there be need that I bear witness now,
I'm glad to say: soul of my soul art thou!
Thine acts are always to my mind,
And thou the richer art, I find.
Thy service to reward, I hold
The green bough higher than my crowns of gold.
To all a true word spoken be:
Dear Son, I much delight in thee.

BOY CHARIOTEER (*to the Crowd*).

The greatest gifts my hand flings out,
See! I have scattered round about.
On divers heads there glows the tongue
Of flame which I upon them flung,—
Leaps back and forth among the shapes,
On this remains, from that escapes,
But very seldom upward streams
In transient flush of mellow beams;
And unto many, ere they mark,
It is extinct and leaves them dark.

CHATTER OF WOMEN.

Upon the chariot that man
Is certainly a charlatan:
There, perched behind, the clown is seen,
From thirst and hunger grown so lean
As one ne'er saw him; if you'd pinch,
He hasn't flesh to feel and flinch.

THE STARVELING.

Disgusting women, off! I know
That when I come, you'd have me go.

When woman fed her own hearth-flame,
Then *Avaritia was my name;*
Then throve the household fresh and green,
For naught went out and much came in.
To chest and press I gave good heed,
And that you'd call a vice, indeed!
But since in later years, the fact is,
Economy the wife won't practise,
And, like the host of spendthrift scholars,
Has more desires than she has dollars,
The husband much discomfort brooks,
For there are debts where'er he looks.
She spends what spoil she may recover
Upon her body, or her lover;
In luxury eats, and to excess
Drinks with the flirts that round her press,
For me that raises money's price:
Male is my gender, Avarice!

LEADER OF THE WOMEN.

With dragons, mean may be the dragon;
It's all, at best, but lying stuff!
He comes, the men to spur and egg on,
And now they're troublesome enough.

CROWD OF WOMEN.

The scarecrow! Knock him from the wagon!
What means the fag, to threaten here?
As if his ugly face we'd fear!
Of wood and pasteboard is each dragon:
Come on—his words shall cost him dear!

HERALD.

Now, by my wand! Be still—let none stir!
Yet for my help there's scarcely need;
See how each grim and grisly monster,
Clearing the space around with speed,
Unfolds his fourfold wings of dread!
The dragons shake themselves in anger,
With flaming throats, and scaly clangor;
The place is clear, the crowd has fled.

(PLUTUS *descends from the chariot.*)

HERALD.

How kingly comes he from above!
He beckons, and the dragons move;
Then from the chariot bring the chest
With gold, and Avarice thereon.
See, at his feet the load they rest!
A marvel 't is, how it was done.

PLUTUS (*to the* CHARIOTEER).

Now thou hast left the onerous burden here,
Thou 'rt wholly free: away to thine own sphere!
Here it is not! Confused and wild, to-day,
Distorted pictures press around our way.
Where clear thy gaze in sweet serenity,
Owning thyself, confiding but in thee,
Thither, where Good and Beauty are unfurled,
To Solitude!—and there create thy world!

BOY CHARIOTEER.

Thus, as an envoy, am I worthy of thee;
Thus, as my next of kindred, do I love thee.
Where thou art, is abundance; where I go
Each sees a splendid profit round him grow.
In inconsistent life each often wavers,
Whether to seek from thee, or me, the favors.
Thy followers may be indolent, 't is true;
Who follows me, has always work to do.
My deeds are never secret and concealed;
I only breathe, and I'm at once revealed.
Farewell, then! Thou the bliss hast granted me;
But whisper low, and I return to thee!

[*Exit, as he came.*

PLUTUS.

'T is time, now, to unchain the precious metals!
The padlocks with the herald's wand I smite:
The chest is opened: look! from iron kettles
It pours like golden blood before your sight.
It boils, and threatens to devour, as fuel,
Melting them, crown and ring and chain and jewel!

ALTERNATE CRIES OF THE CROWD.

See here, and there! they boil and swim;
The chest is filling to the brim!—
Vessels of gold are burning there,
And minted rolls are turning there,
And ducats jingle as they jump!—
O, how my heart begins to thump!—
All my desire I see, and more.
They're rolling now along the floor.—
'T is offered you: don't be a dunce,
Stoop only, and be rich at once!—
Then, quick as lightning we, the rest,
Will take possession of the chest.

HERALD.

What ails ye, fools? What mean ye all?
'T is but a joke of Carnival.
To-night be your desires controlled;
Think you we'd give you goods and gold?
Why, in this game there come to view
Too many counters even, for you.
A pleasant cheat, ye dolts! forsooth
You take at once for naked truth.
What's truth to you? Illusion bare
Surrounds and rules you everywhere.
Thou Plutus-mask, Chief unrevealed,
Drive thou this people from the field!

PLUTUS.

Thy wand thereto is fit and free;
Lend it a little while to me!
I dip it in the fiery brew,—
Look out, ye maskers! all of you.
It shines, and snaps, and sparkles throws;
The burning wand already glows.
Who crowdeth on, too near to me,
Is burned and scorched relentlessly.—
And now my circuit I'll commence.

CRIES AND CROWDING.

Woe's me! We're lost—there's no defence!—-

Let each one fly, if fly he can!—
Back! clear the way, you hindmost man!—
It sparkles fiercely in mine eyes.—
The burning wand upon me lies.—
We all are lost, we all are lost!—
Back, back! ye maskers, jammed and tossed!—
Back, senseless crowd, away from there!—
O, had I wings, I'd take the air.

PLUTUS.

Now is the circle crowded back,
And none, I think, scorched very black.
The throng retires,
Scared by the fires.
As guaranty for ordered law,
A ring invisible I draw.

HERALD.

A noble work is thine, to-night:
I thank thy wisdom and thy might.

PLUTUS.

Preserve thy patience, noble friend,
For many tumults yet impend.

AVARICE.

Thus, if one pleases, pleasantly
May one survey this circle stately;
For, ever foremost, crowd the women greatly,
If aught to stare at, or to taste, there be.
Not yet entirely rusty are my senses!
A woman fair is always fair to me:
And since, to-day, it makes me no expenses,
We'll go a courting confidently.
But in a place so populate
All words to every ear don't penetrate;
So, wisely I attempt, and hope success,
Myself by pantomine distinctly to express.
Hand, foot, and gesture will not quite suffice,
So I employ a jocular device.
Like clay will I the gold manipulate;
One may transform it into any state.

HERALD.

What will the lean fool do? Has he,
So dry a starveling, humor? See,
He kneads the gold as it were dough!
Beneath his hands 't is soft; yet, though
He roll and squeeze it, for his pains
Disfigured still the stuff remains.
He turns to the women there, and they
All scream, and try to get away,
With gestures of disgust and loathing:
The ready rascal stops at nothing.
I fear he takes delight to see
He has offended decency.
I dare not silently endure it:
Give me my wand, that I may cure it!

PLUTUS.

The danger from without he does not see:
Let him alone; his Fool's-hour fast is waning.
There'll be no space for his mad pranks remaining;
Mighty is Law, mightier Necessity.

TUMULT AND SONG.

The savage hosts, with shout and hail,
From mountain-height and forest-vale
Come, irresistibly as Fate:
Their mighty Pan they celebrate.
They know, forsooth, what none can guess,
And in the empty circle press.

PLUTUS.

I know you well, and your illustrious Pan!
Boldly together you've performed your plan.
Full well I know what every one does not,
And clear for you, as duty bids, the spot.
Be Fortune still her favor lending!
The strangest things may here be bred:
They know not whitherward they're wending,
Because they have not looked ahead.

SAVAGE SONG.

Furbished people, tinsel-stuff!

They're coming rude, they're coming rough;
In mighty leap, in wildest race,
Coarse and strong they take their place.

Fauns, pair on pair,
Come dancing down,
With oaken crown
On crispy hair;
The fine and pointed ear is seen,
Leaf-like, the clustering curls between:
A stubby nose, face broad and flat,
The women don't object to that;
For when his paw holds forth the Faun,
The fairest to the dance is drawn.

See now, behind the Satyr skip,
With foot of goat, lean leg and hip,—
Lean and sinewy must they be:
For, chamois-like, on mountains he
Loveth to stand or scamper free.
Then, strong in freedom of the skies,
Child, wife, and man doth he despise,
Who, deep in the valley's smoke and steam
That they live also, snugly dream;
While, pure and undisturbed, alone
The upper world is all his own.

The little crowd comes tripping there;
They don't associate pair by pair.
In mossy garb, with lantern bright,
They move commingling, brisk and light,
Each working on his separate ground,
Like firefly-emmets swarming round;
And press and gather here and there,
Always industrious everywhere.
With the "Good People" kin we own;
As surgeons of the rocks we're known.
Cupping the mountains, bleeding them

From fullest veins, depleting them
Of store of metals, which we pile,
And merrily greet: "Good cheer!" the while.
Well-meant the words, believe us, then!
We are the friends of all good men.
Yet we the stores of gold unseal
That men may pander, pimp, and steal;
Nor iron shall fail his haughty hand
Who universal murder planned:
And who these three Commandments breaks
But little heed o' the others takes.
For that we're not responsible:
We're patient—be you, too, as well!

GIANTS.

The wild men of the woods they're named,
And in the Hartz are known and famed;
In naked nature's ancient might
They come, each one a giant wight,
With fir-tree trunk in brawny hand,
Around the loins a puffy band,
The merest apron of leaf and bough:—
The Pope hath no such guards, I trow.

NYMPHS IN CHORUS.
(*They surround the great* PAN.)

He comes! We scan
The world's great All,
Whose part doth fall
To mighty Pan.
Ye gayest ones, advance to him,
Your maddest measures dance to him!
Since serious and kind is he,
He wills that we should joyous be,
Under the blue, o'er-vaulting roof,
Ever he seemeth slumber-proof;
Yet murmurs of the brooks he knows,
And soft airs lull him to repose.
At midday sleeping, o'er his brow
The leaf is moveless on the bough:
Of healthy buds the balsam there

Pervades the still, suspended air:
The nymph no longer dares to leap,
And where she stands, she falls asleep.
But when, all unexpected, he
Maketh his voice heard terribly,
Like rattling thunder, roar of wave,
Then each one seeks himself to save;
The serried ranks disperse in fright,
The hero trembles in the fight.
Then honor to whom the honor is due,
And hail to him who led us to you!

DEPUTATION OF GNOMES.
(*to the great* PAN).

When the rich possession, shining
Through the rocks in thread and vein,
To the skilful wand's divining
Shows its labyrinthine chain,

We in vaults and caverns spacious,
Troglodytes, contented bide;
While in purest daylight, gracious,
Thou the treasures dost divide.

Now we see, wilt thou believe us,
Here a wondrous fountain run,
Promising with ease to give us
What was hardly to be won.

Lo! It waits for thy attaining:
Then be moved to break the spell!
All the wealth which thou art gaining
Profits all the world as well.

PLUTUS (*to the* HERALD).

We, in the highest sense, must be collected,
And let what *may* come, come, though unexpected
Thy courage has not yet been counted short:
The fearful thing we now shall see will try it;
The world and History will both deny it,
So write it faithfully in thy report!

(Grasping the wand which PLUTUS *holds in his hand.)*

The dwarfs conduct the great Pan nigher,
Yet gently, to the fount of fire.
It bubbles from the throat profound,
Then sinks, retreating, to the ground,
And dark the open crater shows;
And then again it boils and glows.
Great Pan in cheerful mood stands by,
Rejoiced the wondrous things to spy,
And right and left the foam-pearls fly.
How can he in the cheat confide?
He bends and stoops, to look inside.—
But now, behold! his beard falls in:
Whose is that smoothly-shaven chin?
His hand conceals it from our sight.
What follows is a luckless plight;
The beard, on fire, flies back to smite
His wreath and head and breast with flame:
To pain is turned the merry game.
They haste to quench the fire, but none
The swiftly-kindling flames can shun,
That flash and dart on other heads
Till wide the conflagration spreads:
Wrapped in the element, in turn
The masking groups take fire and burn.
But hark! what news is bruited here
From mouth to mouth, from ear to ear?
O evermore ill-fated night,
That brings to us such woe and blight!
To-morrow will proclaim to all
What no one wishes to befall,
  For everywhere the cry I hear:
  "The Emperor suffers pain severe!"
  O were the proclamation wrong!
  The Emperor burns and all his throng
  Accurst be they who him misled,
  With resinous twigs on breast and head,
  To rave and bellow hither so,
  To general, fatal overthrow.

O Youth! O Youth! wilt never thou
Limit thy draught of joy, in season?—
O Majesty, wilt never thou,
Omnipotent, direct with reason?
The mimic woods enkindled are;
The pointed tongues lick upward far
To where the rafters interlace:
A fiery doom hangs o'er the place.
Our cup of misery overflows,
For who shall save us no one knows.
The ash-heap of a night shall hide,
To-morrow, this imperial pride.

PLUTUS.

Terror is enough created;
Now be help inaugurated!
Smite, thou hallowed wand, and make
Earth beneath thee peal and quake!
Thou, the spacious breadth of air,
Cooling vapors breathe and bear!
Hither speed, around us growing,
Misty films and belts o'erflowing,
And the fiery tumult tame!
Trickle, whisper, clouds, be crisper,
Roll in masses, softly drenching,
Mantling everywhere, and quenching!
Ye, the moist, the broadly bright'ning,
Change to harmless summer lightning
All this empty sport of flame!—
When by spirits we're molested,
Then be Magic manifested.

IV.

PLEASURE-GARDEN.

THE MORNING SUN.

The EMPEROR, *his Court, Gentlemen and Ladies:* FAUST,
MEPHISTOPHELES, *becomingly, according to the
mode, not showily dressed: both kneel.*

FAUST.

Sire, pardon'st thou the jugglery of flame?

EMPEROR (*beckoning him to rise*).

I wish more exhibitions of the same.
A-sudden stood I in a glowing sphere;
It almost seemed as if I Pluto were.
There lay, like night, with little fires besprent,
A rocky bottom. Out of many a vent,
Whirling, a thousand savage flames ascended,
Till in a single vault their streamers blended.
The tongues even to the highest dome were shot,
That ever was, and ever then was not.
Through the far space of spiral shafts of flame
The long processions of the people came;
Crowding, till all the circle was o'errun,
They did me homage, as they've ever done.
Some from my Court I knew: to speak with candor,
A Prince I seemed o'er many a salamander.

MEPHISTOPHELES.

That art thou, Sire! Because each element
Fully accepts thy Majesty's intent.
Obedient Fire is tested now by thee:
Where wildest heaving, leap into the Sea,
And scarce the pearly floor thy foot shall tread,
A grand rotunda rises o'er thy head:
Thou seest the green, translucent billows swelling,
With purple edge, for thy delightful dwelling,
Round thee, the central point. Walk thou at will,
The liquid palaces go with thee still!
The very walls rejoice in life, disporting
In arrowy flight, in chasing and consorting:
Sea-marvels crowd around the glory new and fair,
Shoot from all sides, yet none can enter there.
There gorgeous dragons, golden-armored, float;
There gapes the shark, thou laughest in his throat.
However much this Court thy pride may please,
Yet hast thou never seen such throngs as these.
Nor from the loveliest shalt thou long be parted;
The curious Nereids come, the wild, shy-hearted,

To thy bright dwelling in the endless waters,—
Timid and sly as fish the youngest daughters,
The elder cunning: Thetis hears the news
And will, at once, her second Peleus choose.
The seat, then, on Olympus high and free—

EMPEROR.

The spaces of the air I leave to thee:
One all too early must ascend that throne.

MEPHISTOPHELES.

And Earth, high Prince! already is thine own.

EMPEROR.

What fortune brought thee here, for our delights,
Directly from the One and Thousand Nights?
If thou like Scheherazade art rich in stories,
My favor shall insure thee higher glories.
Be ready always, when your world of day,
As often haps, disgusts me every way!

LORD HIGH STEWARD (*enters hastily*).

Highness Serene, I never dared expect
To trumpet forth a fortune so select
As this, supremely blessing me,
Which I announce with joy to thee:
Reckoning on reckoning's balanced squarely;
The usurer's claws are blunted rarely;
I'm from my hellish worry free:
Things can't in Heaven more cheerful be.

GENERAL-IN-CHIEF (*follows hastily*).

Arrears of pay are settled duly,
The army is enlisted newly;
The trooper's blood is all alive,
The landlords and the wenches thrive.

EMPEROR.

How breathe your breasts in broader spaces!
How cheerful are your furrowed faces!
How ye advance with nimble speed!

TREASURER (*appearing*).
Ask these, 't is they have done the deed!

FAUST.
It is the Chancellor's place the matter to present.

CHANCELLOR (*who comes forward slowly*).
In my old days I'm blest, and most content.
So hear and see the fortune-freighted leaf
Which has transformed to happiness our grief.
(*He reads.*)
"To all to whom this cometh, be it known:
A thousand crowns in worth this note doth own.
It to secure, as certain pledge, shall stand
All buried treasure in the Emperor's land:
And 't is decreed, perfecting thus the scheme,
The treasure, soon as raised, shall this redeem."

EMPEROR.
A most enormous cheat—a crime, I fear!
Who forged the Emperor's sign-manual here?
Has there not been a punishment condign?

TREASURER.
Remember! Thou the note didst undersign;
Last night, indeed. Thou stood'st as mighty Pan,
And thus the Chancellor's speech, before thee, ran:
"Grant to thyself the festal pleasure, then
The People's good—a few strokes of the pen!"
These didst thou give: they were, ere night retreated,
By skilful conjurers thousandfold repeated;
And, that a like advantage all might claim,
We stamped at once the series with thy name:
Tens, Thirties, Fifties, Hundreds, are prepared.
Thou canst not think how well the folk have fared.
Behold thy town, half-dead once, and decaying,
How all, alive, enjoying life, are straying!
Although thy name long since the world made glad,
Such currency as now it never had.
No longer needs the alphabet thy nation,
For in this sign each findeth his salvation.

EMPEROR.

And with my people does it pass for gold?
For pay in court and camp, the notes they hold?
Then I must yield, although the thing's amazing.

LORD HIGH STEWARD.

'T was scattered everywhere, like wild-fire blazing,
As currency, and none its course may stop.
A crowd surrounds each money-changer's shop,
And every note is there accepted duly
For gold and silver's worth—with discount, truly.
Thence is it spread to landlords, butchers, bakers:
One half the people feast as pleasure-takers;
In raiment new the others proudly go,—
The tradesmen cut their cloth, the tailors sew.
The crowd "The Emperor's health!" in cellars wishes,
Midst cooking, roasting, rattling of the dishes.

MEPHISTOPHELES.

If one along the lonely terrace stray,
He sees the lady, in superb array,
With brilliant peacock-fan before one eye;
A note she looks for, as she simpers by,
And readier than by wit or eloquence
Before Love's favor falls the last defence.
One is not plagued his purse or sack to carry;
Such notes one lightly in his bosom bears,
Or them with fond epistles neatly pairs:
The priest devoutly in his breviary
Bears his: the soldier would more freely trip,
And lightens thus the girdle round his hip
Your Majesty will pardon, if my carriage
Seems as it might the lofty work disparage.

FAUST.

The overplus of wealth, in torpor bound,
Which in thy lands lies buried in the ground,
Is all unused; nor boldest thought can measure
The narrowest boundaries of such a treasure.
Imagination, in its highest flight,
Exerts itself, but cannot grasp it quite;

Yet minds, that dare explore the secrets soundless,
In boundless things possess a faith that's boundless.

MEPHISTOPHELES.

Such paper, stead of gold and jewelry,
So handy is—one know's one's property:
One has no need of bargains or exchanges,
But drinks of love or wine, as fancy ranges.
If one needs coin, the brokers ready stand,
And if it fail, one digs awhile the land.
Goblet and chain one then at auction sells,
And paper, liquidated thus, compels
The shame of doubters and their scornful wit.
The people wish naught else; they're used to it:
From this time forth, your borders, far and wide,
With jewels, gold, and paper are supplied.

EMPEROR.

You've given our empire this prosperity;
The pay, then, equal to the service be!
The soil intrusted to your keeping, shall you
The best custodians be, to guard its value.
You know the hoards, well-kept, of all the land,
And when men dig, 't is you must give command.
Unite then now, ye masters of our treasure,
This, your new dignity, to wear with pleasure,
And bring the Upper World, erewhile asunder,
In happiest conjunction with the Under!

TREASURER.

No further strife shall shake our joint position;
I like to have as partner the magician.

[*Exit, with* FAUST.

EMPEROR.

Man after man, the Court will I endow:
Let each confess for what he'll spend, and how!

PAGE (*receiving*).

I'll lead a jolly life, enjoy good cheer.

A SECOND (*the same*).

I'll buy at once some trinkets for my dear.

CHAMBERLAIN (*accepting*).
Wines twice as good shall down my throat go trickling

A SECOND (*the same*).
I feel the dice within my pockets tickling.

KNIGHT BANNERET (*reflectively*).
My lands and castle shall be free of debt.

ANOTHER (*the same*).
I'll add to other wealth the wealth I get.

EMPEROR.
I hoped the gifts to bolder deeds would beckon;
But he who knows you, knows whereon to reckon.
I see that, spite of all this treasure-burst,
You stay exactly as you were at first.

FOOL (*approaching*).
You scatter favors: grant me also some!

EMPEROR.
Thou 'rt come to life? 'T would go at once for rum

FOOL.
The magic leaves! I don't quite comprehend.

EMPEROR.
That I believe; for them thou 'lt badly spend.

FOOL.
There others drop: I don't know what to do.

EMPEROR.
Just pick them up! they fall to thy share, too.
[*Exit.*

FOOL.
Five thousand crowns are mine? How unexpected!

MEPHISTOPHELES.
Two-leggéd wine-skin, art thou resurrected?

FOOL.

Much luck I've had, but like this never yet.

MEPHISTOPHELES.

Thou 'rt so rejoiced, it puts thee in a sweat.

FOOL.

But look at this, is 't money's-worth, indeed?

MEPHISTOPHELES.

'T will bring thee what thy throat and belly need.

FOOL.

And cattle can I buy, and house and land?

MEPHISTOPHELES.

Of course! just make an offer once, off-hand!

FOOL.

Castle and wood, and chase, and fishing?

MEPHISTOPHELES.

All!

I'd like upon Your Worship then to call.

FOOL.

To-night as landed owner I shall sit.

[*Exit.*

MEPHISTOPHELES (*solus*).

Who now will doubt that this our Fool has wit?

V.

A GLOOMY GALLERY.

FAUST. MEPHISTOPHELES.

MEPHISTOPHELES.

WHAT wilt thou with me in this gloomy gallery?
Is there not still enough of sport
There, in the crowded, motley Court,—
Not chance for tricks, and fun, and raillery?

FAUST.

Don't tell me that!—In our old days the fun of it
Didst thou wear out, and I'll have none of it.
Thy wandering here and there is planned
Just to evade what I demand.
But I'm tormented something to obtain;
The Marshal drives me, and the Chamberlain.
The Emperor orders, he will instantly
Helen and Paris here before him see,—
The model forms of Man and Woman, wearing,
Distinctly shown, their ancient shape and bearing.
Now to the work! I dare not break my word.

MEPHISTOPHELES.

So thoughtlessly to promise was absurd.

FAUST.

Thou hast not, comrade, well reflected
What comes of having used thy powers:
We've made him rich; 't is now expected
That we amuse his idle hours.

MEPHISTOPHELES.

Thou deem'st the thing is quickly fixed:
Here before steeper ways we're standing;
With strangest spheres wouldst thou be mixed,
And, sinful, addest new debts to the old,—
Think'st Helen will respond to thy commanding
As freely as the paper-ghosts of gold!
With witches'-riches and with spectre-pictures,
And changeling-dwarfs, I'll give no cause for strictures;
But Devil's-darlings, though you may not scold 'em,
You cannot quite as heroines behold 'em.

FAUST.

The old hand-organ still I hear thee play!
From thee one always gets uncertain sense,
The father, thou, of all impediments:
For every means thou askest added pay.
A little muttering, and the thing takes place;
Ere one can turn, beside us here her shade is.

MEPHISTOPHELES.

I've no concern with the old heathen race;
They house within their special Hades.
Yet there's a way.

FAUST.

Speak, nor delay thy history!

MEPHISTOPHELES.

Unwilling, I reveal a loftier mystery.—
In solitude are throned the Goddesses,
No Space around them, Place and Time still less;
Only to speak of them embarrasses.
They are THE MOTHERS!

FAUST (*terrified*).
Mothers!

MEPHISTOPHELES.

Hast thou dread?

FAUST.

The Mothers! Mothers!—a strange word is said.

MEPHISTOPHELES.

It is so. Goddesses, unknown to ye,
The Mortals,—named by us unwillingly.
Delve in the deepest depths must thou, to reach them:
'T is thine own fault that we for help beseech them.

FAUST.

Where is the way?

MEPHISTOPHELES.

No way!—To the Unreachable,
Ne'er to be trodden! A way to the Unbeseechable,
Never to be besought! Art thou prepared?
There are no locks, no latches to be lifted;
Through endless solitudes shalt thou be drifted.
Hast thou through solitudes and deserts fared?

FAUST.

I think 't were best to spare such speeches;

They smell too strongly of the witches,
Of cheats that long ago insnared.
Have I not known all earthly vanities?
Learned the inane, and taught inanities?
When as I felt I spake, with sense as guide,
The contradiction doubly shrill replied;
Enforced by odious tricks, have I not fled
To solitudes and wildernesses dread,
And that I might not live alone, unheeded,
Myself at last unto the Devil deeded!

MEPHISTOPHELES.

And hast thou swum to farthest verge of ocean,
And there the boundless space beheld,
Still hadst thou seen wave after wave in motion,
Even though impending doom they fear compelled.
Thou hadst seen something,—in the beryl dim
Of peace-lulled seas the sportive dolphins swim;
Hadst seen the flying clouds, sun, moon, and star:
Naught shalt thou see in endless Void afar,—
Not hear thy foostep fall, nor meet
A stable spot to rest thy feet.

FAUST.

Thou speak'st, as of all mystagogues the chief,
Who e'er brought faithful neophytes to grief;
Only reversed:—I to the Void am sent,
That Art and Power therein I may augment:
To use me like the cat is thy desire,
To scratch for thee the chestnuts from the fire.
Come on, then! we'll explore, whate'er befall;
In this, thy Nothing, may I find my All!

MEPHISTOPHELES.

I'll praise thee, ere we separate: I see
Thou knowest the Devil thoroughly.
Here, take this key!

FAUST.

That little thing?

MEPHISTOPHELES.

Take hold of it, not undervaluing!

FAUST.

It glows, it shines,—increases in my hand!

MEPHISTOPHELES.

How much 't is worth, thou soon shalt understand.
The Key will scent the true place from all others:
Follow it down!—'t will lead thee to the Mothers.

FAUST (*shuddering*).

The Mothers! Like a blow it strikes me still!
What is the word, to hear which makes me chill?

MEPHISTOPHELES.

Art thou so weak, disturbed by each new word?
Wilt only hear what thou 'st already heard?
To wondrous things art thou so used already,
Let naught, howe'er it sound, make thee unsteady!

FAUST.

Nathless in torpor lies no good for me;
The chill of dread is Man's best quality.
Though from the feeling oft the world may fend us,
Deeply we feel, once smitten, the Tremendous.

MEPHISTOPHELES.

Descend, then! I could also say: Ascend!
'T were all the same. Escape from the Created
To shapeless forms in liberated spaces!
Enjoy what long ere this was dissipated!
There whirls the press, like clouds on clouds unfold-
          ing;
Then with stretched arm swing high the key thou 'rt
          holding!

FAUST (*inspired*).

Good! grasping firmly, fresher strength I win:
My breast expands, let the great work begin!

MEPHISTOPHELES.

At last a blazing tripod tells thee this,
That there the utterly deepest bottom is.
Its light to thee will then the Mothers show,

Some in their seats, the others stand or go,
At their own will: Formation, Transformation,
The Eternal Mind's eternal recreation,
Forms of all creatures,—there are floating free.
They'll see thee not; for only wraiths they see.
So pluck up heart,—the danger then is great,—
Go to the tripod ere thou hesitate,
And touch it with the key!
(FAUST, *with the key, assumes a decidedly command-
ing attitude.* MEPHISTOPHELES, *observing him.*)
                 So, that is right!
It will adhere, and follow thee to light.
Composedly mounting, by thy luck upborne,
Before they notice it, shalt thou return.
When thou the tripod hither hast conveyed,
Then call the hero, heroine, from the shade,—
The first that ever such a deed perfected:
'T is done, and thou thereto hast been selected.
For instantly, by magic process warmed,
To gods the incense-mist shall be transformed.

FAUST.

What further now?

MEPHISTOPHELES.
               Downward thy being strain!
Stamp and descend, stamping thou 'lt rise again.
     (FAUST *stamps, and sinks out of sight.*)
If only, by the key, he something learn!
I'm curious to see if he return.

VI.

BRILLIANTLY LIGHTED HALLS.

EMPEROR AND PRINCES. THE COURT IN MOVEMENT.

CHAMBERLAIN (*to* MEPHISTOPHELES).
THE spirit-scene you've promised, still you owe us;
Our Lord's impatient; come, the phantasm show us!

LORD HIGH STEWARD.

Just now His Gracious Self did question me:
Delay not, nor offend His Majesty!

MEPHISTOPHELES.

My comrade's gone to set the work in motion;
How to begin, he has the proper notion
In secret he the charms must cull,
Must labor with a fervor tragic:
Who would that treasure lift, the Beautiful,
Requires the highest Art, the sage's Magic.

LORD HIGH STEWARD.

What arts you need, is all the same to me;
The Emperor wills that you should ready be.

A BLONDE (*to* MEPHISTOPHELES).

One word, Sir! Here you see a visage fair,—
In sorry summer I another wear!
There sprout a hundred brown and reddish freckles,
And vex my lily skin with ugly speckles.
A cure!

MEPHISTOPHELES.

'T is pity! Shining fair, yet smitten,—
Spotted, when May comes, like a panther-kitten!
Take frog-spawn, tongues of toads, which cohobate,
Under the full moon deftly distillate,
And, when it wanes, apply the mixture:
Next spring, the spots will be no more a fixture.

A BRUNETTE.

To sponge upon you, what a crowd's advancing!
I beg a remedy: a frozen foot
Annoys me much, in walking as in dancing;
And awkwardly I manage to salute.

MEPHISTOPHELES.

A gentle kick permit, then, from my foot!

THE BRUNETTE.

Well,—that might happen, when the two are lovers.

MEPHISTOPHELES.

My kick a more important meaning covers:
Similia similibus, when one is sick.
The foot cures foot, each limb its hurt can palliate;
Come near! Take heed! and, pray you, don't retaliate!

THE BRUNETTE (*screaming*).

Oh! oh! it stings! That was a fearful kick,
Like hoof of horse.

MEPHISTOPHELES.

        But it has cured you, quick.
To dance whene'er you please, you now are able;
To press your lover's foot, beneath the table.

LADY (*pressing forwards*).

Make room for me! Too great is my affliction,
My tortures worse than those described in fiction:
His bliss, till yesterday, was in *my* glances,
But now he turns his back, and spins with *her* ro-
    mances.

MEPHISTOPHELES.

The matter's grave, but listen unto me!
Draw near to him with gentle, soft advances;
Then take this coal and mark him stealthily
On mantle, shoulder, sleeve,—though ne'er so slight,
Yet penitent at once his heart will be.
The coal thereafter you must straightway swallow,
And let no sip of wine or water follow:
He'll sigh before your door this very night.

THE LADY.

It is not poison, sure?

MEPHISTOPHELES (*offended*).

        Respect, where it is due!
To get such coals, you'd travel many a mile:
They're from the embers of a funeral pile,
The fires whereof we once more hotly blew.

PAGE.

I love, yet still am counted adolescent.

MEPHISTOPHELES (*aside*).
I know not whom to listen to, at present.
(*To the Page.*)
Let not the younger girls thy fancies fetter;
Those well in years know how to prize thee better.—
(*Others crowd around him.*)
Already others? 'T is a trial, sooth!
I'll help myself, at last, with naked truth—
The worst device!—so great my misery.
O Mothers! Mothers! let but Faust go free!
(*Gazing around him.*)
The lights are burning dimly in the hall,
The Court is moving onward, one and all:
I see them march, according to degrees,
Through long arcades and distant galleries.
Now they assemble in the ample space
Of the Knights' Hall; yet hardly all find place.
The breadth of walls is hung with arras rich,
And armor gleams from every nook and niche.
Here, I should think, there needs no magic word:
The ghosts will come, and of their own accord.

VII.

HALL OF THE KNIGHTS, DIMLY LIGHTED.

(*The Emperor and Court have entered.*)

HERALD.
MINE ancient office, to proclaim the action,
Is by the spirits' secret influence thwarted:
One tries in vain; such wildering distraction
Can't be explained, or reasonably reported.
The chairs are ranged, the seats are ready all:
The Emporer sits, fronting the lofty wall,
Where on the tapestry the battles he
Of the great era may with comfort see.
Here now are all—Prince, Court, and their belonging,
Benches on benches in the background thronging;
And lovers, too, in these dim hours enchanted,

Beside their loved ones lovingly are planted.
And now, since all have found convenient places,
We're ready: let the spirits show their faces.
Trumpets.

ASTROLOGER.

Begin the Drama! 'T is the Sire's command:
Ye walls, be severed straightway, and expand!
Naught hinders; magic answers our desire:
The arras flies, as shrivelled up by fire;
The walls are split, unfolded: in the gloom
A theatre appears to be created:
By mystic light are we illuminated,
And I ascend to the proscenium.

MEPHISTOPHELES
(*rising to view in the prompter's box.*)

I hope to win, as prompter, general glory;
For prompting is the Devil's oratory.
(*To the Astrologer.*)
Thou know'st the tune and time the stars that lead;
Thou wilt my whispers like a master heed.

ASTROLOGER.

By power miraculous, we here behold
A massive temple of the days of old.
Like Atlas, who erewhile the heavens upbore,
The serried columns stand, an ample store:
Well may they for the weight of stone suffice,
Since two might bear a mighty edifice.

ARCHITECT.

That the antique? As fine it can't be rated;
I'd sooner style it awkward, over-weighted.
Coarse is called noble, and unwieldy, grand:
Give me the slender shafts that soar, expand!
To lift the mind, a pointed arch may boast;
Such architecture edifies us most.

ASTROLOGER.

Receive with reverence the star-granted hours;
Let magic words bind Reason's restless powers,

But in return unbind, to circle free,
The wings of splendid, daring Phantasy!
What you have boldly wished, see now achieved!
Impossible 't is—therefore to be believed.
(FAUST *rises to view on the other side of proscenium.*)
In priestly surplice, crowned, a marvellous man,
He now fulfils what he in faith began.
With him, a tripod from the gulf comes up:
I scent the incense-odors from the cup.
He arms himself, the work to consecrate,
And henceforth it can be but fortunate.

FAUST (*sublimely*).

Ye Mothers, in your name, who set your throne
In boundless Space, eternally alone,
And yet companioned! All the forms of Being,
In movement, lifeless, ye are round you seeing.
Whate'er once was, there burns and brightens free
In splendor—for 't would fain eternal be;
And ye allot it, with all-potent might,
To Day's pavilions and the vaults of Night.
Life seizes some, along his gracious course;
Others arrests the bold Magician's force;
And he, bestowing as his faith inspires,
Displays the Marvellous, that each desires.

ASTROLOGER.

The glowing key has scarcely touched the cup,
And lo! through all the space, a mist rolls up:
It creeps about, and like a cloudy train,
Spreads, rounding, narrowing, parting, closed **again**.
And now, behold a spirit-masterpiece!
Music is born from every wandering fleece.
The tones of air, I know not how they flow;
Where'er they move all things melodious grow.
The pillared shaft, the triglyph even rings:
I think, indeed, the whole bright temple sings.
The vapors settle; as the light film clears,
A beauteous youth, with rhythmic step, appears.
Here ends my task; his name I need not tell:
Who doth not know the gentle Paris well?

LADY.

O, what a youthful bloom and strength I see!

A SECOND.

Fresh as a peach, and full of juice, is he!

A THIRD.

The finely drawn, the sweetly swelling lip!

A FOURTH.

From such a cup, no doubt, you'd like to sip?

A FIFTH.

He's handsome, if a little unrefined.

A SIXTH.

He might be somewhat gracefuller, to my mind.

KNIGHT.

The shepherd I detect; I find him wearing
No traces of the Prince, or courtly bearing.

ANOTHER.

O, yes! half-naked is the youth not bad;
But let us see him first in armor clad!

LADY.

He seats himself, with such a gentle grace!

KNIGHT.

You'd find his lap, perchance, a pleasant place?

ANOTHER.

He lifts his arm so lightly o'er his head.

CHAMBERLAIN.

'T is not allowed: how thoroughly ill-bred!

LADY.

You lords find fault with all things evermore.

CHAMBERLAIN.

To stretch and yawn before the Emperor!

LADY.

He only acts: he thinks he's quite alone.

CHAMBERLAIN.

Even the play should be politely shown.

LADY.

Now sleep falls on the graceful youth so sweetly.

CHAMBERLAIN.

Now will he snore: 't is natural, completely!

YOUNG LADY.

Mixed with the incense-steam, what odor precious
Steals to my bosom, and my heart refreshes?

OLDER LADY.

Forsooth, it penetrates and warms the feeling!
It comes from him.

OLDEST LADY.

          His flower of youth, unsealing,
It is: Youth's fine ambrosia, ripe, unfading,
The atmosphere around his form pervading.
       (HELENA *comes forward.*)

MEPHISTOPHELES.

So, that is she? *My* sleep she would not waste:
She's pretty, truly, but she's not my taste.

ASTROLOGER.

There's nothing more for me to do, I trow;
As man of honor, I confess it now.
The Beauty comes, and had I tongues of fire,—
So many songs did Beauty e'er inspire,—
Who sees her, of his wits is dispossessed,
And who possessed her was too highly blessed.

FAUST.

Have I still eyes? Deep in my being springs
The fount of Beauty, in a torrent pouring!
A heavenly gain my path of terror brings.

The world was void, and shut to my exploring,—
And, since my priesthood, how hath it been graced!
Enduring 't is, desirable, firm-based.
And let my breath of being blow to waste,
If I for thee unlearn my sacred duty!
The form, that long erewhile my fancy captured,
That from the magic mirror so enraptured,
Was but a frothy phantom of such beauty!
'T is Thou, to whom the stir of all my forces,
The essence of my passion's courses,—
Love, fancy, worship, madness,—here I render!

MEPHISTOPHELES (*from the box*).
Be calm!—you lose your rôle, to be so tender!

OLDER LADY.
Tall and well-formed! Too small the head, alone.

YOUNGER LADY.
Just see her foot! A heavier ne'er was shown.

DIPLOMATIST.
Princesses of her style I've often seen:
From head to foot she's beautiful, I ween.

COURTIER.
She near the sleeper steals, so soft and sly.

LADY.
How ugly, near that youthful purity!

POET.
Her beauty's light is on him like a dawn.

LADY.
Endymion and Luna—as they're drawn!

POET.
Quite right! The yielding goddess seems to sink,
And o'er him bend, his balmy breath to drink.
Enviable fate—a kiss!—the cup is full!

DUENNA.

Before all people!—that is more than cool.

FAUST.

A fearful favor to the boy!

MEPHISTOPHELES.
Be still!
Suffer the shade to do whate'er it will!

COURTIER.

She slips away, light-footed: he awakes.

LADY.

Just as I thought! Another look she takes.

COURTIER.

He stares: what haps, to him a marvel is.

LADY.

But none to her, what she before her sees!

COURTIER.

She turns around to him with dignity.

LADY.

I see, she means to put him through his paces:
All men, in such a case, act stupidly.
Then, too, he thinks that first he's won her graces.

KNIGHT.

Majestically fine!—She pleases me.

LADY.

The courtesan! How very vulgar she!

PAGE.

Just where he is, is where I'd like to be!

COURTIER.

Who would not fain be caught in such sweet meshes?

LADY.

Through many a hand hath passed that jewel precious;
The gilding, too, is for the most part gone.

ANOTHER.

She has been worthless from her tenth year on.

KNIGHT.

Each takes the best that chance for him obtains;
I'd be contented with these fair remains.

A LEARNED MAN.

I freely own, though I distinctly see,
'T is doubtful if the genuine one she be.
The Present leads us to exaggeration,
And I hold fast the written, old relation.
I read that, truly, ere her bloom was blighted,
The Trojan gray-beards greatly she delighted.
And here, methinks, it tallies perfectly:
I am not young, yet she delighteth me.

ASTROLOGER.

No more a boy! A bold, heroic form,
He clasps her, who can scarce resist the storm.
With arm grown strong he lifts her high and free:
Means he to bear her off?

FAUST.
          Rash fool, let be!
Thou dar'st? Thou hear'st not? Hold!—I'll be
    obeyed.

MEPHISTOPHELES.

The spectral drama thou thyself hast made!

ASTROLOGER.

A word more! After all we've seen to-day,
I call the piece: *The Rape of Helena.*

FAUST.

What! Rape? Am I for nothing here? To stead me,
Is not this key still shining in my hand?

Through realms of terror, wastes, and waves it led me,
Through solitudes, to where I firmly stand.
Here foothold is! Realities here centre!
The strife with spirits here the mind may venture,
And on its grand, its double lordship enter!
How far she was, and nearer, how divine!
I'll rescue her, and make her doubly mine.
Ye Mothers! Mothers! crown this wild endeavor!
Who knows her once must hold her, and forever!

ASTROLOGER.

What art thou doing, Faust? O, look at him!
He seizes her: the form is growing dim.
He turns the key against the youth, and, lo!
It touches him— Woe's me! Away now! Woe on
    woe!
(*Explosion.* FAUST *lies upon the earth. The Spirits
            dissolve in vapor.*)

MEPHISTOPHELES
    (*taking* FAUST *upon his shoulders*).
You have it now! One's self with fools to hamper,
At last even on the Devil puts a damper.
        Darkness. Tumult.

ACT II.

I.

A HIGH-ARCHED, NARROW, GOTHIC CHAMBER, FORMERLY FAUST'S, UNCHANGED.

MEPHISTOPHELES
(*coming forth from behind a curtain. While he holds
    it up and looks behind him,* FAUST *is seen lying
    stretched out upon an antiquated bed*).
LIE there, ill-starred! seduced, unwise,
    To bonds that surely hold the lover!
Whom Helena shall paralyze
Not soon his reason will recover.
        (*Looking around him.*)

I look about, and through the glimmer
Unchanged, uninjured, all appears:
The colored window-panes, methinks, are dimmer,
The cobwebs have increased with years.
The ink is dry, the paper old and brown,
But each thing in its place I find:
Even the quill is here laid down,
Wherewith his compact with the Devil he signed.
Yea, deeper in, the barrel's red
With trace of blood I coaxed him then to shed.
A thing so totally unique
The great collectors would go far to seek.
Half from its hook the old fur-robe is falling,
That ancient joke of mine recalling,
How once I taught the boy such truth
As still, it may be, nourishes the youth.
The wish returns, with zest acuter,
Aided by thee, thou rough disguise,
Once more to take on airs as college tutor,
As one infallible in one's own eyes.
The *savans* this assurance know:
The Devil lost it, long ago!
(*He shakes the fur which he has taken down: moths,
       crickets, and beetles fly out.*)

CHORUS OF INSECTS.

Welcome, and hail to thee!
Patron, to-day:
We're flying and humming,
We hear and obey.
Singly and silently
Us thou hast sown;
Hither, by thousands,
Father, we've flown.
The imp in the bosom
Is snugly concealed;
But lice in the fur-coat
Are sooner revealed.

MEPHISTOPHELES.

What glad surprise I feel, from this young life bestowed!

One reaps in time, if one has only sowed.
Once more I'll shake the ancient fleeces out:
Still here and there a chance one flies about.—
Off, and around! in hundred thousand nooks
Hasten to hide yourselves—among the books,
There, in the pasteboard's wormy holes,
Here, in the smoky parchment scrolls,
In dusty jars, that broken lie,
And yonder skull with empty eye.
In all this trash and mould unmatched,
Crotchets forever must be hatched.

(*He puts on the fur-mantle.*)

Come, once again upon my shoulders fall!
Once more am I the Principal.
But 't is no good to ape the college;
For where are those who will my claim acknowledge?

(*He pulls the bell, which gives out a shrill, penetrating
sound, causing the halls to tremble and the doors to
fly open.*)

FAMULUS
(*tottering hither down the long, dark gallery*).

What a sound! What dreadful quaking!
Stairs are rocking, walls are shaking;
Through the colored windows brightening
I behold the sudden lightning;
Floors above me crack and rumble,
Lime and lumber round me tumble,
And the door, securely bolted,
Is by magic force unfolded.—
There! How terrible! a Giant
Stands in Faust's old fur, defiant!
As he looks, and beckons thither,
I could fall, my senses wither.
Shall I fly, or shall I wait?
What, O what shall be my fate!

MEPHISTOPHELES (*beckoning*).
Come hither, Friend! Your name is Nicodemus.

FAMULUS.
Most honored Sir, such is my name—*Oremus!*

MEPHISTOPHELES.

Dispense with that!

FAMULUS.

O joy! you know me yet.

MEPHISTOPHELES.

Old, and a student still,—I don't forget,
Most mossy Sir! Also a learned man
Continues study, since naught else he can.
'T is thus one builds a moderate house of cards;
The greatest minds ne'er end them, afterwards.
Your master is a skilful fellow, though:
The noble Doctor Wagner all must know.
The first in all the learned world is he,
Who now together holds it potently,
Wisdom increasing, daily making clearer.
How thirst for knowledge listener and hearer!
A mighty crowd around him flocks.
None for the rostrum e'er were meeter:
The keys he holds as doth Saint Peter,
The Under and the Upper he unlocks.
His light above all others sparkles surer,
No name or fame beside him lives:
Even that of Faust has grown obscurer;
'T is he alone invents and gives.

FAMULUS.

Pardon, most honored Sir! if I am daring
To contradict you, in declaring
All that upon the subject has no bearing;
For modesty is his allotted part.
The incomprehensible disappearing
Of that great man to him is most uncheering;
From his return he hopes new strength and joy of
 heart.
As in the days of Doctor Faust, the room,
Since he's away, all things unchanged,
Waits for its master long estranged.
To venture in, I scarce presume.—
What stars must govern now the skies!
It seemed as if the basement quivered;

The door-posts trembled, bolts were shivered:
You had not entered, otherwise.

MEPHISTOPHELES.

Where may his present dwelling be?
Lead me to him! Bring him to me!

FAMULUS.

His prohibition is so keen!
I do not dare to intervene.
For months, his time unto the great work giving,·
In most secluded silence he is living.
The daintiest of distinguished learners,
His face is like a charcoal-burner's,
From nose to ears all black and deadened;
His eyes from blowing flames are reddened:
Thus he, each moment, pants and longs,
And music make the clattering tongs.

MEPHISTOPHELES.

An entrance why should he deny me?
I'll expedite his luck, if he'll but try me!
(*The* FAMULUS *goes off*: MEPHITOPHELES *seats himself
with gravity.*)
Scarce have I taken my position here,
When there, behind, I see a guest appear.
I know him; he is of the school new-founded,
And his presumption will be quite unbounded.

BACCALAUREUS (*storming along the corridor*).
Doors and entrances are open!
Well,—at last there's ground for hoping
That no more, in mouldy lumber,
Death-like, doth the Living slumber,
To himself privations giving,
Till he dies of very living!

All this masonry, I'm thinking,
To its overthrow is sinking;
And, unless at once we hurry,
Us will crash and ruin bury.

Daring though I be, 't were murther
Should I dare to venture further.

What is that I see before me?
Here, (what years have rolled o'er me!)
Shy and unsophisticated,
I as honest freshman waited;
Here I let the gray-beards guide me,
Here their babble edified me!

Out of dry old volumes preaching,
What they knew, they lied in teaching;
What they knew themselves believed not,
Stealing life, that years retrieved not.
What!—in yonder cell benighted
One still sits, obscurely lighted!

Nearer now, I see, astounded,
Still he sits, with furs surrounded,—
Truly, as I saw him last,
Roughest fleeces round him cast!
Then adroit he seemed to be,
Not yet understood by me:
But to-day 't will naught avail him—
Oh, I'll neither fear nor fail him!

If, ancient Sir, that bald head, sidewards bending,
Hath not been dipped in Lethe's river cold,
See, hitherward your grateful scholar wending,
Outgrown the academic rods of old.
You're here, as then when I began;
But *I* am now another man.

MEPHISTOPHELES.

I'm glad my bell your visit brought me.
Your talents, then, I rated high;
The worm, the chrysalid soon taught me
The future brilliant butterfly.
Your curly locks and ruffle-laces
A childish pleasure gave; you wooed the graces.
A queue, I think, you've never worn?

But now your head is cropped and shorn.
Quite bold and resolute you appear.
But don't go, *absolute*, home from here!

BACCALAUREUS.

Old master, in your old place leaning,
Think how the time has sped, the while!
Spare me your words of double meaning!
We take them now in quite another style.
You teased and vexed the honest youth;
You found it easy then, in truth,
To do what no one dares, to-day.

MEPHISTOPHELES.

If to the young the simple truth we say,
The green ones find it nowise pleasant play;
But afterwards, when years are over,
And they the truth through their own hide discover,
Then they conceive, themselves have found it out:
"The master was a fool!" one hears them shout.

BACCALAUREUS.

A rogue, perhaps! What teacher will declare
The truth to us, exactly fair and square?
Each knows the way to lessen or exceed it,
Now stern, now lively, as the children need it.

MEPHISTOPHELES.

Beyond a doubt, there is a time to learn;
But you are skilled to teach, I now discern.
Since many a moon, some circles of the sun,
The riches of experience you have won.

BACCALAUREUS.

Experience! mist and froth alone!
Nor with the mind at all coequal:
Confess, what one has always known
Is not worth knowing, in the sequel!

MEPHISTOPHELES (*after a pause*).

It's long seemed so to me. I was a fool:
My shallowness I now must ridicule.

BACCALAUREUS.

I'm glad of that! I hear some reason yet—
The first old man of sense I ever met!

MEPHISTOPHELES.

I sought for hidden treasures, grand and golden,
And hideous coals and ashes were my share.

BACCALAUREUS.

Confess that now your skull, though bald and olden,
Is worth no more than is yon empty, there!

MEPHISTOPHELES (*amiably*).

Know'st thou, my friend, how rude thou art to me?

BACCALAUREUS.

One lies, in German, would one courteous be.

MEPHISTOPHELES

(*wheeling his chair still nearer to the proscenium, to
the spectators*).

Up here am I deprived of light and air:
Shall I find shelter down among you there?

BACCALAUREUS.

It is presumptuous, that one will try
Still to be something, when the time's gone by.
Man's life lives in his blood, and where, in sooth,
So stirs the blood as in the veins of youth?
There living blood in freshest power pulsates,
And newer life from its own life creates.
Then something's done, then moves and works the man;
The weak fall out, the sturdy take the van.
While half the world beneath *our* yoke is brought,
What, then, have you accomplished? Nodded—
        thought—
Dreamed, and considered—plan, and always plan!
Age is an ague-fever, it is clear,
With chills of moody want and dread;
When one has passed his thirtieth year,
One then is just the same as dead.
'T were best, betimes, to put you out o' the way.

MEPHISTOPHELES.

The Devil, here, has nothing more to say.

BACCALAUREUS.

Save through my will, no Devil can there be.

MEPHISTOPHELES (*aside*).

The Devil, though, will trip thee presently!

BACCALAUREUS.

This is Youth's noblest calling and most fit!
The world was not, ere I created it;
The sun I drew from out the orient sea;
The moon began her changeful course with me;
The Day put on his shining robes. to greet me;
The Earth grew green, and burst in flower to meet me,
And when I beckoned, from the primal night
The stars unveiled their splendors to my sight.
Who, save myself, to you deliverance brought
From commonplaces of restricted thought?
I, proud and free, even as dictates my mind,
Follow with joy the inward light I find,
And speed along, in mine own ecstasy,
Darkness behind, the Glory leading me!

[*Exit.*

MEPHISTOPHELES.

Go hence, magnificent Original!—
What grief on thee would insight cast!
Who can think wise or stupid things at all,
That were not thought already in the Past?
Yet even from him we're not in special peril;
He will, erelong, to other thoughts incline:
The must may foam absurdly in the barrel,
Nathless it turns at last to wine.
    (*To the younger parterre, which does not applaud.*)
My words, I see, have left you cold;
For you, my children, it may fall so:
Consider now, the Devil's old;
To understand him, be old also!

II.

LABORATORY.

*After the manner of the Middle Ages; extensive, pon-
derous apparatus for fantastic purposes.*
WAGNER (*at the furnace*).

THE loud bell chimes with fearful clangor,
  The sooty walls feel the vibration;
Soon must the long suspense be ended
Of my most earnest expectation.
It shines, the darknesses are rended:
Within the phial's inmost chamber
It gleams, as doth a living ember,—
Yea, a carbuncle, burning, bright'ning,
It rays the darkness with its lightning.
Now white and clear the lustres blend!
O that I hold, nor lose it more!
Ah, God! what rattles at the door?

MEPHISTOPHELES (*entering*).
Welcome! I mean it as a friend.

WAGNER (*anxiously*).
Be welcome to the planet of the hour!
(*Whispering.*)
Yet breath and speech suspend! A work of power,
A splendid work, will soon be here displayed.

MEPHISTOPHELES (*whispering*).
What is it, then?

WAGNER (*whispering*).
A man is being made.

MEPHISTOPHELES.
A man? And what enamored pair
Have you within the chimney hidden?

WAGNER.
Nay, God forbid! This procreation is most rare:

Of the old, senseless mode we're now well ridden.
The tender point, whence Life commenced its course,
The outward stress of gracious inward force,
Which took and gave, itself delineating,
First near, then foreign traits assimilating,
We now of all its dignity divest:
The beast therein may further find a zest,
But Man must learn, with his great gifts, to win
Henceforth a purer, loftier origin.

(*Turning towards the furnace.*)

It brightens,—see! Sure, now, my hopes increase
That if, from many hundred substances,
Through mixture—since on mixture all depends—
The human substance gently be compounded,
And by a closed retort surrounded,
Distilled, and fed, and slowly founded,
Then in success the secret labor ends.

(*Again turning towards the furnace.*)

'T will be! the mass is working clearer!
Conviction gathers, truer, nearer!
The mystery which for Man in Nature lies
We dare to test, by knowledge led;
And that which she was wont to organize
We crystallize, instead.

MEPHISTOPHELES.

Who lives, learns many secrets to unravel;
For him, upon this earth, there's nothing new can be:
I've seen already, in my years of travel,
Much crystallized humanity.

WAGNER

(*up to this time continuously attentive to the phial*).

It mounts, it lightens, grows,—'t is won!
A moment more, and it is done!
Insane, at first, appears a great intent;
We yet shall laugh at chance in generation;
A brain like this, for genuine thinking meant,
Will henceforth be a thinker's sure creation.

(*Rapturously inspecting the phial.*)

The glass vibrates with sweet and powerful tone;
It darkens, clears: it *must* arrive at being!
And now in delicate shape is shown
A pretty manikin, moving, living, seeing!
What more can we, what more the world demand?
The secret, solved, all men may reach:
Hark! as the ringing tones expand,
They form a voice, result in speech.

HOMUNCULUS
(*in the phial, to* WAGNER).
How goes it, Daddy? It was then no jest!
Come, press me tenderly upon thy breast!
But not too hard, for fear the glass might shatter!
This is the quality of matter:
For what is natural, scarce the world has place;
What's artificial, needs restricted space.

(*To* MEPHISTOPHELES.)
Thou rogue, Sir Cousin! here I find thee, too?
And at the proper time! My thanks are due:
A lucky fortune led thee here to me;
Since I exist, then I must active be.
I'd fain begin my work without delay:
Thou art adroit in shortening my way.

WAGNER.
But first, a word! I'm shamed that answers fail me;
For old and young with problems so assail me.
Now, for example, none e'er comprehended
How soul and body wedded are and blended,—
Hold fast, as if defying separation
Yet never cease their mutual irritation.
Therefore—

MEPHISTOPHELES.
Desist! I'd rather ask him why
The man and wife agree so wretchedly.
To thee, my friend, the thing will ne'er be clear:
There's work to do: for that the little fellow's here.

HOMUNCULUS.

What's to be done?

MEPHISTOPHELES (*pointing to a side-door*).
Thy talents here employ!

WAGNER (*still gazing at the phial*).
Forsooth, thou art the very loveliest boy!
(*The side-door opens:* FAUST *is seen stretched out
upon a couch.*)

HOMUNCULUS (*astonished*).
Significant!—
(*The phial slips out of* WAGNER'S *hands, hovers over*
FAUST, *and shines upon him.*)
Fair scenery!—Waters, moving
In forest shadows: women there, undressing,
The loveliest forms!—the picture is improving.
One, marked by beauty, splendidly expressing
Descent from Gods or high heroic races,
Now dips her foot in the translucent shimmer:
The living flame of her sweet form displaces
The yielding crystal, cool around the swimmer.
But what a sound of wings! What rapid dashing
Across the glassy pool, what fluttering, splashing!
The maidens fly, alarmed; but only she,
The queen, looks on, composed and terror-free
And sees with proud and womanly delight
The swan-prince press her knee with plumage white,
Importunately tame: he grows acquainted.—
But all at once floats up a vapor pale,
And covers with its closely-woven veil
The loveliest picture ever dreamed or painted.

MEPHISTOPHELES.
How much hast thou to tell,—what stories merry!
So small thou art, so great a visionary!
Nothing see I!—

HOMUNCULUS.
Of course. Thou, from the North,

And in the age of mist brought forth,
In knighthood's and in priestcraft's murky den,
How should thy sight be clearer, then?
In gloom alone art thou at home.

            (*Gazing around.*)

Brown masonry, repellent, crumbling slowly,
Arch-pointed, finical, fantastic, lowly!—
If this man wakes, another danger's nigh;
At once upon the spot he'll die.
Wood-fountains, swans, and naked beauties,
Such was his dream of presage fair:
How should these dark surroundings suit his
Desires, when them *I* scarce can bear?
Away with him!

MEPHISTOPHELES.
        I hail the issue's chances.

HOMUNCULUS.
Command the warrior to the fight,
Conduct the maiden to the dances,
And all is finished, as is right.
Just now—there breaks on me a light—
'T is Classical Walpurgis-Night;
Whate'er may come, it is the best event,
So bring him to his proper element!

MEPHISTOPHELES.
The like of that I never heard one mention.

HOMUNCULUS.
How should it have attracted your attention?
Only romantic ghosts are known to you;
A genuine phantom must be classic too.

MEPHISTOPHELES.
But whitherward shall then we travel, tell me!
Your antique cronies in advance repel me.

HOMUNCULUS.
Northwestwards, Satan, is thy park and pale,
But we, this time, southeastwards sail.

Peneus, there, the great plain wanders through,
By thickets, groves, and silent coves, and meadow
    grasses;
The level stretches to the mountain passes,
And o'er it lies Pharsalus, old and new.

MEPHISTOPHELES.

Alas! have done! Bring not that fell collision
Of tyrant and of slave before my vision!
I'm tired of that: for scarcely is it done
Than they the same thing have again begun;
And no one marks that he's the puppet blind
Of sly Asmōdi, lurking there behind.
They fight, we're told their freedom's right to save;
But, clearlier seen, 't is slave that fights with slave.

HOMUNCULUS.

Leave unto me their fractiousness and clatter.
Each must protect himself, as best he can,
From boyhood up, and thus becomes a man.
How this one shall recover, is our matter.
Hast thou a method, let it tested be!
But hast thou none, so leave the case to me!

MEPHISTOPHELES.

There's many a Brocken-method I might try,
But pagan bolts, I find, the way deny.
The Grecian race was little worth, alway;
It dazzles with the senses' freer play,
To cheerful sins the heart of man entices;
While ours are ever counted gloomy vices.
Now, what shall be?

HOMUNCULUS.

          Shyness was ne'er thy blame.
When I to thee Thessalian witches name,
I've not said nothing, that I know.

MEPHISTOPHELES (*lustfully*).

Thessalian witches! Well! The persons, those,

Whom I inquired for, long ago.
Night after night beside them to repose,
I think would hardly suit: but so,
A mere espial, trial,—

HOMUNCULUS.
Here! cast o'er
The knight your magic mantle, and infold him!
The rag will still, as heretofore,
Upon his airy course—and thine—uphold him.
I'll light the way.

WAGNER (*anxiously*).
And I?

HOMUNCULUS.
Eh? You
Will stay at home, most weighty work to do.
Unfold your ancient parchments, and collect
Life's elements as your recipes direct,
One to the other with due caution fitting.
The *What* consider, more the *How* and *Why!*
Meanwhile, about the world at random flitting,
I may detect the dot upon the "I."
The lofty aim will then accomplished be;
Such an endeavor merits such requital:
Gold, honor, glory, healthy forces vital,
And science, too, and virtue,—possibly.
Farewell!

WAGNER (*sorrowfully*).
Farewell! It doth depress my heart:
I fear, already, we forever part.

MEPHISTOPHELES.
Down to Peneus, with his aid!
Sir Cousin is a deft attendant.
(*Ad spectatores.*)
Upon the creatures we have made
We are, ourselves, at last, dependent.

III.

CLASSICAL WALPURGIS-NIGHT

1.

THE PHARSALIAN FIELDS.

Darkness.

ERICHTHO.

TO this night's awful festival, as oft before,
I enter here, Erichtho, I, the gloomy one:
Not so atrocious as the evil poets draw,
In most superfluous slander—for they never cease
Their blame or praises . . . Over-whitened I behold
The vale, with waves of tents that glimmer gray afar,
The after-vision of that fatal, fearful night.
How oft is it repeated!—will forever be
Forever re-enacted! No one grants the realm
Unto another: unto him whose might achieved
And rules it, none; for each, incompetent to rule
His own internal self, is all too fain to sway
His neighbor's will, even as his haughty mind inclines.
But here a lesson grand was battled to the end,
How force resists and grapples with the greater force.
The lovely, thousand-blossomed wreath of Freedom
rends,
And bends the stubborn laurel round the Ruler's brow.
Here, of his days of early greatness Pompey dreamed:
Before the trembling balance Cæsar yonder watched!
It will be weighed: the world knows unto whom it
turned.
The watch-fires flash and glow, spendthrift of ruddy
flame;
Reflections of the squandered blood the earth exhales,
And, lured by rare and marvellous splendor of the
night,
The legion of Hellenic legends gathers here.
Round all the fires uncertain hover, or at ease
Sit near them, fabulous forms of ancient days. . . .

The moon, imperfect, truly, but of clearest beam,
Arises, scattering mellow radiance everywhere:
Vanish the phantom tents, the fires are burning blue.

But o'er my head what unexpected meteor!
It shines, illuminates the sphere of earth below.
I scent the Living! therefore it becomes me not
Them to approach, I being harmful unto them:
An evil name it brings me, and it profits naught.
Already now it sinks: discreetly I withdraw.

[*Exit*

The Airy Travellers above.

HOMUNCULUS.
Once again the circle follow,
O'er the flames and horrors hover!
Ghostly 't is in vale and hollow,
Spectral all that we discover.

MEPHISTOPHELES.
If, as through my window nightly
In the grewsome North, I see
Spectres hideous and unsightly,
Here is home, as there, to me.

HOMUNCULUS.
See! a tall one there is striding
On before us, in the shade.

MEPHISTOPHELES.
Through the air she saw us gliding,
And it seems she is afraid.

HOMUNCULUS.
Let her stride! The knight be taken
Now, and set upon the strand:
Here to life again he'll waken,
Seeking it in fable-land.

FAUST (*as he touches the earth*).
Where is she?—

HOMUNCULUS.

It's more than we can tell,
But to inquire would here be well.
Thou 'rt free to hasten, ere the day,
From flame to flame, and seek her so:
Who to the Mothers found his way
Has nothing more to undergo.

MEPHISTOPHELES.

I also claim my share in the excursion;
Yet know no better plan for our diversion,
Than that each one, amid these fires,
Should seek such fortunes as he most desires.
Then, as a sign to reunite us,
Let, little one, thy lantern sound and light us!

HOMUNCULUS.

Thus shall it shine, and thus shall ring!
(*The glass shines and rings powerfully.*)
And now, away to many a marvellous thing!

FAUST (*solus*).

Where is she?—But no further question make!
If this were not the soil that bore her feet,
If not the wave that to her coming beat,
Yet 't is the air that knows the tongue she spake.
Here, by a marvel! Here, on Grecian land!
I felt at once the earth whereon I stand.
Through me, the sleeper, fresher spirit stealing,
I rise refreshed, Antæus in my feeling.
Together here I find the strangest store;
Let me this labyrinth of flames explore.

[*Goes away.*

MEPHISTOPHELES (*prying around*).

And as among these fires I wander, aimless,
I find myself so strange, so disconcerted:
Quite naked most, a few are only shirted;
The Griffins insolent, the Sphinxes shameless,
And what not all, with pinions and with tresses,
Before, behind, upon one's eyesight presses!—

Indecency, 't is true, is our ideal,
But the Antique is too alive and real;
One must with modern thought the thing bemaster,
And in the fashion variously o'erplaster:—
Disgusting race! Yet I, perforce, must meet them,
And as new guest with due decorum greet them.—
Hail, then, Fair Ladies! Graybeards wise, good cheer.

GRIFFIN (*snarling*).

Not graybeards! Graybeards? No one likes to hear
One call him *gray*. For in each word there rings
The source, wherefrom its derivation springs.
Gray, growling, grewsome, grinning, graves, and
     grimly
Etymologically accord, nor dimly,
And make us grim.

MEPHISTOPHELES.

              And yet, why need you stiffen?
You like the *grif* in your proud title, "Griffin."

GRIFFIN
(*as above, and continuously so*).

Of course! for this relation is found fit;
Though often censured, oftener praised was it.
Let one but *grip* at maidens, crowns, and gold:
Fortune is gracious to the Griper bold.

ANTS
(*of the colossal kind*).

You speak of gold, much had ourselves collected;
In rocks and caverns secretly we trapped it:
The Arimaspean race our store detected,—
They're laughing now, so far away they've snapped it.

THE GRIFFINS.

We soon shall force them to confess.

THE ARIMASPEANS

But not in this free night of jubilee.
Before the morrow all will squandered be;
This time our efforts will obtain success.

MEPHISTOPHELES
(*who has seated himself between the* SPHINXES).
How soon I feel familiar here, among you!
I understand you, one and all.

SPHINX.
Our spirit-tones, when we have sung you,
Become, for you, material.
Now name thyself, till we shall know thee better.

MEPHISTOPHELES.
With many names would men my nature fetter.
Are Britons here? So round the world they wheel,
To stare at battle-fields, historic traces,
Cascades, old walls, and classic dreary places;
And here were something worthy of their zeal.
Their Old Plays also testify of me;
Men saw me there as "Old Iniquity."

SPHINX.
How did they hit on that?

MEPHISTOPHELES.
I know not, verily.

SPHINX.
Perhaps! Hast thou in star-lore any power?
What say'st thou of the aspects of the hour?

MEPHISTOPHELES (*looking up*).
Star shoots on star, the cloven moon doth ride
In brilliance; in this place I'm satisfied:
I warm myself against thy lion's hide.
It were a loss to rise from out these shades:—
Propose enigmas, or at least charades!

SPHINX.
Express thyself, and 't will a riddle be.
Try once thine own analysis: 't were merry.
"To both Devout and Wicked necessary:
To those, a breast-plate for ascetic fighting;

To these, boon-comrade, in their pranks uniting;
And both amusing Zeus, the fun-delighting."

FIRST GRIFFIN (*snarling*).
I like not him!

SECOND GRIFFIN (*snarling more gruffly*).
What will the fellow here?

BOTH.
The Nasty One is not of us, 't is clear!

MEPHISTOPHELES (*brutally*).
Think'st thou, perhaps, thy guest has nails to scratch,
That with thy sharper talons cannot match?
Just try it once!

SPHINX (*gently*).
Stay, shouldst thou find it well;
But from our ranks thou wilt thyself expel.
In thine own land thou 'rt wont thyself to pamper,
Yet here, I think, thy spirits feel a damper.

MEPHISTOPHELES.
Thine upper part entices; naught is fairer;
But, further down, the beast excites my terror.

SPHINX.
Bitter, False one, will be thy expiation;
Our claws are sound and worthy proof,
But thou with withered horse's-hoof,
Art ill at ease in our association.
(*The* SIRENS *prelude above.*)

MEPHISTOPHELES.
On yonder poplars by the river,
What are the birds that swing above?

SPHINX.
Beware! The very best that ever
Existed, they have lured to love.

SIRENS.

Ah, why vitiate your senses,
Where those Uglinesses darken?
We, in crowds, come hither: hearken
How the accordant strain commences,
Meet for Sirens' soft pretences!

SPHINXES
(*mocking them, in the same melody*).
Let them to descend be bidden!
In the branches they have hidden
Hideous falcon-claws they're wearing,
And you'll feel their cruel tearing,
Once you lend them willing ear.

SIRENS.

Banish hate and envy rather!
We the purest pleasures gather,
Under Heaven's auspicious sphere!
On the earth and on the ocean,
We, with cheerful beckoning motion,
Bid the wanderer welcome here.

MEPHISTOPHELES.

These are of novelties the neatest,
Where from the throat and harp-string sweetest
The tones around each other twine.
They're lost on me, these tinkling trickles;
The sound my ear-drum pats and tickles,
But cannot reach this heart of mine.

SPHINXES.

Speak not of heart! Fool, so to call it!
An old and wrinkled leathern wallet
Would better suit that face of thine.

FAUST (*approaching*).
How strange! I, satisfied, behold these creatures,—
In the Repulsive, grand and solid features:
A fate propitious I behold advance.
Whither transports me now this solemn glance?

(*Pointing to the* SPHINXES).
Once before these took Œdipus his stand:
(*Pointing to the* SIRENS.)
These made Ulysses write in hempen band:
(*Pointing to the* ANTS.)
By these the highest treasure was amassed:
(*Pointing to the* GRIFFINS.)
By these 't was held inviolate and fast:
Fresh spirit fills me, face to face with these—
Grand are the Forms, and grand the Memories!

MEPHISTOPHELES.

Once thou hadst cursed such crude antiques,
But now, it seems, they've comfort given;
For when a man his sweetheart seeks,
Welcome to him are monsters, even.

FAUST (*to the* SPHINXES).

Ye woman-forms, give ear, and say
Hath one of you seen Helena?

SPHINXES.

Before her day our line expired in Greece;
Our very last was slain by Hercules:
Yet ask of Chiron, if thou please.
He gallops round throughout this ghostly night,
And if he halt for thee, thy chance is bright.

SIRENS.

Thou art not to failure fated!
How Ulysses, lingering, learned us,
Nor, regardless passing, spurned us,
Manifold hath he narrated:
All to thee shall be confided,
Seekest thou our meads, divided
By the dark-green arms of Ocean.

SPHINX.

Let not thyself thus cheated be!
Not like Ulysses bound,—but we
Will with good counsel thee environ:

If thou canst find the noble Chiron,
Thou 'lt learn what I have promised thee.

[FAUST *goes away.*

MEPHISTOPHELES (*ill-temperedly*).

What croaks and flaps of wings go past!
One cannot see, they fly so fast,
In single file, from first to last:
A hunter would grow tired of these.

SPHINX.

The storm-wind like, that winter harrows,
Reached hardly by Alcides' arrows,
They are the swift Stymphalides;
And not ill-meant their greetings creak,
With goose's foot and vulture's beak.
They fain would join us in our places,
And show themselves as kindred races.

MEPHISTOPHELES (*as if intimidated*).

Some other brute is hissing shrill.

SPHINX.

Be not afraid, though harsh the pæan!
They are the hydra-heads, the old Lernæan,
Cut from the trunk, yet think they're something still.
But say, what means your air distressed?
Why show your gestures such unrest?
Where will you go? Then take your leave!
That chorus, there, I now perceive,
Turns like a weathercock your neck. Advance!—
Greet as you will each lovely countenance!
They are the Lamiæ, wenches vile,
With brazen brows and lips that smile,
Such as the satyr-folk have found so fair:
A cloven foot may venture all things there.

MEPHISTOPHELES.

But stay you here, that I again may find you?

SPHINX.

Yes! Join the airy rabble, there behind you!

From Egypt we, long since, with all our peers,
Accustomed were to reign a thousand years.
If for our place your reverence be won,
We rule for you the days of Moon and Sun.
    We sit before the Pyramids
    For the judgment of the Races,
    Inundation, War, and Peace,—
    With eternal changeless faces.

2.

PENEUS

(surrounded with NYMPHS *and Tributary Streams).*

PENEUS.

STIR yourselves, ye whispering rushes,
  Rustle, slender willow-bushes,
  Sister reeds, breathe softer, crisper,
  Trembling poplar-branches, whisper
  To the interrupted dream!
  Fearful premonitions wake me,
  Secret shudders thrill and shake me
  In my rippling, sleeping stream.

FAUST *(advancing to the river).*

Here, behind the vines that dangle
O'er the thicket's bowery tangle,
If I heard aright, were noises
Similar to human voices.
Babbling seemed the wave to patter,
And the breeze in sport to chatter.

NYMPHS *(to* FAUST).

  For thee were it better
  To lie here, reviving
  In coolness thy body,
  Outwearied with striving,—
  The rest, that eludes thee,
  To taste, and be free:
  We'll rustle and murmur,
  And whisper to thee.

FAUST.

I am awake! Let them delay me,
The incomparable Forms!—and sway me,
As yonder to my sight confessed!
How strangely am I moved, how nearly!
Are they but dreams? or memories, merely?
Already once was I so blest.
Beneath the swaying bushes hiding,
The full, fresh waves are softly gliding;
They scarcely rustle on their path:
A hundred founts from all sides hasten,
To fill a pure and sparkling basin,
The hollowed level of a bath.
The fair young limbs of women trouble
The watery glass that makes them double,
And doubles, thus, the eye's delight:
In joyous bath each other aiding,
Or boldly swimming, shyly wading,
Then cry, and splash, and foamy fight.
It were enough, the picture viewing,—
My healthy eyesight here renewing,—
Yet I desire the still unseen.
My gaze would pierce through yonder cover,
Whose leafy wealth is folded over
The vision of the stately Queen.·

Strange! across the crystal skimming,
From the coves the swans are swimming,
Moving in majestic state:
Floating calmly and united,
But how proud and self-delighted,
Head and neck they lift elate! . . .
One, his feathers proudly pluming,
Boldly on his grace presuming,
Leads the others in the race;
With his whitest plumage showing
Wave-like on the wave he's throwing,
Speeds he to the sacred place. . . .
The others back and forth together
Swim on with smoothly shining feather,
And soon, in mimic battle met,

Shall chase aside the maids affrighted,
Till, for their own protection slighted,
Their bounden service they forget.

NYMPHS.

Sisters, bend and lay the ear
On the turf beside the river!
Sound of hoofs, if right I hear,
Swift approaching, seems to shiver.
Would I knew whose rapid flight
Brings a message to the Night!

FAUST.

As I think, the earth is ringing
From a charger, hither springing.
See there! See there!
A fortune comes, most fair:
Shall I attain its blessing?
O, marvel past expressing!
A rider trots towards us free:
Spirit and strength in him I see,—
Upon a snow-white steed careering. . . .
I know him now, I hail with awe
The famous son of Philyra!—
Halt, Chiron, halt! I've something for thy hearing.

CHIRON.

What then? What is it?

FAUST.

Thy course delay!

CHIRON.

I rest not.

FAUST.

Take me with thee, then, I pray!

CHIRON.

Mount! and I thus can ask, at leisure,
Whither thy way. Thou standest on the shore;
I'll bear thee through the flood, with pleasure.

FAUST (*mounting*).
Whither thou wilt. I thank thee evermore. . . .
The mighty man, the pedagogue, whose place
And fame it was, to teach a hero-race,—
The splendid circle of the Argonauts,
And all whose deeds made quick the Poet's thoughts.

CHIRON.
We will not further speak of these!
As Mentor even Pallas is not venerated;
And, after all, they manage as they please,
As if they'd not been educated.

FAUST.
The leech, who knoweth flower and fruit,
Whose lore can sound the deepest root,—
Who heals the sick, and soothes the wounded place,
Him, here, in mind and body I embrace!

CHIRON.
When heroes, near me, felt the smart,
My helpful knowledge failed them seldom;
But, at the last, I left mine art
To priest and simple-gathering beldam.

FAUST.
Thy speech the true great man betrays,
Who cannot hear a word of praise;
His modesty would fain confound us
To think his equals still were round us.

CHIRON.
Thou seemest skilled to feign such matter—
People and Prince alike to flatter.

FAUST.
But surely thou wilt grant to me
That thou the greatest of thy time didst see,
Upon their paths of proud achievement trod,
And lived thy days, a serious demigod.
Among those grand, heroic forms of old,
Whom didst thou for the best and worthiest hold?

CHIRON.

Of those beneath the Argonauts' bright banner,
Each worthy was in his peculiar manner,
And by the virtue of his strength selective
Sufficed therein, where others were defective.
Castor and Pollux were as victors hailed,
Where beauty and the grace of youth prevailed:
Decision, the swift deed for others' aid,
Gave the fair crown before the Boreads laid:
Reflective, prudent, strong, in council wise,
So Jason ruled, delight of women's eyes:
Then Orpheus, gentle, silent, brooding, lowering,
But when he struck the lyre, all-overpowering.
Sharp-sighted Lynceus, who by day and dark
Through shoreward breakers steered the sacred bark.
Danger is best endured where men are brothers;
When one achieves, then praise him all the others.

FAUST.

But Hercules thy speech is wronging—

CHIRON.

Ah, me! awaken not my longing! . . .
I had not seen, in Fields Elysian,
How Phœbus, Arês, Hermes, shine;
But there arose before my vision
A form that all men called divine.
A king by birth, as ne'er another,
A youth magnificent to view;
Though subject to his elder brother,
And to the loveliest women, too.
No second such hath Gæa granted,
Or Hebe led to Heaven again;
For him the songs are vainly chanted,
The marble hewn for him in vain.

FAUST.

Though ever to his form addicted,
His grace the sculptors could not wreak.
The fairest Man hast thou depicted,
Now of the fairest Woman speak!

CHIRON.

What!—Little worth is woman's beauty,
So oft an image dumb we see:
I only praise, in loving duty,
A being bright and full of glee.
For Beauty in herself delighteth;
And irresistibly she smiteth
When sweetly she with Grace uniteth,
Like Helena, when her I bore.

FAUST.

Her didst thou bear?

CHIRON.
                                This back she pressed.

FAUST.

Was I not wild enough, before?
And now such seat, to make me blest!

CHIRON.

Just so she grasped me by the hair
As thou dost.

FAUST.
                        O, I scarcely dare
To trust my senses!—tell me more!
She is my only aspiration!
Whence didst thou bear her—to what shore?

CHIRON.

Not difficult is the relation.
'T was then, when came the Dioscuri bold
To free their sister from the robbers' hold;
But these, accustomed not to be subdued,
Regained their courage and in rage pursued.
The swamps below Eleusis did impede
The brothers' and the sister's flying speed:
The brothers waded: splashing through the reed,
I swam: then off she sprang, and pressing me
On the wet mane, caressing me,
She thanked with sweetly-wise and conscious tongue.
How charming was she!—dear to age, so young!

FAUST.

But seven years old!—

CHIRON.

         Philologists, I see,
Even as they cheat themselves, have cheated thee.
'T is curious with your mythologic dame:
The Poet takes her when he needs her name;
She grows not old, stays ever young and warm,
And of the most enticing form;
Seduced in youth, in age enamoring still,—
Enough! no time can bind the Poet's will.

FAUST.

Then let no bonds of Time be thrown around her!
Even as on Pheræ's isle Achilles found her,
Beyond the bounds of Time. What blessing rare,
In spite of Fate such love to win and wear!
And shall not I, by mightiest desire,
Unto my life that sole fair form acquire,
That shape eternal, peer of Gods above,
Tender as grand, sublime as sweet with love?
Thou saw'st her once; *to-day* I saw her beam,
The dream of Beauty, beautiful as Dream!
My soul, my being, now is bound and chained;
I cannot live, unless she be attained.

CHIRON.

Thou, Stranger! feel'st, as man, such ecstasy;
Among us, Spirits, mad thou seem'st to be.
Yet, as it haps, thy fortune now is omened;
For every year, though only for a moment,
It is my wont to call at Manto's dwelling,—
She, Esculapius' child, whose prayers are swelling
Unto her father, that, his fame to brighten,
The brains of doctors he at last enlighten,
And them from rashly dealing death may frighten.
I like her best of all the guild of Sibyls,—
Helpful and kind, with no fantastic fribbles;
She hath the art, if thou the time canst borrow,
With roots of power to give thee healing thorough.

FAUST.

But I will not be healed! my aim is mighty:
I will not be, like others, meanly flighty!

CHIRON.

The noble fountain's cure neglect thou not:
But quick dismount! We've reached the spot.

FAUST.

And whither, in this dreary night, hast thou
To land through pebbly rivers brought me now?

CHIRON.

Here Rome and Greece in battle tried their powers;
Here flows Peneus, there Olympus towers,—
The greatest realm that e'er was lost in sand.
The monarch flies, the conquering burghers stand.
Look up and see, in moonlight shining clear,
The memorable, eternal Temple near!

MANTO (*dreaming within*).
From horse-hoofs tremble
The sacred steps of the Temple!
The Demigods draw near.

CHIRON.
Quite right!
Open your eyes, and see who's here!

MANTO (*awaking*).
Welcome! Thou dost not fail, I see.

CHIRON.
And still thy temple stands for thee!

MANTO.
And speedest thou still unremitting?

CHIRON.
And thou in peaceful calm art sitting,
While I rejoice in restless heels?

MANTO.

I wait, and Time around me wheels.
And he?

CHIRON.

The vortex of this night
Hath whirled him hither to thy sight.
Helen, with mad, distracted senses,
Helen he'd win by all pretences,
And knows not how or where the task commences;
But he deserves the Esculapian cure.

MANTO.

To whom the Impossible is lure
I love.
(CHIRON *is already far away.*)
Rash one, advance! there's joy for thee!
This dark way leads thee to Persephone.
Under Olympus' hollow foot,
Secret, she waits prohibited salute.
I smuggled Orpheus in to her, of old:
Use *thy* chance better! On!—be bold!
[*They descend.*

3.

ON THE UPPER PENEUS, AS BEFORE.

SIRENS.

PLUNGE in cool Peneus' wave!
There 't is well to sport in swimming,
Songs with chorded voices hymning,
That the ill-starred folk we save.
Health is none where water fails!
Let our hosts, with sounding pæan,
Hasten to the blue Ægæan,
Where each joy shall swell our sails.
(*Earthquake.*)
Back the frothy wave is flowing,
Now no longer downward going;
Shakes the bed, the waters roar,
Cracks and smokes the stony shore.

Let us fly! Come, every one!
By this marvel profit none.
Leave, ye guests, this wild commotion
For the cheerful sports of Ocean,
Shining, where the quivering reaches,
Lightly heaving, bathe the beaches,—
There, where Luna's double splendor
Freshens us with night-dews tender.
There the freest life delights us;
Here the threatening Earthquake frights us:
Who is prudent, haste away!
Fearful is it, here to stay.

SEISMOS
(*growling and jolting in the depths*).
Once again the force applying,
Bravely with the shoulders prying,
We to get above are trying,
Where to us must all give way.

SPHINXES.
What a most repulsive shaking,
Terrible and hideous quaking!
What a quivering and shocking,
Hither rolling, thither rocking!
What vexation and dismay!
But we shall not change our station,
Were all Hell in agitation. ·. . .
Now behold a dome upswelling,
Wonderful! 'T is *he,* compelling,—
He, the hoary, antiquated,
He who Delos' isle created,
Bidding it from ocean break,
For the childed woman's sake.
He, with all his force expended,
Rigid arms and shoulders bended,
Like an Atlas in his gesture
Pushes up the earth's green vesture,
Loam and grit, and sand and shingle,
Where the shore and river mingle:
Thus our valley's bosom quiet

Cross-wise tears he, in his riot.
In unwearied force defiant,
He, a caryatid-giant,
Bears a fearful weight of boulders,
Buried still below his shoulders;
But no further shall be granted,
For the Sphinxes here are planted.

SEISMOS.

The work alone I've undertaken;
The credit will be given to me:
Had I not jolted, shoved, and shaken,
How should this world so beauteous be?
How stood aloft your mountains ever,
In pure and splendid blue of air,
Had I not heaved with huge endeavor
Till they, like pictures, charm you there?
When, where ancestral memory brightens,
Old Night and Chaos saw me sore betrayed,
And in the company of Titans
With Pelion and Ossa as with balls we played,
None could in ardent sport of youth surpass us,
Until, outwearied, at the last,
Even as a double cap, upon Parnassus
His summits wickedly we cast.
Apollo, now, upon that mount of wonder
Finds with the Muses his retreat:
For even Jove, and for his bolts of thunder,
I heaved and held the lofty seat.
Thus have I forced the fierce resistance
And struggled upward from the deep;
And summon now to new existence
The joyous dwellers of the steep.

SPHINXES.

'T is true, the hill would seem primeval,
And warranted of old to stand,
Had we not witnessed its upheaval,
Toiling and towering from the land.
A bushy forest, spreading, clothes its face,
And rocks on rocks are pressing to their place.

A Sphinx, therefrom, is by no fear o'ertaken:
We shall not let our sacred seats be shaken.

GRIFFINS.

Gold in spangle, leaf, and spark
Glimmers through the fissures dark.
Quick, lest others should detect it,
Haste, ye Emmets, and collect it!

CHORUS OF EMMETS.

Upward have thrown it,
As they, the giant ones,
Quick-footed, pliant ones,
Climb it and own it!
Rapidly in and out!
In each such fissure
Is every crumb about
Wealth for the wisher!
Seek for them greedily,
Even the slightest:
Everywhere speedily
Gather the brightest!
Diligent be, and bold—
Swarm to the fountain:
Only bring in the Gold!
Heed not the Mountain!

GRIFFINS.

Come in! come in!—the treasure heap!
Our claws upon it we shall keep.
The most efficient bolts they are;
The greatest wealth they safely bar.

PYGMIES.

Verily, here we sit securely;
How it happened, is not clear.
Ask not whence we came; for surely
'T is enough that we are here.
Unto Life's delighted dwelling
Suitable is every land;
Where a rifted rock is swelling,

Also is the Dwarf at hand.
Male and female, busy, steady,
We as models would suffice:
Who can tell if such already
Labored so in Paradise?
Here our lot as best we measure,
And our star of fate is blest:
Mother Earth brings forth with pleasure.
In the East as in the West.

DACTYLS.

If she, in a single night,
The Pygmies brought to light,
Pygmies of all she'll create yet,
And each find his mate yet!

PYGMY-ELDERS.

Be ye, in haste,
Conveniently placed!
Labor, and lead
Strength unto speed!
Peace is yet with ye,
Build now the smithy,—
The host be arrayed
With armor and blade!
Emmets, laborious,
Working victorious,
Scorning to settle,
Furnish us metal!
Dactyls, your host,
Smallest and most,
Hear the requiring,
Bring wood for firing!
Heap in the chambers
Fuel, untiring:
Furnish us embers!

GENERALISSIMO.

With arrow and bow,
Encounter the foe!
By yonder tanks

The heron-ranks,
The countless-nested,
The haughty-breasted,
At one quick blow
Shoot, and bring low!
All together,
That we may feather
Our helmets so.

EMMETS AND DACTYLS.

Who now will save us!
We bring the iron,
And chains enslave us.
To break our fetters
Were now defiant;
We bide our season,—
Meanwhile, be pliant!

THE CRANES OF IBYCUS.

Murder-cries and moans of dying!
Startled wings that flap in flying!
What lament, what pain and fright
Pierces to our airy height!
All have fallen in the slaughter,
Reddening with their blood the water;
Pygmy-lust, misformed and cruel,
Robs the heron of his jewel.
On their helms the plumage waves,—
Yonder fat-paunched, bow-legged knaves!
Comrades of our files of motion,
Serried wanderers of ocean,
You we summon to requital
In a cause to you so vital.
Strength and blood let no one spare!
Endless hate to them we swear!

(*They disperse, croaking in the air.*)

MEPHISTOPHELES (*on the plain*).

With ease the Northern witches I controlled,
But o'er these foreign sprites no power I hold.
The Blocksberg is a most convenient place;

Howe'er one strays, one can his path retrace.
Dame Ilse watches for us from her stone,
And Henry sits upon his mountain-throne:
The Snorers snarl at Elend—snorting peers,—
And all is finished for a thousand years.
But here, who knows if, even where he stand,
Beneath his feet may not puff up the land?
I cheerily wander through a level glade,
And, all at once, behind me heaved, is made
A mountain—scarcely to be called so, true;
Yet high enough the Sphinxes from my view
To intercept. . . . Still many a fire flares out
Adown the vale, the mad concern about. . . .
Still dance and hover, beckoning and retreating,
The gay groups round me, with their knavish greeting
But gently now! For spoiled by stealthy pleasure,
One always seeks to snatch some dainty treasure.

LAMIÆ.

(drawing MEPHISTOPHELES *after them).*

Quicker and quicker!
And further take him!
Then hesitating,
Chattering and prating!
'T is fun to make him—
Old, sinful Tricker!—
Follow behind us:
To penance comes he
With halt-foot clumsy;
He marches hobbling,
And forwards wobbling·
His leg he trails
In haste to find us;
We fly—he fails.

MEPHISTOPHELES *(standing still).*

Accurséd fate! Deceived, as oft!
Since Adam's time seduced and scoffed!
Though old we grow, not wisely schooled:
Enough already I've been fooled!
We know, how wholly worthless is the **race**,

With body corseted and painted face;
Of health responsive own they not a tittle,
Where'er one grasps them, every limb is brittle.
The thing is known, and patent to our glances,
And yet, whene'er the trollops pipe, one dances.

LAMIÆ (*pausing*).

Halt! he reflects; his steps delay:
Turn back to meet him, lest he get away!

MEPHISTOPHELES (*striding forwards*).

Forwards! the doubt, my strength benumbing,
I won't encourage foolishly;
For were the witches not forthcoming,
Why, who the devil would Devil be!

LAMIÆ (*very graciously*).

Round this hero lightly moving,
Let his heart, the choice approving,
One of us select for loving!

MEPHISTOPHELES.

True, in this uncertain lustre,
Seem ye fair maids, in a cluster;
Fain would I to you be juster.

EMPUSA (*pressing forwards*).

Not me, too? I'm also fittted
In your train to be admitted!

LAMIÆ.

She's one too many; for, in short,
She always ruins all our sport.

EMPUSA (*to* MEPHISTOPHELES).

Empusa, with the ass's foot,
Thy cousin dear, gives thee salute!
Only a horse's hoof is thine,
And yet, Sir Cousin, greeting fine!

MEPHISTOPHELES.

Strangers I here anticipated,

And find, alas! my near--related:
The old tale—instances by dozens—
From Hartz to Hellas always cousins!

EMPUSA.

I act with promptness and decision;
In many forms could meet thy vision
Yet in thy honor now, instead,
Have I put on the ass's head.

MEPHISTOPHELES.

Great things, I see, are here portended,
Thus with the race as kinsman blended:
Let come what may, since I have known her—
The ass's head—I'd fain disown her.

LAMIÆ.

Leave her, the Ugly! She doth scare
Whatever lovely seems and fair;
Whate'er was lovely, fair to see,
When *she* comes, ceases so to be.

MEPHISTOPHELES.

These cousins also,—soft, delicious,
Are one and all to me suspicious:
I fear, beneath their cheeks of roses
Some metamorphosis reposes.

LAMIÆ.

But try—take hold! For we are many,
And if thou hast a lucky penny,
Secure thyself the highest prize!
What means thy wanton organ-grinding?
A wretched wooer 't is, we're finding,
Yet swagger'st thus, and seem'st so wise! . .
Now one of us will he lay hand on,
So by degrees your masks abandon,
And show your natures to his eyes!

MEPHISTOPHELES.

The fairest here have I selected. . . .
       (Clasping her.)

O, what a broomstick, unexpected!
                (*Grasping another.*)
And this one? . . . Vilest countenance!

LAMIÆ.

Think not thou 'rt worth a better chance!

MEPHISTOPHELES.

That little one, she warms my gizzard. . . .
But through my hand she slips, a lizard;
Her smooth braids, snaky-like, intwine.
I try the tall one, yet she worse is,—
I only grasp a Bacchic thyrsus,
The head a scaly cone of pine.
What follows next? Behold a fat one:
Perhaps I'll find delight in *that* one,
So, once for all, the chance renew!
The Turks, for one so puffy, flabby,
Would pay a price by no means shabby . . .
But, ah! the puff-ball bursts in two!

LAMIÆ.

Now scatter widely, hovering, feigning,
In lightning-like, dark flight enchaining
The interloping witch's-son!
Uncertain circles, awful, poiseless!
Horrid bat-wings, flying noiseless!
He 'scapes too cheaply, when it's done.

MEPHISTOPHELES (*shaking himself*).

I've not become, it seems, a great deal·shrewder;
The North's absurd, 't is here absurder, ruder,
The spectres here preposterous as there,
People and poets shallow ware.
This masquerade resembles quite—
As everywhere—a dance of appetite.
I sought a lovely masked procession,
And caught such things, I stood aghast. . . .
I'd give myself a false impression,
If this would only longer last.
                (*Losing himself among the rocks.*)

Where am I then? and whither sped?
There was a path; 't is now a dread.
By level ways I've wandered hither,
Where rubble now is piled together.
I clamber up and down in vain;
Where shall I find my Sphinx again?
I had not dreamed so mad a sight,—
A mountain in a single night!
A bold witch-journey, to my thought:
Their Blocksberg with them they have brought.

OREAD (*from the natural rock*).

Come up to me! My mountain old
In its primeval form behold!
Revere the steep and rocky stairs, ascending
Where Pindus' offshoots with the plain are blending!
Unshaken, thus I heaved my head
When o'er my shoulders Pompey fled.
Beside me this illusive rock
Will vanish at the crow of cock.
I see such fables oft upthrown,
And suddenly again go down.

MEPHISTOPHELES.

Honor to thee, thou reverend Head,
With strength of oak engarlanded!
The clearest moonlight never cleaves
The darkness of your crowded leaves.
I see between the bushes go
A light, with unpretending glow.
How all things fit and balance thus!
'T is verily Homunculus.
Now whence thy way, thou little lover?

HOMUNCULUS.

From place to place I flit and hover,
And, in the best sense, I would fain exist,
And most impatient am, my glass to shatter:
But what till now I've witnessed, is 't
Then strange if I mistrust the matter?
Yet I'll be confidential, if thou list:

I follow two Philosophers this way.
'T was "Nature!" "Nature!"—all I heard them say;
I'll cling to them, and see what they are seeing,
For they must understand this earthly being,
And I shall doubtless learn, in season,
Where to betake me with the soundest reason.

MEPHISTOPHELES.

Then do it of thy own accord!
For here, where spectres from their hell come,
Is the philosopher also welcome.
That so his art and favor delectate you,
At once a dozen new ones he'll create you.
Unless thou errest, thou wilt ne'er have sense;
Wouldst thou exist, thyself the work commence!

HOMUNCULUS.

Good counsel, also, is not to reject.

MEPHISTOPHELES.

Then go thy way! We further will inspect.
                                   [*They separate.*

ANAXAGORAS (*to* THALES).

Thy stubborn mind will not be rightened:
What else is needful, that thou be enlightened?

THALES.

To every wind the billows yielding are;
Yet from the cliff abrupt they keep themselves **afar.**

ANAXAGORAS.

By fiery vapors rose this rock you're seeing.

THALES.

In moisture came organic life to being.

HOMUNCULUS (*between the two*).

To walk with you may I aspire?
To come to being is my keen desire.

ANAXAGORAS.

Hast thou, O Thales! ever in a night
Brought forth from mud such mountain to the light?

THALES.

Nature, the living current of her powers,
Was never bound to Day and Night and Hours;
She makes each form by rules that never fail,
And 't is not Force, even on a mighty scale.

ANAXAGORAS.

But here it *was!*—Plutonic fire, the shaper!
Explosive force of huge Æolian vapor
Broke through the level Earth's old crust primeval,
And raised the new hill with a swift upheaval!

THALES.

What further shall therefrom result? The hill
Is there: 't is well!—so let it stand there still!
In such a strife one loses leisure precious,
Yet only leads the patient folk in leashes.

ANAXAGORAS.

The Mountain's rocky clefts at once
Are peopled thick with Myrmidons,
With Pygmies, Emmets, Fingerlings,
And other active little things.

(*To* HOMUNCULUS.)
To greatness hast thou ne'er aspired,
But lived an eremite retired;
Canst thou persuade thy mind to govern,
I'll have thee chosen as their sovereign.

HOMUNCULUS.

What says my Thales?

THALES.

       —Will not recommend:
For small means only unto small deeds tend,
But great means make the small man great

See there! The Cranes, with purpose heinous!—
The troubled populace they menace,
And they would menace thus the king.
With pointed beaks and talons ample
The little men they pierce and trample:
Doom comes already thundering.
It was a crime, the heron-slaughter,
Beset amid their peaceful water;
But from that rain of arrows deadly
A fell revenge arises redly,
And calls the kindred o'er the flood
To spill the Pygmies' guilty blood.
What use for shield and helm and spear?
Or for the dwarfs the heron-feather?
Dactyl and Emmet hide together:
Their cohorts scatter, seek the rear!

ANAXAGORAS

(after a pause, solemnly).

Though I the subterranean powers approve,
Yet help, in this case, must be sought above. . . .
O thou aloft, in grace and vigor vernal,
Tri-named, tri-featured, and eternal,
By all my people's woe I cry to thee,
Diana, Luna, Hecaté!
Thou breast-expanding One, thou deeply-pondering,
Thou calmly-shining One, majestic wandering,
The fearful craters of thy shade unseal,
And free from spells thine ancient might reveal!

(Pause.)

Am I too swiftly heard?
Has then my cry
To yonder sky,
The course of Nature from its orbit stirred?

And greater, ever greater, drawing near,
Behold the Goddess' orbéd throne appear,
Enormous, fearful in its grimness,
With fires that redden through the dimness! . .

No nearer! Disk of dread, tremendous,
Lest thou, with land and sea, to ruin send us!
Then were it true, Thessalian Pythonesses
With guilty spells, as Song confesses,
Once from thy path thy steps enchanted,
Till fatal gifts by thee were granted? . . .
The shield of splendor slowly darkles,
Then suddenly splits, and shines, and sparkles!
What rattling and what hissing follow,
With roar of winds and thunders hollow!—
Before thy throne I speak my error. . . .
O, pardon! *I* invoked the terror.
                    (*Casts himself upon his fate.*)

THALES.

How many things can this man see and hear?
What happed, is not to me entirely clear;
I've not, like him, experienced it.
The Hours are crazy, we'll admit;
For Luna calmly shines, and free,
In her high place, as formerly.

HOMUNCULUS.

Look yonder where the Pygmies fled!
The round Hill has a pointed head.
I felt a huge rebound and shock;
Down from the moon had fallen the rock,
And then, without the least ado,
Both foe and friend it smashed and slew.
I praise such arts as these, that show
Creation in a night fulfilled;
That from above and from below
At once this mountain-pile could build.

THALES.

Be still! 'T was but imagined so.
Farewell, then, to the ugly brood!
That thou wast not their king, is good.
Off to the cheerful festals of the Sea!
There as a marvellous guest, they'll honor thee.
                    [*They depart.*

MEPHISTOPHELES
(*climbing up the opposite side*).
Here must I climb by steep and rocky stairways,
And roots of ancient oaks—the vilest rare ways!
Upon my Hartz, the resinous atmosphere
Gives hint of pitch, to me almost as dear
As sulphur is,—but here, among these Greeks,
For such a smell one long and vainly seeks;
And curious am I—for 't is worth the knowing—
To find wherewith they keep their fires of Hell a-going.

DRYAD.
At home, be wise as it befits thee there;
Abroad, thou hast no cleverness to spare.
Thou shouldst not homeward turn thy mind, but here
The honor of the ancient oaks revere.

MEPHISTOPHELES.
One thinks on all relinquished there;
Use made it Paradise, and keeps it fair.
But say, what is 't, in yonder cave
Obscure, a crouching triple-shape resembling?

DRYAD.
The Phorkyads! Go there, if thou art brave;
Address them, if thou canst, untrembling!

MEPHISTOPHELES.
Why not! . . I something see, and am dumbfounded!
Proud as I am, I must confess the truth:
I've never seen their like, in sooth,—
Worse than our hags, an Ugliness unbounded!
How can the Deadly Sins then ever be
Found ugly in the least degree,
When one this triple dread shall see?
We would not suffer them to dwell
Even at the dreariest door of Hell;
But here, in Beauty's land, the Greek,
They're famed, because they're called *antique*. . . .
They stir, they seem to scent my coming;
Like vampire-bats, they're squeaking, twittering,
        humming.

THE PHORKYADS.

Give me the eye, my sisters, that it spy
Who to our temple ventures now so nigh.

MEPHISTOPHELES.

Most honored Dame! Approaching, by your leave,
Grant that your triple blessing I receive.
I come, though still unknown, yet, be it stated,
If I mistake not, distantly related.
Old, reverend Gods, already did I see;
To Ops and Rhea have I bowed the knee;
The Parcæ even—your sisters—yesterday,
Or day before, they came across my way;
And yet the like of you ne'er met my sight:
Silent am I, and ravished with delight.

THE PHORKYADS.

This spirit seems to have intelligence.

MEPHISTOPHELES.

I am amazed no poet has the sense
To sing your praises,—say, how can it be
That we no pictures of your beauty see?
Should not, through you, the chisel strive to wean us
From shapes like those of Juno, Pallas, Venus?

THE PHORKYADS.

Sunken in solitude and stillest night,
The mind of us ne'er took so far a flight.

MEPHISTOPHELES.

How should it, then? since here, concealed from view,
None ever see you, none are seen by you!
But choose those dwelling-places, and be known,
Where Art and Splendor share an equal throne;
Where swift, with double tread, day after day,
A marble block as hero walks away;
Where—

THE PHORKYADS.

Cease, and rouse in us no longer vision!
What profit, if we knew them with precision?—

We, born in night, akin to gloom alone,
Unto ourselves almost, to others quite, unknown.

MEPHISTOPHELES.

In such a case there's little more to say,
But one one's self to others can convey.
One eye supplies you three, one tooth as well,
So were it mythologically possible
In two the being of the Three to cover,
And unto me the third fair form make over,
A short time, only.

ONE
Will it do, forsooth?

THE OTHERS.

We'll try it!—but without or eye or tooth.

MEPHISTOPHELES.

Now just the best thing have you taken away.
How shall I then the image stern display?

ONE.

'T is easily done: just close one eye,
And let thy one side-tusk be seen thereby:
In profile, thus, with not a trait diminished,
Thy sisterly resemblance will be finished.

MEPHISTOPHELES.

So be it, then!

THE PHORKYADS.
So be it!

MEPHISTOPHELES
(*as* PHORKYAD *in profile*).
Me behold,
The much-beloved son of Chaos old!

THE PHORKYADS.

Daughters of Chaos are we, by good right.

MEPHISTOPHELES.

Disgrace! They'll call me now hermaphrodite.

THE PHORKYADS.

In our new sister-triad what a beauty!
Two eyes have we, two teeth, for further duty.

MEPHISTOPHELES.

Now from all eyes I'll hide this visage fell,
To fright the devils in the pool of Hell.

[*Exit.*

4.

ROCKY COVES OF THE ÆGEAN SEA.

The Moon delaying in the Zenith.

SIRENS
(*couched upon the cliffs around, fluting and singing*).

THOUGH erewhile, by spells nocturnal
   Thee Thessalian hags infernal
Downward drew, with guilt intended,—
Look, from where thine arch is bended,
On the multitudinous, splendid
Twinkles of the billowy Ocean!
Shine upon the throngs in motion
O'er the waters, wild and free!
To thy service vowed are we:
Fairest Luna, gracious be!

NEREIDS AND TRITONS
(*as Wonders of the Sea*).

Call with clearer, louder singing,
Through the Sea's broad bosom ringing,
Call the tenants of the Deep!
When the storm swept unimpeded
We to stillest depths receded;
Forth at sound of song we leap.
See! delighted and elated,
We ourselves have decorated,
With our golden crowns have crowned us,
With our spangled girdles bound us,
Chains and jewels hung around us!
All are spoils which you purvey!

Treasures, here in shipwreck swallowed,
You have lured, and we have followed
You, the Dæmons of our bay.

SIRENS.

In the crystal cool, delicious,
Smoothly sport the happy fishes,
Pliant lives that nothing mar;
Yet, ye festive crowds that gather,
We, to-day, would witness, rather,
That ye more than fishes are.

NEREIDS AND TRITONS.

We, before we hither wandered,
Thoroughly the question pondered:
Sisters, Brothers, speed afar!
Briefest travel, light endurance,
Yield the validest assurance
That we more than fishes are.

[*They depart.*

SIRENS.

Off! they have left the place,
Steering away to Samothrace,
Vanished with favoring wind.
What is their purpose there, in the **dreary**
Domain of the lofty Cabiri?
Gods are they, but the strangest crew,
Ever begetting themselves anew,
And unto their own being blind.

In thy meridian stay,
Luna!—graciously delay,
That the Night still embrace us,
And the Day not chase us!

THALES
(*on the shore, to* HOMUNCULUS).
I fain would lead thee unto Nereus old.
Not distant are we from his cavern cold,
But stubbornness is his delight,
The peevish and repulsive wight.

Howe'er the human race has tried,
The Grumbler's never satisfied:
Yet he the Future hath unsealed,
And men thereto their reverence yield,
And give him honor in his station.
Many his benefits have tasted.

HOMUNCULUS.

Then let us try, without more hesitation!
My glass and flame will not at once be wasted.

NEREUS.

Are human voices those that reach mine ear?
At once my wrath is kindled, keen and clear.
Aspiring forms, that high as Gods would ramble,
Yet ever damned their own selves to resemble.
In ancient years could I divinely rest,
Yet was impelled to benefit the Best;
And when, at last, I saw my deeds completed,
It fully seemed as were the work defeated.

THALES.

And yet we trust thee, Graybeard of the Sea!
Thou art the Wise One: drive us not from thee!
Behold this Flame, in man's similitude:
It yields itself unto thy counsel good.

NEREUS.

What! Counsel? When did ever men esteem it?
Wise words in hard ears are but lifeless lore.
Oft as the Act may smite them when they scheme it,
The People are as self-willed as before.
How warned I Paris, in paternal trust,
Before a foreign woman woke his lust!
Upon the Grecian strand he stood so bold;
I saw in spirit, and to him foretold
The smoky winds, the overwhelming woe,
Beams all a-blaze, murder and death below,—
Troy's judgment-day, held fast in lofty rhyme,
A terror through a thousand years of time!
My words seemed sport unto the reckless one:
His lust he followed: fallen was Ilion,—

A giant carcass, stiff, and hacked with steel,
To Pindus' eagles 't was a welcome meal.
Ulysses, too! did I not him presage
The wiles of Circe and the Cyclops' rage?
His paltering mind, his crew's inconstant strain,
And what not all?—and did it bring him gain?
Till him, though late, the favoring billow bore,
A much-tossed wanderer, to the friendly shore.

THALES.

Such conduct, truly, gives the wise man pain,
And yet the good man once will try again.
An ounce of gratitude, his help repaying,
Tons of ingratitude he sees outweighing.
And nothing trifling now we beg of thee;
The boy here wishes to be born, and be.

NEREUS.

Let not my rarest mood be spoiled, I pray!
Far other business waits for me to-day.
I've hither bidden, by the wave and breeze,
The Graces of the Sea, the Dorides.
Olympus bears not, nor your lucent arch,
Such lovely forms, in such a lightsome march:
They fling themselves, in wild and wanton dalliance,
From the sea-dragons upon Neptune's stallions,
Blent with the element so freely, brightly,
That even the foam appears to lift them lightly.
In Venus' chariot-shell, with hues of morn,
Comes Galatea, now the fairest, borne;
Who, since that Cypris turned from us her face,
In Paphos reigns as goddess in her place.
Thus she, our loveliest, long since came to own,
As heiress, templed town and chariot-throne.
Away! the father's hour of rapture clips
Hate from the heart, and harshness from the lips.
Away to Proteus! Ask that wondrous man
Of Being's and of Transformation's plan!

[*He retires towards the sea.*

THALES.

We, by this step, gain nothing: one may meet

Proteus, and straight he melts, dissolving fleet.
Though he remains, he only says
That which confuses and astonishes.
However, of such counsel thou hast need;
So, at a venture, let us thither speed!

[*They depart.*

SIRENS (*on the rocks above*).
What is 't, that, far advancing,
Glides o'er the billows dancing?
As, when the winds are shifted,
Shine snowy sails, uplifted,
So shine they o'er the waters,
Transfigured Ocean-daughters.
We'll clamber down, and, near them,
Behold their forms, and hear them.

NEREIDS AND TRITONS.
What in our hands we bear you
Much comfort shall prepare you.
Chelone's buckler giant
Shines with its forms defiant:—
They're Gods that we are bringing
High songs must you be singing!

SIRENS.
Small to the sight,
Great in their might,—
Saviours of the stranded,
Ancient Gods, and banded.

NEREIDS AND TRITONS.
We bring you the Cabiri
To festals calm and cheery;
For where their sway extendeth
Neptune the realm befriendeth.

SIRENS.
We yield to your claim;
When a shipwreck came,
Irresistibly you
Protected the crew.

NEREIDS AND TRITONS.

Three have we brought hither,
The fourth refused us altogether:
He was the right one, said he,—
Their only thinker ready.

SIRENS.

One God the other God
Smites with the scoffer's rod:
Honor all grace they bring,
Fear all evil they fling!

NEREIDS AND TRITONS.

Seven are they, really.

SIRENS.

Where, then, stay the other three?

NEREIDS AND TRITONS.

The truth we cannot gather:
Ask on Olympus, rather!
There pines the eighth, forgotten,
By no one ever thought on!
In grace to us entreated,
But not yet all completed.

These incomparable, unchainable,
Are always further yearning,
With desire and hunger burning
For the unattainable!

SIRENS.

These are our ways:
The God that sways
Sun, Moon, or other blaze,
We worship: for it pays.

NEREIDS AND TRITONS.

Highest glory for us behold,
Leading these festals cheery!

SIRENS.

The heroes of the ancient time
Fail of their glory prime,
Where and howe'er it may unfold;
Though they have won the fleece of Gold,—
Ye, the Cabiri!
  (*Repeated as full chorus.*)
Though they have won the fleece of Gold,—
We! Ye! the Cabiri!
(*The* NEREIDS *and* TRITONS *move past.*)

HOMUNCULUS.

These Malformations, every one,
Had earthen pots for models:
Against them now the wise men run,
And break their stubborn noddles.

THALES.

That is the thing one wishes, just!
The coin takes value from its rust.

PROTEUS (*unperceived*).

This pleases me, the old fable-ranger!
The more respectable, the stranger.

THALES.

Where art thou, Proteus?

PROTEUS
(*speaking ventriloqually, now near, now at a distance*).
                    Here! and here!

THALES.

I pardon thee thine ancient jeer.
Cheat not a friend with vain oration:
Thou speak'st, I know, from a delusive station.

PROTEUS (*as if at a distance*).

Farewell!

THALES (*softly to* HOMUNCULUS).
      He is quite near: shine brilliantly!
For curious as a fish is he;

And in whatever form he hide,
A flame will make him hither glide.

HOMUNCULUS.
At once a flood of light I'll fling,
Yet softly, lest the glass should spring.

PROTEUS
(*in the form of a giant tortoise*).
What shines so fair, so graciously?

THALES (*covering* HOMUNCULUS).
Good! If thou wishest, canst thou nearer see.
Be not annoyed to take a little trouble,
And show thyself on man's foundation double.
What we disclose, to whomsoe'er would see it,
With our will only, by our favor, be it!

PROTEUS (*in a noble form*).
Still world-wise pranks thou failest to forget.

THALES.
To change thy form remains thy pleasure yet.
(*He uncovers* HOMUNCULUS.)

PROTEUS (*astonished*).
A shining dwarf! The like I ne'er did see!

THALES.
He asks thy counsel, he desires to be.
He is, as I myself have heard him say,
(The thing's a marvel!) only born half-way.
He has no lack of qualities ideal,
But far too much of palpable and real.
Till now the glass alone has given him weight,
And he would fain be soon incorporate.

PROTEUS.
Thou art a genuine virgin's-son:
Finished, ere thou shouldst be begun!

THALES (*whispering*).
Viewed from another side, the thing seems critical:
He is, methinks, hermaphroditical!

PROTEUS.

Then all the sooner 't will succeed:
Let him but start, 't will be arranged with speed.
No need to ponder here his origin;
On the broad ocean's breast must thou begin!
One starts there first within a narrow pale,
And finds, destroying lower forms, enjoyment:
Little by little, then, one climbs the scale,
And fits himself for loftier employment.

HOMUNCULUS.

Here breathes and blows a tender air;
And I delight me in the fragrance rare.

PROTEUS.

Yea, verily, my loveliest stripling!
And farther on, far more enjoyable.
Around yon narrow spit the waves are rippling,
The halo bright and undestroyable!
There to the host we'll nearer be,
Now floating hither o'er the sea.
Come with me there!

THALES.
I'll go along.

HOMUNCULUS.
A spirit-purpose, triply strong!

5.

TELCHINES OF RHODES.

*On Sea-Horses and Sea-Dragons, wielding Neptune's
Trident.*

CHORUS.

WE'VE forged for old Neptune the trident that
urges
To smoothness and peace the refractory surges.
When Jove tears the clouds of the tempest asunder,

'T is Neptune encounters the roll of the thunder:
The lightnings above may incessantly glow,
But wave upon wave dashes up from below,
And all that, between them, the terrors o'erpower,
Long tossed and tormented, the Deep shall devour;
And thence he hath lent us his sceptre to-day.—
Now float we contented, in festal array.

SIRENS.

You, to Helios consecrated,
To the bright Day's blessing fated,—
You to this high Hour we hail:
Luna's worship shall prevail!

TELCHINES.

O loveliest Goddess by night over-vaulted!
Thou hearest with rapture thy brother exalted:
To listen to Rhodes thou wilt lean from the skies;
To him, there, the pæans eternally rise.
When the day he begins, when he ends its career,
His beam is the brightest that falls on us here.
The mountains, the cities, the sea and the shore,
Are lovely and bright to the God they adore:
No mist hovers o'er us, and should one appear,
A beam and a breeze, and the Island is clear!
There Phœbus his form may by hundreds behold,—
Colossal, as youth, as the Gentle, the Bold;
For we were the first whose devotion began
To shape the high Gods in the image of Man.

PROTEUS.

But leave them to their boasting, singing!
Beside the holy sunbeams, bringing
All life, their dead works are a jest.
They melt and cast, with zeal impassioned,
And what they once in bronze have fashioned,
They think it's something of the best.
These proud ones are at last made lowly:
The forms of Gods, that stood and shone,
Were by an earthquake overthrown,
And long since have been melted wholly.

This earthly toil, whate'er it be,
Is never else than drudgery:
A better life the waves declare thee,
And now to endless seas shall bear thee
Proteus-Dolphin.

           (*He transforms himself.*)
         'T is done! Behold!
Unto thy fairest fortune waken:
Upon my back shalt thou be taken,
And wedded to the Ocean old.

THALES.

Yield to the wish so wisely stated,
And at the source be thou created!
Be ready for the rapid plan!
There, by eternal canons wending,
Through thousand, myriad forms ascending,
Thou shalt attain, in time, to Man.

   (HOMUNCULUS *mounts the Proteus-Dolphin.*)

PROTEUS.

In spirit seek the watery distance!
Boundless shall there be thine existence,
And where to move, thy will be free.
But struggle not to higher orders!
Once Man, within the human borders,
Then all is at an end for thee.

THALES.

That's as it haps: 't is no ill fate
In one's own day to be true man and great.

PROTEUS (*to* THALES).

Some one, perchance, of thine own kind!
Their lives continue long, I find;
For with thy pallid phantom-peers
I've seen thee now for many hundred years.

SIRENS (*on the rocks*).

See! what rings of cloudlets, gliding
Round the moon, in circles play!

They are doves whom Love is guiding,
With their wings as white as day.
Paphos hither sends them fleetly,
All her ardent birds, to us,
And our festival completely
Crowns with purest rapture, thus!

NEREUS (*advancing to* THALES).

Though some nightly wanderer's vision
Deem yon ring an airy spectre,
We, the spirits, with decision
Entertain a view correcter:
They are doves, whose convoy gathers
Round my daughter's chariot-shell,
With a flight of wondrous spell,
Learned in old days of the fathers.

THALES.

That I also think is best,
Which the true man comfort gives,
When in warm and peaceful nest
Something holy for him lives.

PSYLLI AND MARSI
(*on sea-bulls, sea-heifers and sea-rams*).

In hollow caves on Cyprus' shore,
By the Sea-God still unbattered,
Not yet by Seismos shattered,
By eternal winds breathed o'er,
And still, as in days that are measured,
Contented and silently pleasured,
The chariot of Cypris we've treasured.
By the murmurs, the nightly vibrations,
O'er the waves and their sweetest pulsations,
Unseen to the new generations,
The loveliest daughter we lead.
We fear not, as lightly we hie on,
Either Eagle or wing-lifted Lion,
Either Crescent or Cross,
Though the sky it emboss,—
Though it changefully triumphs and flashes,

In defeat to forgetfulness dashes,
Lays the fields and the cities in ashes!
Straightway, with speed,
The loveliest of mistresses forth we lead.

SIRENS.

Lightly moved, with paces graver,
Circle round the car again;
Line on line inwoven, waver
Snake-like in a linking chain,—
Stalwart Nereids, come, enring us,
Rudest women, wild and free;
Tender Dorides, ye bring us
Her, the Mother of the Sea,—
Galatea, godlike woman,
Worthiest immortality,
Yet, like those of lineage human,
Sweet with loving grace is she.

DORIDES
(*in chorus, mounted on dolphins, passing* **NEREUS**).
Lend us, Luna, light and shadow,
Show this youthful flower and fire!
For we bring beloved spouses,
Praying for them to our sire.
(*To* NEREUS.)
They are boys, whom we have rescued
From the breaker's teeth of dread;
They, on reeds and mosses bedded,
Back to light and life we led:
Now must they, with glowing kisses,
Thank us for the granted blisses;
On the youths thy favor shed!

NEREUS.

Lo, now! what double gains your deed requite!
You show compassion, and you take delight.

DORIDES.

If thou praisest our endeavor,
Father, grant the fond request,—
Let us hold them fast forever
On each young, immortal breast.

NEREUS.

Take joy in what you've finely captured,
And shape to me the youthful crew;
I cannot grant the boon enraptured
Which only Zeus can give to you.
The billows, as they heave and rock you,
Allow to love no firmer stand,
So, when these fancies fade and mock you,
Send quietly the youths to land.

DORIDES.

Fair boys, we must part, forsooth;
Yet we love you, we vow it!
We have asked for eternal truth,
But the Gods will not allow it.

THE YOUTHS.

We sailor-boys, if still you would
Give love, as first you gave it,
We've never had a life so good,
And would not better have it!
(GALATEA *approaches on her chariot of shell.*)

NEREUS.

'T is thou, O my darling!

GALATEA.

O, Sire! what delight!
Linger, ye dolphins! I cling to the sight.

NEREUS.

Already past, they swiftly wander
On, in circling courses wheeling!
What care they for the heart's profoundest feeling?
Ah, would they took me with them yonder!
Yet a single glance can cheer
All the livelong barren year.

THALES.

Hail! All hail! with newer voices:
How my spirit rejoices,

By the True and the Beautiful penetrated!
From Water was everything first created!
Water doth everything still sustain!
Ocean, grant us thine endless reign!
If the clouds thou wert sending not,
The swelling streams wert spending not,
The winding rivers bending not,
And all in thee were ending not,
Could mountains, and plains, and the world itself, be?
The freshest existence is nourished by thee!

ECHO
(*chorus of the collective circles*).
The freshest existence flows ever from thee!

NEREUS.
They turn and wheel again, afar;
No longer face to face they are.
In linking circles, wide extending,—
In their festive dances blending,—
The countless cohorts now appear.
But Galatea's chariot-shell
Still I see, and see it well:
It shines like a star
Through the crowds intwining.
Love from the tumult still is shining!
Though ne'er so far,
It shimmers bright and clear,
Ever true and near.

HOMUNCULUS.
This softly heaving brine on,
Whatever I may shine on
Is all with beauty crowned.

PROTEUS.
Within this moisture living,
Thy lamp now first is giving
A clear and splendid sound.

NEREUS.
What mystery new, 'mid the crowds that are wheeling,
Is now to our vision its wonders revealing?

What flames round the shell at the feet of the Queen?—
Now flaring in force, and now shining serene,
As if by the pulses of love it were fed.

THALES.

Homunculus is it, by Proteus misled! . .
And these are the signs of imperious yearning,
The presage of swelling, impatiently spurning:
He'll shiver his glass on the glittering throne—
He glows and he flashes, and now he hath flown!

SIRENS.

What fiery marvel the billows enlightens,
As one on the other is broken and brightens?
It flashes, and wavers, and hitherward plays!
On the path of the Night are the bodies ablaze,
And all things around are with flames overrun:
Then Eros be ruler, who all things begun!

　　　　Hail, ye Waves! Hail, Sea unbounded,
　　　　　By the holy Fire surrounded!
　　　　Water, hail! Hail, Fire, the splendid!
　　　　Hail, Adventure rarely ended!

ALL TOGETHER.

　　　　Hail, ye Airs that softly flow!
　　　　Hail, ye caves of Earth below!
　　　　Honored now and evermore
　　　　Be the Elemental Four!

ACT III.

BEFORE THE PALACE OF MENELAUS IN
SPARTA.

HELENA *enters, with the* CHORUS *of Captive Trojan
Women.* PANTHALIS, *Leader of the Chorus.*

HELENA.

I MUCH admired and much reviled,—I, Helena,
,Come from the strand where we have disembarked
　　but now,
Still giddy from the restless rocking of the waves

Of Ocean, which from Phrygian uplands hitherwards
On high, opposing backs—Poseidon's favor won
And Euros' strength—have borne us to our native bay.
Below there, with the bravest of his warriors, now
King Menelaus feels the joy of his return;
But thou, O bid me welcome back, thou lofty House
Which Tyndarus, my father, on the gentle slope,
Returning from the Hill of Pallas, builded up;
And when I here with Clytemnestra sister-like,
With Castor and with Pollux gayly sporting, grew,
Before all Sparta's houses nobly was adorned.
Ye valves of yon dark iron portals, ye I hail!
Once through your festive and inviting opening
It happened that to me, from many singled out,
The coming of the bridegroom Menelaus shone.
Unfold again for me, that I the King's command
Fulfil with strictness, as unto a spouse is meet:
Give entrance now, and let all things be left behind
Which hitherto have stormed upon me, full of doom!
For, since this place all unsuspicious I forsook
For Cytheræa's fane, as holy duty called,
But there the robber seized me, he the Phrygian,—
Happened have many things, which people far and
    wide
So fain relate, but which so fain hears not the one
Of whom the legend rose, and to a fable grew.

CHORUS.

Disdain thou not, O beautiful Dame,
Possession proud of the highest estate!
For the greatest fortune is thine alone,
The fame of beauty that towers o'er all.
The name of the hero heralds his path,
Thence proudly he strides;
Yet bends at once the stubbornest man,
And yields to all-conquering Beauty's might.

HELENA.

Enough, with mine own spouse have I been hither
    shipped,
And now by him beforehand to his city sent;

Yet what his purposes may be, I fail to guess.
Do I come here as wife? Or do I come as queen?
Or come, an offering for the Prince's bitter pain,
And for the long-endured misfortune of the Greeks?
For they, the Immortals, verily fixed my Fame and
      Fate
Ambiguously, attendants twain of doubtful worth
To Beauty, who upon this very threshold stand
With gloomy and with threatening presence at my side.
Then, even, in the hollow ship, but seldom looked
My spouse on me, nor ever word of comfort spake:
As if he brooded evil, fronting me he sat.
But now, when speeding towards the strand of that
      deep cove
Eurotas makes, scarce had the foremost vessels' prows
The land saluted, than he spake, as urged the Gods:
"Here, in their ordered rank, my warriors disembark;
Them shall I muster, ranged along the ocean-strand.
But thou go ever onwards, up the hallowed banks
Of fair Eurotas, dowered with gifts of plenteous fruit,
Guiding the stallions o'er the bloom of watery meads,
Till there, on that most lovely plain thy journey ends,
Where Lacedemon, once a fruitful spreading field,
Surrounded by austerest mountains, built its seat.
Set thou thy foot within the high-towered princely
      House,
And muster well the maids, whom there behind I left,
Together with the old and faithful Stewardess.
Let her display to thee the wealth of treasures stored,
Even as thy father them bequeathed, and I myself,
In war and peace accumulating, have amassed.
All things shalt thou in ancient order find: because
It is the Ruler's privilege, that he all things
In faithful keeping find, returning to his house,—
Where'er he may have left it, each thing in its place;
For power to change in aught possesses not the slave."

CHORUS.

Let now the splendid, accumulate wealth
Rejoice and cheer thee, in eye and heart!
For the gleam of chain and the glory of crown

Are lying idly in haughty repose:
But enter thou in and challenge them all,
And they will respond.
I rejoice to witness Beauty compete
With gold and pearl and the jewel-stone.

HELENA.

Thereafter further came my lord's imperious speech:
"Now when all things in order thou inspected hast,
Then take so many tripods as thou needful deem'st,
And vessels manifold, such as desires at hand
Who offers to the Gods, fulfilling holy use,—
The kettles, also bowls, the shallow basin's disk;
The purest water from the sacred fountain fill
In lofty urns; and further, also ready hold
The well-dried wood that rapidly accepts the flame;
And let the knife, well-sharpened, fail not finally;
Yet all besides will I relinquish to thy care."
So spake he, urging my departure; but no thing
Of living breath did he, who ordered thus, appoint,
That shall, to honor the Olympian Gods, be slain.
'T is critical; and yet I banish further care,
And let all things be now to the high Gods referred,
Who that fulfil, whereto their minds may be disposed,
Whether by men 't is counted good, or whether bad;
In either case we mortals, we are doomed to bear.
Already lifted oft the Offerer the axe
In consecration o'er the bowed neck of the beast,
And could not consummate the act; for enemies
Approaching, or Gods intervening, hindered him.

CHORUS.

What shall happen, imagin'st thou not.
Queen, go forwards
With courage!
Blessing and evil come
Unexpected to men:
Though announced, yet we do not believe.
Burned not Ilion, saw we not also
Death in the face, shamefullest death?
And are we not here,

With thee companioned, joyously serving,
Seeing the dazzling sun in the heavens,
And the fairest of earth, too,—
Kindest one, thee,—we, the happy?

HELENA.

Let come, what may! Whate'er awaits me, it beseems
That I without delay go up in the Royal House,
Which, long my need and yearning, forfeited almost,
Once more hath risen on my sight, I know not how.
My feet no longer bear me with such fearlessness
Up the high steps, which as a child I sprang across.

CHORUS.

Cast ye, O sisters! ye
Sorrowful captives,
All your trouble far from ye!
Your mistress's joy partake,
Helena's joy partake,
Who the paternal hearth
Delightedly now is approaching,
Truly with late-returning
But with firmer and surer feet!

Praise ye the sacredest,
Still re-establishing
And home-bringing Immortals!
How the delivered one
Soars as on lifted wings
Over asperities, while in vain
The prisoned one, yearningly,
Over the fortress-parapet
Pineth with outspread arms!

But a God took hold of her,
The Expatriate,
And from Ilion's ruins
Hither hath borne her again,
To the ancient, the newly embellished
Paternal house,
From unspeakable

Raptures and torments,
Early youthful days,
Now refreshed, to remember.

PANTHALIS (*as* LEADER OF THE CHORUS).

Forsake ye now the joy-encompassed path of Song,
And toward's the portal's open valves your glances
    turn!
What, Sisters, do I see? Returneth not the Queen
With swift and agitated step again to us?
What is it now, great Queen, what could encounter thee
To move and shake thee so, within thy house's halls,
Instead of greeting? Thou canst not conceal the thing;
For strong repulsion written on thy brow I see.
And noble indignation, struggling with amaze.

HELENA

(*who has left the wings of the portal open, excitedly*).

A common fear beseemeth not the child of Zeus;
No lightly-passing hand of terror touches her;
But that fell Horror, which the womb of ancient Night
With first of things delivered, rolled through many
    forms,
Like glowing clouds that from the mountain's fiery
    throat
Whirl up expanding, even heroes' breasts may shake.
Thus terribly have here to-day the Stygian Gods
Mine entrance in the house betokened, and I fain,
Even as a guest dismissed, would take myself away
From this oft-trodden threshold I so longed to tread.
But, no! hither have I retreated to the light;
Nor further shall ye force me, Powers, be who ye may!
Some consecration will I muse: then, purified,
The hearth-fire may the wife so welcome, as the lord.

LEADER OF THE CHORUS.

Discover, noble Dame, unto thy servants here,
Who reverently assist thee, what hath come to pass.

HELENA.

What I beheld, shall ye with your own eyes behold,

If now that shape the ancient Night hath not at once
Re-swallowed to the wonders of her deepest breast.
But I with words will yet declare it, that ye know.
When solemnly, my nearest duty borne in mind,
The Royal House's gloomy inner court I trod,
Amazed I saw the silent, dreary corridors.
No sound of diligent labor, going forwards, met
The ear, no signs of prompt and busy haste the eye;
And not a maid appeared to me, no stewardess
Such as is wont to greet the stranger, friendly-wise.
But when towards the ample hearth-stone I advanced,
I saw, beside the glimmering ashes that remained,
A veiled and giant woman seated on the ground,
Not like to one who sleeps, but one deep-sunk in
        thought.
With words of stern command I summoned her to work,
The stewardess surmising, who meanwhile, perchance,
My spouse with forethought there had stationed when
        he left;
But she, still crouched together, sat immovable.
Stirred by my threats at last, she lifted the right arm
As if from hearth and hall she beckoned me away.
I turned indignantly from her, and swiftly sped
Unto the steps whereon aloft the Thalamos
Adorned is set, and near thereto the treasure-room:
But suddenly from the floor the wondrous figure
        sprang,
Barring my way imperiously, and showed herself
In haggard height, with hollow, blood-discolored eyes,
A shape so strange that eye and mind confounded are.
But to the winds I speak: for all in vain doth Speech
Fatigue itself, creatively to build up forms.
There look, yourselves! She even ventures forth to
        light!
Here are we masters, till the lord and king shall come.
The horrid births of Night doth Phœbus, Beauty's
        friend,
Drive out of sight to caverns, or he binds them fast.

(PHORKYAS *appears on the threshold, between the*
                    door-posts.)

CHORUS.
Much my experience, although the tresses,
Youthfully clustering, wave on my temples;
Many the terrible things I have witnessed,
Warriors lamenting, Ilion's night,
When it fell.

Through the beclouded, dusty and maddened
Throngs of the combatants, heard I the Gods then
Terribly calling, heard I the iron
Accents of Discord clang through the field,
City-wards.

Ah, yet stood they, Ilion's
Ramparts; but ever the fiery glow
Ran from neighbor to neighbor walls,
Ever extending from here and there,
With the roar of its own storm,
Over the darkening city.

Flying saw I, through smoke and flame,
And the tongues of the blinding fire,
Fearful angering presence of Gods,
Stalking marvellous figures,
Giant-great, through the gloomy
Fire-illuminate vapors.

Saw I, or was it but
Dread of the mind, that fashioned
Forms so affrighting? Never can
Justly I say it? Yet that I Her,
Horrible, here with eyes behold,
Is to me known and certain:
Even to my hand were palpable,
Did not the terror restrain me,
Holding me back from the danger.

Which one of Phorkys'
Daughters then art thou?
Since I compare thee
Unto that family.

Art thou, perchance, of the Graiæ,
One of the dreaded gray-born,
One eye and tooth only
Owning alternately?

Darest thou, Monster,
Here beside Beauty,
Unto high Phœbus'
Vision display thee?
Step thou forth, notwithstanding!
For the Ugly beholds he not,
Even as his hallowed glances
Never beheld the shadow.

Yet a sorrowful adverse fate,
Us mortals compelleth, alas!
To endure the unspeakable eye-pain
Which She, the accurst, reprehensible,
Provokes in the lovers of Beauty.

Yes, then hearken, if thou brazenly
Us shalt encounter, hear the curse,—
Hear the threat of every abuse
From the denouncing mouths of the Fortunate,
Whom the Gods themselves have fashioned!

PHORKYAS.

Old is the saw, and yet its sense is high and true,
That Shame and Beauty ne'er together, hand in hand,
Pursued their way across the green domains of Earth.
Deep-rooted dwells in both such force of ancient hate,
That wheresoever on their way one haps to meet
The other, each upon her rival turns her back:
Then forth again vehemently they hasten on,
Shame deep depressed, but Beauty insolent and bold,
Till her at last the hollow night of Orcus takes,
If Age hath not beforehand fully tamed her pride.
So now I find ye, shameless ones, come from abroad
With arrogance o'erflowing, as a file of cranes
That with their hoarse, far-sounding clangor high in
    air,

A cloudy line, slow-moving, send their creaking tones
Below, the lone, belated wanderer to allure
That he look up; but, nothwithstanding, go their way,
And he goes his: and likewise will it be, with us.
Who, then, are you, that round the Royal Palace high
Like Mænads wild, or like Bacchantes, dare to rave?
Who, then, are you, that you the House's stewardess
Assail and howl at, as the breed of dogs the moon?
Think ye from me 't is hidden, of what race ye are?
Ye brood, in war begotten and in battle bred,
Lustful of man, seducing no less than seduced,
Emasculating soldiers', burghers' strength alike!
Methinks, to see your crowd, a thick cicada-swarm
Hath settled on us, covering the green-sown fields.
Devourers ye of others' toil! Ye snatch and taste,
Destroying in its bud the land's prosperity!
Wares are ye, plundered, bartered, and in market sold!

HELENA.

Who rates the servant-maids in presence of the Dame
Audaciously invades the Mistress' household-right:
Her only it becometh to commend what is
Praiseworthy, as to punish what is blamable.
Content, moreover, am I with the service which
They gave me, when the lofty strength of Ilion
Beleaguered stood, and fell in ruin: none the less
When we the sorrowful and devious hardships bore
Of errant travel, where each thinks but of himself.
Here, too, the like from this gay throng do I expect:
Not what the slave is, asks the lord, but how he serves.
Therefore be silent, cease to grin and jeer at them!
If thou the Palace hitherto hast guarded well
In place of Mistress, so much to thy credit stands;
But now that she herself hath come, shouldst thou retire
Lest punishment, in place of pay deserved, befall!

PHORKYAS.

To threaten the domestics is a right assured,
Which she, the spouse august of the God-prospered
king,
By many years of wise discretion well hath earned.

Since thou, now recognized, thine ancient station here
Again assum'st, as Queen and Mistress of the House,
Grasp thou the reigns so long relaxed, be ruler now,
Take in thy keep the treasure, and ourselves thereto!
But first of all protect me, who the eldest am,
From this pert throng, who with thee, Swan of Beauty
    matched,
Are only stumpy-winged and cackling, quacking geese.

LEADER OF THE CHORUS.
How ugly, near to Beauty, showeth Ugliness!

PHORKYAS.
How silly, near to understanding want of sense!
(*Henceforth the* CHORETIDS *answer in turn, stepping
    singly forth from the* CHORUS.)

CHORETID I.
Of Father Erebus relate, relate of Mother Night!

PHORKYAS.
Speak thou of Scylla, sister-children of one flesh!

CHORETID II.
Good store of hideous monsters shows thy family tree!

PHORKYAS.
Go down to Orcus! There thy tribe and kindred seek!

CHORETID III.
Those who dwell there are all by far too young for thee.

PHORKYAS.
On old Tiresias try thy lascivious arts!

CHORETID IV.
Orion's nurse was great-great-grandchild unto thee!

PHORKYAS.
Thee harpies, I suspect, did nurse and feed on filth.

CHORETID V.
Wherewith dost thou such choice emaciation feed?

PHORKYAS.
Not with the blood, for which thou all too greedy art.

CHORETID VI.
Thou, hungering for corpses, hideous corpse thyself!

PHORKYAS.
The teeth of vampires in thy shameless muzzle shine!

LEADER OF THE CHORUS.
Thine shall I stop, when I declare thee who thou art.

PHORKYAS.
Then name thyself the first! The riddle thus is solved.

HELENA.
Not angered, but in sorrow, do I intervene,
Prohibiting the storm of this alternate strife!
For nothing more injurious meets the ruling lord
Than quarrels of his faithful servants, underhand.
The echo of his orders then returns no more
Accordantly to him in swiftly finished acts,
But, roaring wilfully, encompasses with storm
Him, self-confused, and chiding to the empty air.
Nor this alone: in most unmannered anger ye
Have conjured hither pictures of the shapes of dread,
Which so surround me, that to Orcus now I feel
My being whirled, despite these well-known native
    fields.
Can it be memory? Was it fancy, seizing me?
Was all that, I? and am I, now? and shall I hence-
    forth be
The dream and terror of those town-destroying ones?
I see the maidens shudder: but, the eldest, thou
Composedly standest—speak a word of sense to me!

PHORKYAS.
Whoe'er the fortune manifold of years recalls,
Sees as a dream at last the favor of the Gods.
But thou, so highly dowered, so past all measure helped,
Saw'st in the ranks of life but love-desirous men,

To every boldest hazard kindled soon and spurred.
Thee early Theseus snatched, excited by desire,
Like Heraclês in strength, a splendid form of man.

HELENA.

He bore me forth, a ten-year-old and slender roe,
And shut me in Aphidnus' tower, in Attica.

PHORKYAS.

But then, by Castor and by Pollux soon released,
The choicest crowd of heroes, wooing, round thee
pressed.

HELENA.

Yet most my secret favor, freely I confess,
Patroclus won, the likeness of Pelides he.

PHORKYAS.

Wed by thy father's will to Menelaus then,
The bold sea-rover, the sustainer of his house.

HELENA.

My sire the daughter gave him, and the government:
Then from our wedded nearness sprang Hermione.

PHORKYAS.

Yet when he boldly claimed the heritage of Crete,
To thee, the lonely one, too fair a guest appeared.

HELENA.

Why wilt thou thus recall that semi-widowhood,
And all the hideous ruin it entailed on me?

PHORKYAS.

To me, a free-born Cretan, did that journey bring
Imprisonment, as well,—protracted slavery.

HELENA.

At once he hither ordered thee as stewardess,
Giving in charge the fortress and the treasure-stores.

PHORKYAS.

Which thou forsookest, wending to the towered town
Of Ilion, and the unexhausted joys of love.

HELENA.

Name not those joys to me! for sorrow all too stern
Unendingly was poured upon my breast and brain.

PHORKYAS.

Nathless, they say, dost thou appear in double form;
Beheld in Ilion,—in Egypt, too, beheld.

HELENA.

Make wholly not confused my clouded, wandering
    sense!
Even in this moment, who I am I cannot tell.

PHORKYAS.

And then, they say, from out the hollow Realm of
    Shades
Achilles yet was joined in passion unto thee,
Who earlier loved thee, 'gainst all ordinances of Fate!

HELENA.

To him, the Vision, I, a Vision, wed myself:
It was a dream, as even the words themselves declare.
I vanish hence, and to myself a Vision grow.
    (*She sinks into the arms of the* SEMICHORUS.)

CHORUS.

Silence! silence!
False-seeing one, false-speaking one!
Out of the hideous, single-toothed
Mouth, what should be exhaled from
Such abominable horror-throat!
For the Malevolent, seeming benevolent,—
Wolf's wrath under the sheep's woolly fleece,—
Fearfuller far is unto me than
Throat of the three-headed dog.
Anxiously listening stand we here.
When? how? where shall break again forth

Further malice
From the deeply-ambushed monster?

Now, stead of friendly words and consoling,
Lethe-bestowing, gratefully mild,
Stirrest thou up from all the Past
Evillest more than good things,
And darkenest all at once
Both the gleam of the Present
And also the Future's
Sweetly glimmering dawn of hope!

Silence! silence!
That the Queen's high spirit,
Nigh to forsake her now,
Hold out, and upbear yet
The Form of all forms
Which the sun shone on ever.

(HELENA *has recovered, and stands again in the centre.*)

PHORKYAS.

Forth from transient vapors comes the lofty sun of
this bright day,
That, obscured, could so delight us, but in splendor
dazzles now.
As the world to thee is lovely, thou art lovely unto us;
Though as ugly they revile me, well I know the
Beautiful.

HELENA.

Tottering step I from the Void that—dizzy, fainting,—
round me closed;
And again would fain be resting, for so weary are my
limbs.
Yet to Queens beseemeth chiefly, as to all men it
beseems,
Calm to be, and pluck up courage, whatsoe'er may
menace them.

PHORKYAS.

Standing now in all thy greatness, and in all thy
beauty, here,

Says thine eye that thou commandest: what command'st thou? speak it out!

PHORKYAS.

Be prepared, for much neglected in your quarrel, to
atone!
Haste, a sacrifice to furnish, as the king hath ordered
me!

HELENA.

PHORKYAS.
All is ready in the palace—vessels, tripods, sharpened
axe,
For the sprinkling, fumigating: show to me the victim now!

HELENA.
This the king not indicated.

PHORKYAS.
Spake it not? O word of woe!

HELENA.
What distress hath overcome thee?

PHORKYAS.
Queen, the offering art thou!

HELENA.
I?

PHORKYAS.
And these.

CHORUS.
Ah, woe and sorrow!

PHORKYAS.
Thou shalt fall beneath the axe.

HELENA.
Fearful, yet foreboded! I, alas!

PHORKYAS.
There seemeth no escape.

CHORUS.

Ah! and what to us will happen?

PHORKYAS.

    She will die a noble death;
But upon the lofty beam, upholding rafter-frame and
  roof,
As in birding-time the throstles, ye in turn shall struggling hang!
(HELENA *and the* CHORUS *stand amazed and alarmed,
  in striking, well-arranged groups.*)

PHORKYAS.

Ye Phantoms!—like to frozen images ye stand,
In terror thus from Day to part, which is not yours.
Men, and the race of spectres like you, one and all,
Renounce not willingly the bright beams of the sun;
But from the end may none implore or rescue them.
All know it, yet 't is pleasant unto very few.
Enough! ye all are lost: now speedily to work!
(*She claps her hands: thereupon appear in the door-
  way muffled dwarfish forms, which at once carry
  out with alacrity the commands expressed.*)
This way, ye gloomy, sphery-bodied monster throng!
Roll hitherwards! ye here may damage as ye will.
The altar portable, the golden-horned, set up!
The axe let shimmering lie across the silver rim!
The urns of water fill! For soon, to wash away,
Shall be the black blood's horrible and smutching
  stains.
Here spread the costly carpets out upon the dust,
That so the offering may kneel in queenly wise,
And folded then, although with severed head, at once
With decent dignity be granted sepulture!

LEADER OF THE CHORUS.

The Queen is standing, sunk in thought, beside us here,
The maidens wither like the late-mown meadow grass;
Methinks that I, the eldest, in high duty bound,
Should words exchange with thee, primeval eldest
  thou!

Thou art experienced, wise, and seemest well-disposed,
Although this brainless throng assailed thee in mistake.
Declare then, if thou knowest, possible escape!

PHORKYAS.

'T is easy said. Upon the Queen it rests alone,
To save herself, and ye appendages with her.
But resolution, and the swiftest, needful is.

CHORUS.

Worthiest and most reverend of the Parcæ, wisest
　　　sibyl thou,
Hold the golden shears yet open, then declare us Day
　　　and Help!
We already feel discomfort of the soaring, swinging,
　　　struggling;
And our limbs in dances first would rather move in
　　　joyous cadence,
Resting afterwards on lovers' breasts.

HELENA.

Let these be timid! Pain I feel, but terror none;
Yet if thou know'st of rescue, grateful I accept!
Unto the wise, wide-seeing mind is verily shown
The Impossible oft as possible. Then speak, and say!

CHORUS.

Speak and tell us, tell us quickly, how escape we now
　　　the fearful,
Fatal nooses, that so menace, like the vilest form o'
　　　necklace,
Wound about our tender throats? Already, in antici-
　　　pation,
We can feel the choking, smothering—if thou, Rhea,
　　　lofty Mother
Of the Gods, to mercy be not moved.

PHORKYAS.

Have you then patience, such long-winded course of
　　　speech
To hear in silence? Manifold the stories are.

CHORUS.

Patience enough! Meanwhile, in hearing, still we live.

PHORKYAS.

Whoso, to guard his noble wealth, abides at home,
And in his lofty dwelling well cements the chinks
And also from the pelting rain secures the roof,
With him, the long days of his life, shall all be well:
But whosoe'er his threshold's holy square-hewn stone
Lightly with flying foot and guilty oversteps,
Finds, when he comes again, the ancient place, indeed,
But all things altered, if not utterly o'erthrown.

HELENA.

Wherefore declaim such well-known sayings here, as
    these?
Thou wouldst narrate: then stir not up annoying
    themes!

PHORKYAS.

It is historic truth, and nowise a reproach.
Sea-plundering, Menelaus steered from bay to bay;
He skirted as a foe the islands and the shores,
Returning with the booty, which in yonder rusts.
Then ten long years he passed in front of Ilion;
But for the voyage home how many know I not.
And now how is it, where we stand by Tyndarus'
Exalted House? How is it with the regions round?

HELENA.

Has then Abuse become incarnated in thee,
That canst not open once thy lips, except to blame?

PHORKYAS.

So many years deserted stood the valley-hills
That in the rear of Sparta northwards rise aloft,
Behind Taygetus; whence, as yet a nimble brook,
Eurotas downward rolls, and then, along our vale
By reed-beds broadly flowing, nourishes your swans.
Behind there in the mountain-dells a daring breed
Have settled, pressing forth from the Cimmerian
    Night,
And there have built a fortress inaccessible,

Whence land and people now they harry, as they
    please.

HELENA.

Have they accomplished that? Impossible it seems.

PHORKYAS.

They had the time: it may be twenty years, in all.

HELENA.

Is one a Chief? and are they robbers many—leagued?

PHORKYAS.

Not robbers are they; yet of many one is Chief:
I blame him not, although on me he also fell.
He might, indeed, have taken all; yet was content
With some *free-gifts*, he said: tribute he called it not.

HELENA.

How looked the man?

PHORKYAS.

        By no means ill: he pleased me well.
Cheerful and brave and bold, and nobly-formed is he,
A prudent man and wise, as few among the Greeks.
They call the race Barbarians; yet I question much
If one so cruel be, as there by Ilion
In man-devouring rage so many heroes were;
His greatness I respected, did confide in him.
And then, his fortress! That should ye yourselves
    behold!
'T is something other than unwieldy masonry,
The which your fathers, helter-skelter tumbling,
    piled,—
Cyclopean like the Cyclops, stones undressed at once
On stones undressed upheaving: there, however, there
All plumb and balanced is, conformed to square and
    rule.
Behold it from without! It rises heavenward up
So hard, so tight of joint, and mirror-smooth as steel.
To climb up there—nay, even your Thought itself
    slides off!
And mighty courts of ample space within, enclosed

Around with structures of all character and use.
There you see pillars, pillarets, arches great and small,
Balconies, galleries for looking out and in,
And coats of arms.

CHORUS.
What are they?

PHORKYAS.

Ajax surely bore
A twisted serpent on his shield, as ye have seen.
The Seven also before Thebes had images,
Each one upon his shield, with many meanings rich.
One saw there moon and star on the nocturnal sky,
And goddesses, and heroes, ladders, torches, swords,
And whatsoe'er afflicting threateneth good towns.
Such symbols also bore our own heroic band,
In shining tints, bequeathed from eldest ancestry.
You see there lions, eagles, likewise claws and beaks,
Then buffalo-horns, with wings and roses, peacock's-
tails,
And also bars—gold, black and silver, blue and red.
The like of these in halls are hanging, row on row,—
In halls unlimited and spacious as the world:
There might ye dance!

CHORUS.
But tell us, are there dancers there?

PHORKYAS.
Ay, and the best!—a blooming, gold-haired throng of
boys,
Breathing ambrosial youth! So only Paris breathed,
When he approached too nearly to the Queen.

HELENA.

Thou fall'st
Entirely from thy part: speak now the final word!

PHORKYAS.
'Tis thou shalt speak it: say with grave distinctness,
Yes!
Then straight will I surround thee with that fortress.

CHORUS.

                                        Speak,
O speak the one brief word, and save thyself and us!

HELENA.

What! Shall I fear King Menelaus may transgress
So most inhumanly, as thus to smite myself?

PHORKYAS.

Hast thou forgotten how he thy Deiphobus,
Brother of fallen Paris, who with stubborn claim
Took thee, the widow, as his fere, did visit with
Unheard-of mutilation? Nose and ears he cropped,
And otherwise disfigured: 't was a dread to see.

HELENA.

That did he unto him: he did it for my sake.

PHORKYAS.

Because of him he now will do the like to thee.
Beauty is indivisible: who once possessed
Her wholly, rather slays than only share in part.
   (*Trumpets in the distance*: *the* CHORUS *starts in
                        terror.*)
Even as the trumpet's piercing clangor gripes and
        tears
The ear and entrail-nerves, thus Jealousy her claws
Drives in the bosom of the man, who ne'er forgets
What once was his, but now is lost, possessed no more

CHORUS.

Hear'st thou not the trumpets pealing? see'st thou not
        the shine of swords?

PHORKYAS.

King and Lord, be welcome hither! willing reckoning
        will I give.

CHORUS.

What of us?

PHORKYAS.

   You know it clearly, see her death before your eyes;
There, within, your own shall follow: nay, there is no
        help for you!

Pause.

HELENA.

What I may venture first to do, have I devised.
A hostile Dæmon art thou, that I feel full well,
And much I fear thou wilt convert the Good to Bad.
But first to yonder fortress now I follow thee;
What then shall come, I know: but what the Queen
thereby
As mystery in her deepest bosom may conceal,
Remain unguessed by all! Now, Ancient, lead the
way!

CHORUS.

O how gladly we go,
Hastening thither!
Chasing us, Death,
And, rising before us,
The towering castle's
Inaccessible ramparts.
Guard us as well may they
As Ilion's citadel-fort,
Which at last alone
Fell, through contemptible wiles!

(*Mists arise and spread, obscuring the background,
also the nearer portion of the scene, at pleasure.*)

How is it? how?
Sisters, look around!
Was it not cheerfullest day?
Banded vapors are hovering up
Out of Eurotas' holy stream;
Vanished e'en now hath the lovely
Reed-engarlanded shore from the sight,
Likewise the free, gracefully-proud,
Silently floating swans,
Mated in joy of their swimming,
See I, alas! no more.

Still—but still
Crying, I hear them,
Hoarsely crying afar!

Ominous, death-presaging!
Ah, may to us the tones not also,
Stead of deliverance promised,
Ruin announce at the last!—
Us, the swan-like and slender,
Long white-throated, and She,
Our fair swan-begotten.
Woe to us, woe!

All is covered and hid
Round us with vapor and cloud:
Each other behold we not!
What happens? do we advance?

Hover we only with
Skipping footstep along the ground?
Seest thou naught? Soars not even, perchance,
Hermes before us? Shines not the golden wand,
Bidding, commanding us back again
To the cheerless, gray-twilighted,
Full of impalpable phantoms,
Over-filled, eternally empty Hades?

Yes, at once the air is gloomy, sunless vanish now the
    vapors,
Gray and darkly, brown as buildings. Walls present
    themselves before us,
Blank against our clearer vision. Is 't a court? a moat,
    or pitfall?
Fear-inspiring, any way! and Sisters, ah, behold us
    prisoned,—
Prisoned now, as ne'er before!
(*Inner court-yard of a Castle, surrounded with rich,
    fantastic buildings of the Middle Ages.*)

LEADER OF THE CHORUS.

Precipitate and foolish, type of women ye!
Dependent on the moment, sport of every breeze
That blows mischance or luck! and neither ever ye
Supported calmly. One is sure to contradict
The others fiercely, and cross-wise the others her:

Only in joy and pain ye howl and laugh alike.
Be silent now, and hearken what the Mistress here,
High-thoughted, may determine for herself and us!

HELENA.

Where art thou, Pythoness? Whatever be thy name,
Step forth from out these arches of the gloomy keep!
If thou didst go, unto the wondrous hero-lord
Me to announce, preparing thus reception fit,
Then take my thanks, and lead me speedily to him!
I wish the wandering closed, I wish for rest alone.

LEADER OF THE CHORUS.

In vain thou lookest, Queen, all ways around thee
here;
That fatal shape hath vanished hence, perhaps re-
mained
There in the mists, from out whose bosom hither-
wards—
I know not how—we came, swiftly, without a step.
Perhaps, indeed, she strays, lost in the labyrinth
Of many castles wondrously combined in one,
Seeking august and princely welcome from the lord.
But see! up yonder moves in readiness a crowd:
In galleries, at windows, through the portals, comes
A multitude of servants, hastening here and there;
And this proclaims distinguished welcome to the
guest.

CHORUS.

My heart is relieved! O, yonder behold
How so orderly downward with lingering step
The crowd of the youths in dignity comes,
In regular march! Who hath given command
That they marshal in ranks, and so promptly disposed,
The youthfullest boys of the beautiful race?
What shall most I admire? Is 't the delicate gait,
Or the curls of the hair on the white of the brow,
Or the twin-rounded cheeks, blushing red like the
peach,
And also, like them, with the silkiest down?
Fain therein would I bite, yet I fear me to try;

For, in similar case, was the mouth thereupon
Filled—I shudder to tell it!—with ashes.

> But they, the fairest,
> Hither they come:
> What do they bear?
> Steps to the throne
> Carpet and seat,
> Curtain and tent,
> Or similar gear;
> Waving around, and
> Cloudy wreaths forming
> O'er the head of our Queen;
> For she already ascendeth,
> Invited, the sumptuous couch.
> Come forward, now,
> Step by step,
> Solemnly ranged!
> Worthy, O, threefold worthy her,
> May such a reception be blessed!

(*All that is described by the* CHORUS *takes place by degrees. After the boys and squires have descended in a long procession,* FAUST *appears above, at the head of the staircase, in knightly Court costume of the Middle Ages, and then comes down slowly and with dignity.*)

LEADER OF THE CHORUS
(*observing him attentively*).

If now, indeed, the Gods to this man have not lent—
As oft they do to men—a brave, transcendent form,
A winning presence, stately dignity of mien,
For temporary service, all he undertakes
Will always bring him triumph, whether in fight with
    men,
Or in the minor wars with fairest ladies waged.
Him, verily, to hosts of others I prefer,
Whom, highly-famed withal, I have myself beheld.
With slow and solemn step, by reverence restrained,
I see the Prince approach: turn thou thy head, O
    Queen!

FAUST

(*approaching*: *a man in fetters at his side*).

Instead of solemn greeting, as beseems,
Or reverential welcome, bring I thee,
Fast-bound in welded fetters, here, the knave
Whose duty slighted cheated me of mine.
Kneel down, thou Culprit, that this lofty Dame
May hear the prompt confession of thy guilt!
This, Sovereign Mistress, is the man select
For piercing vision, on the turret high
Stationed to look around, the space of heaven
And breadth of earth to read with sharpest glance,
If here or there perchance come aught to view,—
Between the stronghold and the circling hills
If aught may move, whether the billowy herds
Or waves of arméd men : those we protect,
Encounter these. To-day—what negligence!
Thou comest, he proclaims it not: we fail
In honorable reception, most deserved,
Of such high guest. Now forfeited hath he
His guilty life, and should have shed the blood
Of death deserved; but only thou shalt mete
Pardon or punishment, at thy good will.

HELENA.

So high the power, which thou hast granted me,
As Mistress and as Judge, although it were
(I may conjecture) meant but as a test,—
Yet now I use the Judge's bounden right
To give the Accused a hearing: speak then, thou!

LYNCEUS, THE WARDER OF THE TOWER.

Let me kneel, and let me view her,
Let me live, or let me die!
For enslaved, devoted to her,
This God-granted Dame, am I.

Watching for the Morn's advancing
Where her pathways eastward run,
All at once, a sight entrancing,
In the South arose the sun.

There to look, the Wonder drew me:
Not the glens, the summits cold,
Space of sky or landscape gloomy,—
Only Her did I behold.

Beam of sight to me was given,
Like the lynx on highest tree;
But in vain I've urged and striven,
'T was a dream that fettered me.

Could I know, or how be aided?
Think of tower or bolted gate?
Vapors rose and vapors faded,
And the Goddess came in state!

Eye and heart did I surrender
To the softly-shining spell:
Blinding all with Beauty's splendor,
She hath blinded me, as well.

I forgot the warder's duty
And the trumpet's herald-call:
Threaten to destroy me! Beauty
Bindeth angers, frees her thrall.

HELENA.

The Evil which I brought, I dare no more
Chastise. Ah, woe to me! What fate severe
Pursues me, everywhere the breasts of men
So to infatuate, that nor them, nor aught
Besides of worth, they spare? Now plundering,
Seducing, fighting, hurried to and fro,
Heroes and Demigods, Gods, Demons even,
Hither and thither led me, sore-perplexed.
Sole, I the world bewildered, doubly more;
Now threefold, fourfold, woe on woe I bring.
Remove this guiltless man, let him go free!
The God-deluded merits no disgrace.

FAUST.

Amazed, O Queen, do I behold alike

The unerring archer and the stricken prey.
I see the bow, wherefrom the arrow sped
That wounded him. Arrows on arrows fly,
And strike me. I suspect the feathered hum
Of bolts cross-fired through all the courts and towers.
What am I now? At once rebellious thou
Makest my faithfullest, and insecure
My walls. Thence do I fear that even my hosts
Obey the conquering and unconquered Dame.
What else remains, but that I give to thee
Myself, and all I vainly fancied mine?
Let me, before thy feet, in fealty true,
Thee now acknowledge, Lady, whose approach
Won thee at once possession and the throne!

LYNCEUS
(*with a chest, and men who follow, bearing others*).

Thou seest me, Queen, returned and free!
The wealthy begs a glance from thee:
Thee he beheld, and feeleth, since,
As beggar poor, yet rich as prince.

What was I erst? What now am I?
What shall I will?—what do, or try?
What boots the eyesight's sharpest ray?
Back from thy throne it bounds away.

Forth from the East we hither pressed,
And all was over with the West:
So long and broad the people massed,
The foremost knew not of the last.

The foremost fell, the second stood;
The third one's lance was prompt and good;
Each one a hundred's strength supplied:
Unnoted, thousands fell and died.

We onward pressed, in stormy chase;
The lords were we from place to place;
And where, to-day, *I* ruled as chief,
The morrow brought another thief.

We viewed the ground, but viewed in haste:
The fairest woman one embraced,
One took the oxen from the stall;
The horses followed, one and all.

But my delight was to espy
What rarest was, to mind and eye;
And all that others might amass
To me was so much withered grass.

I hunted on the treasure-trail
Where'er sharp sight could me avail:
In every pocket did I see,
And every chest was glass to me.

And heaps of gold I came to own,
With many a splendid jewel-stone:
The emeralds only worthy seem
Greenly upon thy breast to gleam.

'Twixt lip and ear let swaying sleep
The pearly egg of Ocean's deep;
Such place the rubies dare not seek,
They're blanched beside the rosy cheek.

And thus, the treasure's offering
I here before thy presence bring:
Laid at thy feet, be now revealed
The spoils of many a bloody field!

Though I have brought of chests a store,
Yet iron caskets have I more.
Let me attend thee, do thy will,
And I thy treasure-vaults will fill.

For scarcely didst thou mount the throne,
Than bowed to own and bent to own
Thy Beauty's sway, that very hour,
Wisdom, and Wealth, and soverign Power.

All such I held secure, as mine;
Now freed therefrom, behold it thine!

I deemed its worth and value plain;
Now see I, it was null and vain.

What I possessed from me doth pass,
Dispersed like mown and withered grass.
One bright and beauteous glance afford,
And all its worth is straight restored!

FAUST.

Remove with speed the burden boldly won,
Not blamed, indeed, but neither with reward.
All is her own already, which the keep
Within it holds; and special offer thus
Is useless. Go, and pile up wealth on wealth
In order fit! Present the show august
Of splendors yet unseen! The vaulted halls
Make shine like clearest heaven! Let Paradise
From lifeless pomp of life created be!
Hastening, before her footsteps be unrolled
The flower-embroidered carpets! Let her tread
Fall on the softest footing, and her glance,
Gods only bear undazed, on proudest pomp!

LYNCEUS.

What the lord commands is slight;
For the servants, labor light:
Over wealth and blood and breath
This proud Beauty governeth.
Lo! thy warrior-throngs are tame;
All the swords are blunt and lame;
Near the bright form we behold
Even the sun is pale and cold;
Near the riches of her face
All things empty, shorn of grace.

HELENA (*to* FAUST).

Fain to discourse with thee, I bid thee come
Up hither to my side! The empty place
Invites its lord, and thus secures me mine.

FAUST.

First, kneeling, let the dedication be

Accepted, lofty Lady! Let me kiss
The gracious hand that lifts me to thy side.
Confirm me as co-regent of thy realm,
Whose borders are unknown, and win for thee
Guard, slave and worshipper, and all in one!

HELENA.

I hear and witness marvels manifold;
Amazement takes me, much would I inquire.
Yet now instruct me wherefore spake the man
With strangely-sounding speech, friendly and strange:
Each sound appeared as yielding to the next,
And, when a word gave pleasure to the ear,
Another came, caressing then the first.

FAUST.

If thee our people's mode of speech delight,
O thou shalt be enraptured with our song,
Which wholly satisfies both ear and mind!
But it were best we exercise it now:
Alternate speech entices, calls it forth.

HELENA.

Canst thou to me that lovely speech impart?

FAUST.

'T is easy: it must issue from the heart;
And if the breast with yearning overflow,
One looks around, and asks—

HELENA.

                                        Who shares the glow.

FAUST.

Nor Past nor Future shades an hour like this;
But wholly in the Present—

HELENA.

                                        Is our bliss.

FAUST.

Gain, pledge, and fortune in the Present stand:
What confirmation does it ask?

HELENA.

My hand.

CHORUS.

Who would take it amiss, that our Princess
Granteth now to the Castle's lord
Friendliest demonstration?
For, indeed, collectively are we
Captives, as ofttimes already,
Since the infamous downfall
Of Ilion, and the perilous,
Labyrinthine, sorrowful voyage.

Women, to the love of men accustomed,
Dainty choosers are they not,
But proficients skilful;
And unto golden-haired shepherds,
Perchance black, bristly Fauns, too,
Even as comes opportunity,
Unto the limbs in their vigor
Fully award they an equal right.

Near, and nearer already sit
They, to each other drawn,
Shoulder to shoulder, knee to knee;
Hand in hand, they bend and sway
Over the throne's
Softly-pillowed, luxurious pomp.
Majesty here not withholds its
Secretest raptures,
Wilfully, boldly revealed
Thus to the eyes of the people.

HELENA.

I feel so far away, and yet so near;
And am so fain to say: "Here am I! here."

FAUST.

I scarcely breathe; I tremble; speech is dead:
It is a dream, and day and place have fled.

HELENA.

I seem as life were done, and yet so new,
Blent thus with thee,—to thee, the Unknown, true!

FAUST.

To probe this rarest fate be not impelled!
Being is duty, though a moment held.

PHORKYAS (*violently entering*).
Spell in lovers' primers sweetly!
Probe and dally, cosset featly,
Test your wanton sport completely!
But there is not time, nor place.
Feel ye not the gloomy presage?
Hear ye not the trumpet's message?
For the ruin comes apace.
Menelaus with his legions
Storms across the hither regions;
Call to battle all your race!
By the victors execrated,
Like Deiphobus mutilated,
Thou shalt pay for woman's grace:
First shall dangle every light one,
At the altar, then, the Bright One
Find the keen axe in its place!

FAUST.

Disturbance rash! repulsively she presses in;
Not even in danger meet is senseless violence.
Ill message makes the fairest herald ugly seem;
Thou, Ugliest, delightest but in evil news.
Yet this time shalt thou not succeed; with empty
          breath
Stir, shatter thou the air! There is no danger here,
And unto us were danger but an idle threat.

(*Signals, explosions from the towers, trumpets and
    cornets, martial music. A powerful armed force
    marches past.*)

No! hero-bands, none ever braver,
At once shalt thou assembled see:
He, sole, deserves the ladies' favor,
Whose arm defends them gallantly.

(*To the leaders of the troops, who detach themselves
    from the columns, and come forwards.*)

With rage restrained, in silence banded,
And certain of the victory-feast,
Ye, Northern blossoms, half expanded,
Ye, flowery fervors of the East!

The light upon their armor breaking,
They plundered realm on realm, at will:
They come, and lo! the earth is quaking;
They march away, it thunders still!

In Pylos we forsook the waters;
The ancient Nestor is no more,
And soon our lawless army scatters
The troops of kings on Grecian shore.

Back from these walls, no more delaying,
Drive Menelaus to the sea!
There let him wander, robbing, slaying,
As was his wish and destiny.

I hail you Dukes, as forth ye sally
Beneath the rule of Sparta's Queen!
Now lay before her mount and valley,
And you shall share the kingdom green!

Thine, German, be the hand that forges
Defence for Corinth and her bays:
Achaïa, with its hundred gorges,
I give thee, Goth, to hold and raise.

Towards Elis, Franks, direct your motion;
Messene be the Saxon's state:
The Norman claim and sweep the ocean,
And Argolis again make great!

Then each shall dwell in homes well-dowered,
And only outer foemen meet;
Yet still by Sparta over-towered,
The Queen's ancestral, ancient seat.

Each one shall she behold, abiding

In lands that lack no liberal right;
And at her feet ye'll seek, confiding,
Your confirmation, law and light!

(FAUST *descends from the throne*: *the Princes form a circle around him, in order to receive special commands and instructions.*)

CHORUS.

Who for himself the Fairest desires,
First of all things, let him
Bravely and wisely a weapon acquire!
Flattering, indeed, he may conquer
What on earth is the highest;
But he quietly may not possess.
Wily sneaks entice her away,
Robbers boldly abduct her from him:
This to hinder be he prepared!

Therefore now our Prince I praise,
Holding him higher than others,
Since he wisdom and strength combines,
So that the strong men obedient stand,
Waiting his every beckon.
They his orders faithfully heed,
Each for the profiting of himself
As for the Ruler's rewarding thanks,
And for the highest renown of both.

For who shall tear her away
Now, from the mighty possessor?
His is she, and to him be she granted,
Doubly granted by us, whom he,
Even as her, within by sure walls hath surrounded,
And without by a powerful host.

FAUST.

The gifts they've won by our concession,—
In fee to each a wealthy land,—
Are grand and fair: grant them possession!
We in the midst will take our stand.

And they in rivalry protect thee,
Half-Island, girdled by the sea
With whispering waves,—whose soft hill-chains con-
    nect thee
With the last branch of Europe's mountain-tree!

This land, before all lands in splendor,
On every race shall bliss confer,—
Which to my queen in glad surrender
Yields, as it first looked up to her,

When, 'mid Eurotas' whispering rushes
She burst from Leda's purple shell,
So blinding in her beauty's flushes,
That mother, brothers, felt the spell!

This land, which seeks thy sole direction,
Its brightest bloom hath now unfurled:
Prefer thy fatherland's affection
To what is wholly thine, the world!

And though upon its ridgy backs of mountains
The Sun's cold arrow smites each cloven head,
Yet, where the rock is greened by falling fountains,
The wild-goat nibbles and is lightly fed.

The springs leap forth, the streams united follow;
Green are the gorges, slopes, and meads below:
On hundred hillsides, cleft with many a hollow,
Thou seest the woolly herds like scattered snow.

Divided, cautious, graze with measured paces
The cattle onward to the dizzy edge,
Yet for them all are furnished sheltered places,
Where countless caverns arch the rocky ledge.

Pan guards them there, and nymphs of life are dwell-
    ing
In bushy clefts, that moist and freshest be;
And yearningly to higher regions swelling,
The branches crowd aloft of tree on tree.

Primeval woods! the strong oak there is regnant,
And bough crooks out from bough in stubborn state;
The maple mild, with sweetest juices pregnant,
Shoots cleanly up, and dallies with its weight.

And motherly, in that still realm of shadows,
The warm milk flows, for child's and lambkin's lips:
At hand is fruit, the food of fertile meadows,
And from the hollow trunk the honey drips.

Here comfort is in birth transmitted;
To cheek and lip here joy is sent:
Each is immortal in his station fitted,
And all are healthy and content.

And thus the child in that bright season gaineth
The father-strength, as in a dream:
We wonder; yet the question still remaineth,
If they are men, when Gods they seem.

So was Apollo shepherd-like in feature,
That other shepherds were as fair and fleet;
For where in such clear orbit moveth Nature,
All worlds in inter-action meet.
            (*Taking his seat beside her.*)
Thus hath success my fate and thine attended;
Henceforth behind us let the Past be furled!
O, feel thyself from highest God descended!
For thou belongest to the primal world.

Thy life shall circumscribe no fortress frowning!
Still, in eternal youth, stands as it stood,
For us, our stay with every rapture crowning,
Arcadia in Sparta's neighborhood.

To tread this happy soil at last incited,
Thy flight was towards a joyous destiny!
Now let our throne become a bower unblighted,
Our bliss become Arcadian and free!

[*The scene of action is completely transformed.
   Against a range of rocky caverns close bowers are*

*constructed. A shadowy grove extends to the foot
of the rocks which rise on all sides.* FAUST *and*
HELENA *are not seen: the* CHORUS *lies scattered
about, sleeping.*]

PHORKYAS.

How long these maidens have been sleeping, know I
    not:
If they allowed themselves to dream what now mine
    eyes
So clearly saw, is equally unknown to me.
Therefore, I wake them. They, the Young, shall be
    amazed,—
Ye also, Bearded Ones, who sit below and wait,—
Solution of these marvels finally to see.
Awake! arise! and shake from off your locks the dew,
The slumber from your eyes! Listen, and cease to
    blink!

CHORUS.

Speak and tell us, quickly tell us, all the wonders that
    have happened!
We shall hear with greater pleasure, if belief we can-
    not give it,
For both eye and mind are weary, to behold these
    rocks alone.

PHORKYAS.

Children, you have hardly rubbed your eyes, and are
    you weary now?
Hear me, then! Within these caverns, in the grottos
    and the arbors,
Screen and shelter have been lent, as unto twain
    idyllic lovers,
To our Lord and to our Lady.

CHORUS.

How? within there?

PHORKYAS.

Separated
From the world, me only did they summon to their
    quiet service.

Honored thus, I stood beside them, but, as fit in one
  so trusted,
Looked around at something other, turning here and
  there at random,—
Seeking roots, and bark, and mosses, being skilled in
  healing simples,—
And the twain were left alone.

CHORUS.

Speakest thou as if within were spaces roomy as the
  world is:
Wood and meadow, lakes and rivers,—what a fable
  dost thou spin!

PHORKYAS.

Certainly, ye Inexperienced! Those are unexplored
  recesses:
Hall on hall, and court on court succeeding, musingly
  I tracked.
All at once a laughter echoes through the spaces of
  the caverns;
As I look, a Boy is leaping from the mother's lap to
  father's,
From the father to the mother: the caressing and the
  dandling,
Teasing pranks of silly fondness, cry of sport and
  shout of rapture,
They, alternate, deafen me.
He, a Genius naked, wingless, like a Faun without the
  beasthood,
Leaps upon the solid pavement; yet the pavement
  now reacting,
Sends him flying high in air, and at the second bound
  or third, he
Seems to graze the vaulted roof.
Cries, disquieted, the mother: "Leap repeatedly, at
  pleasure,
But beware of flying! for prohibited is flight to thee."
And thus warns the faithful father: "Dwells in earth
  the force elastic
Which thee upwards thus impelleth; touch but with
  thy toe the surface,

Like the son of Earth, Antæus, straightway art thou
    strong again."

So he springs upon the rocky masses, from a dizzy
    cornice

To another, and around, as springs a ball when sharply
    struck.

Yet, a-sudden, in a crevice of the hollow gulf he's van-
    ished,

And it seemeth we have lost him! Mother mourns, and
    father comforts,

Shoulder-shrugging, anxiously I stand. But now,
    again, what vision!

Are there treasures yonder hidden? Garments striped
    with broidered blossoms

Hath he worthily assumed.

Tassels from his shoulders swaying, fillets flutter round
    his bosom,

In his hand the golden lyre, completely like a little
    Phœbus,

Cheerily to the brink he steps, the jutting edge: we
    stand astounded,

And the parents in their rapture clasp each other to
    the heart.

What around his head is shining? What it is, were
    hard to warrant,

Whether golden gauds, or flame of all-subduing
    strength of soul.

So he moves with stately gesture, even as boy himself
    proclaiming

Future Master of all Beauty, all the melodies eternal

Throbbing in his flesh and blood; and you shall thus,
    delighted, hear him,—

Thus shall you behold him, with a wonder never felt
    before!

CHORUS.

Call'st thou a marvel this,
Creta's begotten?
Poetic-didactical word
Hast thou listened to never?
Never yet hearkened Ionia's

Never received also Hellas'
Godlike, heroical treasure
Of ancient, primitive legends?

All that ever happens
Now in the Present
Mocks like a mournful echo
The grander days of the Fathers.
Not comparable is thy story
Unto that loveliest falsehood,
Than Truth more credible,
Sung of the Son of Maia!

This strong and delicate, yet
Scarcely delivered suckling,
Swathe ye in purest downy bands,
Bind ye in precious diapered stuffs,
As is the gossiping nurse's
Unreasonable notion!
Strongly and daintily draws, no less,
Now the rogue the flexible,
Firm yet elastic body
Cunningly out, and leaveth the close,
Purple, impeding shell
Quietly there in its place,
Like the completed butterfly,
Which from the chilly chrysalid
Nimbly, pinion-unfolding, slips,
Boldly and wilfully fluttering through
Sunshine-pervaded ether.
So he, too, the sprightliest:
That unto thieves and jugglers—
All the seekers of profit, as well,—
He the favorable Dæmon was,
Did he speedily manifest
By the skilfullest artifice.
Straight from the Ruler of Ocean stole
He the trident,— from Arês himself
Slyly the sword from the scabbard;
Arrows and bow from Phœbus, and then
Tongs that Hephæstos was using.

Even from Zeus, the Father, bolts had he
Filched, had the fire not scared him.
Eros, also, he overcame
In leg-tripping wrestling match;
Then from Cypris, as she caressed him,
Plundered the zone from her bosom.

[*An exquisite, purely melodious music of stringed
instruments resounds from the cavern. All become
attentive, and soon appear to be deeply moved.
From this point to the pause designated, there is a
full musical accompaniment.*]

PHORKYAS.

Hark! the music, pure and golden;
Free from fables be at last!
All your Gods, the medley olden,
Let depart! their day is past.

You no more are comprehended;
We require a higher part:
By the heart must be expended
What shall work upon the heart.
        (*She retires towards the rocks.*)

CHORUS.

If the flattering music presses,
Fearful Being, to thine ears,
We, restored to health, confess us
Softened to the joy of tears.

Let the sun be missed from heaven,
When the soul is bright with morn!
What the world has never given
Now within our hearts is born.

(HELENA. FAUST. EUPHORION *in the costume already
described.*)

EUPHORION.

Hear ye songs of childish pleasure,
Ye are moved to playful glee;

Seeing me thus dance in measure,
Leap your hearts parentally.

HELENA.

Love, in human wise to bless us,
In a noble Pair must be;
But divinely to possess us,
It must form a precious Three.

FAUST.

All we seek has therefore found us;
I am thine and thou art mine!
So we stand as Love hath bound us:
Other fortune we resign.

CHORUS.

Many years shall they, delighted,
Gather from the shining boy
Double bliss for hearts united:
In their union what a joy!

EUPHORION.

Let me be skipping,
Let me be leaping!
To soar and circle,
Through ether sweeping,
Is now the passion
That me hath won.

FAUST.

But gently! gently!
Not rashly faring;
Lest plunge and ruin
Repay thy daring,
Perchance destroy thee,
Our darling son!

EUPHORION.

I will not longer
Stagnate below here!
Let go my tresses,
My hands let go, here!

Let go my garments!
They all are mine.

HELENA.

O think! Bethink thee
To whom thou belongest!
How it would grieve us,
And how thou wrongest
The fortune fairest,—
Mine, His, and Thine!

CHORUS.

Soon shall, I fear me,
The sweet bond untwine!

HELENA AND FAUST.

Curb, thou Unfortunate!
For our desiring,
Thine over-importunate
Lofty aspiring!
Rurally quiet,
Brighten the plain!

EUPHORION.

Since you will that I try it,
My flight I restrain.
(*Winding in dance through the* CHORUS, *and drawing
them with him.*)
Round them I hover free;
Gay is the race:
Is this the melody?
Move I with grace?

HELENA.

Yes, that is featly done:
Lead them through, every one,
Mazes of art!

FAUST.

Soon let it ended be!
Sight of such jugglery
Troubles my heart.

CHORUS

(*with* EUPHORION, *dancing nimbly and singing, in interlinking ranks*).

When thou thine arms so fair
Charmingly liftest,
The curls of thy shining hair
Shakest and shiftest;
When thou, with foot so light,
Brushest the earth in flight,
Hither and forth again
Leading the linkéd chain,
Then is thy goal in sight,
Loveliest Boy!
All of our hearts in joy
Round thee unite.
> *Pause.*

EUPHORION.

Not yet repose,
Ye light-footed roes!
Now to new play
Forth, and away!
I am the hunter,
You are the game.

CHORUS.

Wouldst thou acquire us,
Be not so fast!
We are desirous
Only, at last,
Clasping thy beauty,
Kisses to claim!

EUPHORION.

Through groves and through hedges!
O'er cliffs and o'er ledges!
Lightly what fell to me,
That I detest:
What I compel to me
Pleases me best.

HELENA AND FAUST.

How perverse, how wild he's growing!
Vain to hope for moderation;
Now it sounds like bugles blowing,
Over vale and forest pealing:
What disorder! What a brawl!

CHORUS
(*entering singly, in haste*).

Forth from us with swiftness ran he!
Spurning us with scornful feeling,
Now he drags from out the many
Here, the wildest one of all.

EUPHORION (*bearing a young* MAIDEN).

Here I drag the little racer,
And by force will I embrace her;
For my bliss and for my zest
Press the fair, resisting breast,
Kiss the mouth, repellent still,—
Manifest my strength and will.

MAIDEN.

Let me go! This frame infoldeth
Also courage, strength of soul:
Strong as thine, our will upholdeth,
When another would control.
I am in a strait, thou deemest?
What a force thine arm would claim!
Hold me, Fool, and ere thou dreamest
I will scorch thee, in my game.
(*She turns to flame and flashes up in the air.*)
To the airy spaces follow,
Follow me to caverns hollow,
Snatch and hold thy vanished aim!

EUPHORION
(*shaking off the flames*).

Rocks all around me here,
Over the forests hung!
Why should they bound me here?

Still am I fresh and young.
Tempests are waking now,
Billows are breaking now:
Both far away I hear;
Fain would be near.
(*He leaps ever farther up the rocks.*)

HELENA, FAUST, AND CHORUS.
Chamois-like, dost thou aspire?
Fearful of the fall are we.

EUPHORION.
I must clamber ever higher,
Ever further must I see.

Now, where I am, I spy!
Midst of the Isle am I:
Midst of Pelops' land,
Kindred in soul, I stand!

CHORUS.
Bide thou by grove and hill,
Peacefully, rather!
We from the vineyards will
Grapes for thee gather,—
Grapes from the ridges tanned,
Figs, and the apple's gold:
Ah! yet the lovely land,
Loving, behold!

EUPHORION.
Dream ye the peaceful day?
Dream, then, who may!
War! is the countersign:
Victory—word divine!

CHORUS.
Who peace and unity
Scorneth, for war's array,
With impunity
Slays his hope of a better day.

EUPHORION.

They, who this land have led
Through danger and dread,
Free, boundlessly brave,
Lavish of blood they gave,—
May they, with glorious
Untamable might,
Make us victorious,
Now, in the fight!

CHORUS.

Look aloft! he seeks the Farness,
Yet to us not small he seems.
As for battle, as in harness,
He like steel and silver gleams.

EUPHORION.

Walls and towers no more immuring,
Each in vigor stands confessed!
Fortress firm and most enduring
Is the soldier's iron breast.

Would ye dwell in freemen's houses?
Arm, and forth to combat wild!
See, as Amazons, your spouses,
And a hero every child!

CHORUS.

Hallowed Poesy,
Heavenward mounting, see!
Shining, the fairest star,
Farther, and still more far!
Yet, from the distance blown,
Hear we the lightest tone,
And raptured are.

EUPHORION.

No, 't is no child which thou beholdest—
A youth in arms, with haughty brow!
And with the Strongest, Freest, Boldest,
His soul is pledged, in manly vow.

I go!
For, lo!
The path to Glory opens now.

HELENA AND FAUST.

Thou thy being scarcely learnest,
Scarcely feel'st the Day's glad beam,
When from giddy steeps thou yearnest
For the place of pain supreme!
Are then we
Naught to thee?
Is the gracious bond a dream?

EUPHORION.

And hear ye thunders on the ocean?
From land the thunder-echoes call?
In dust and foam, with fierce commotion,
The armies shock, the heroes fall!
The command
Is, sword in hand,
To die: 't is certain, once for all.

HELENA, FAUST, AND CHORUS.

What a horror! We shall rue it!
Ah, is Death command to thee?

EUPHORION.

Shall I from the distance view it?
No! the fate be shared by me!

THE ABOVE.

Danger his arrogance brings:
Fatally bold!

EUPHORION.

Yes!—and a pair of wings
See me unfold!
Thither! I must!—and thus!
Grant me the flight!

[*He casts himself into the air: the garments bear him
a moment, his head is illuminated, and a streak of
light follows.*]

CHORUS.

Icarus! Icarus!
Sorrowful sight!

[*A beautiful Youth falls at the feet of the parents.
We imagine that in the dead body we perceive a
well-known form; yet the corporeal part vanishes
at once, and the aureole rises like a comet towards
heaven. The garment, mantle, and lyre remain
upon the ground.*]

HELENA AND FAUST.

Joy is followed, when scarce enjoyed,
By bitterest moan.

EUPHORION (*from the depths*).

Leave me here, in the gloomy Void,
Mother, not thus alone!
                    Pause.

CHORUS [*Dirge.*]

Not alone! where'er thou bidest;
For we know thee what thou art.
Ah! if from the Day thou hidest,
Still to thee will cling each heart.
Scarce we venture to lament thee,
Singing, envious of thy fate;
For in storm and sun were lent thee
Song and courage, fair and great.

Ah! for earthly fortune fashioned,
Strength was thine, and proud descent:
Early erring, o'er-impassioned,
Youth, alas! from thee was rent.
For the world thine eye was rarest,
All the heart to thee was known:
Thine were loves of women fairest,
And a song thy very own.

Yet thou rannest uncontrolledly
In the net the fancies draw,
Thus thyself divorcing boldly

As from custom, so from law;
Till the highest thought expended
Set at last thy courage free:
Thou wouldst win achievement splendid,
But it was not given to thee.

Unto whom, then? Question dreary,
Destiny will never heed;
When in evil days and weary,
Silently the people bleed.
But new songs shall still elate them:
Bow no longer and deplore!
For the soil shall generate them,
As it hath done heretofore.

Complete pause. The music ceases.

HELENA (*to* FAUST).

Also in me, alas! an old word proves its truth,
That Bliss and Beauty ne'er enduringly unite.
Torn is the link of Life, no less than that of Love;
So, both lamenting, painfully I say: Farewell!
And cast myself again—once only—in thine arms.
Receive, Persephone, receive the boy and me.

(*She embraces* FAUST: *her corporeal part disappears,
her garment and veil remain in his arms.*)

PHORKYAS (*to* FAUST).

Hold fast what now alone remains to thee!
The garment let not go! Already twitch
The Demons at its skirts, and they would fain
To the Nether Regions drag it! Hold it fast!
It is no more the Goddess thou hast lost,
But godlike is it. For thy use employ
The grand and priceless gift, and soar aloft!
'T will bear thee swift from all things mean and low
To ether high, so long thou canst endure.
We'll meet again, far, very far from here.

(HELENA'S *garments dissolve into clouds, surround*
FAUST, *lift him aloft in the air, and move away
with him.*)

PHORKYAS

(*takes up* EUPHORION'S *tunic, mantle, and lyre from the earth, steps forward to the proscenium, holds aloft these remains, and speaks*).

> Good leavings have I still discovered!
> The Flame has vanished where it hovered,
> Yet for the world no tears I spend.
> Enough remains to start the Poets living,
> And envy in their guilds to send;
> And, if their talents are beyond my giving,
> At least the costume I can lend.

(*She seats herself upon a column in the proscenium.*)

PANTHALIS.

Now hasten, maidens! we are from the magic freed,
The old Thessalian trollop's mind-compelling spell,—
Freed from the jingling drone of much-bewildering
    sound,
The ear confusing, and still more the inner sense.
Down, then, to Hades! since beforehand went the
    Queen,
With solemn step descending. Now, upon the track,
Let straightway follow her the step of faithful maids!
Her shall we find beside the unfathomed, gloomy King.

CHORUS.

> Queens, of course, are satisfied everywhere:
> Even in Hades take they highest rank,
> Proudly associate with their peers,
> With Persephone closely allied:
> We, however, in the background
> Of the asphodel-besprinkled meadows,
> With the endless rows of poplars
> And the fruitless willows ever mated,—
> What amusement, then, have we?
> Bat-like to squeak and twitter
> In whispers uncheery and ghostly!

LEADER OF THE CHORUS.

Who hath not won a name, and seeks not noble works,
Belongs but to the elements: away then, ye!

My own intense desire is with my Queen to be;
Service and faith secure the individual life.

[*Exit.*

ALL.
Given again to the daylight are we,
Persons no more, 't is true,—
We feel it and know it,—
But to Hades return we never!
Nature, the Ever-living,
Makes to us spirits
Validest claim, and we to her also.

A PART OF THE CHORUS.
We, in trembling whispers, swaying rustle of a thousand branches
Sweetly rocked, will lightly lure the rills of life, the
rootborn, upwards
To the twigs; and, or with foliage or exuberant gush
of blossoms,
Will we freely deck their flying hair for prosperous
airy growth.
Then, when falls the fruit, will straightway gather
gladdened herds and people,
Swiftly coming, briskly pressing, for the picking and
the tasting:
All, as if before the early Gods, will then around us
bend.

A SECOND PART.
We, beside these rocks, upon the far-off shining,
glassy mirror,
Coaxingly will bend and fluctuate, moving with the
gentle waters;
We to every sound will hearken, song of bird or reedy
piping;
Though the dreadful voice of Pan, a ready answer
shall we give:
Comes a murmur, we re-murmur,—thunder, we our
thunders waken
In reverberating crashes, doubly, trebly, tenfold flung!

A THIRD PART.

Sisters, we, of nimbler fancy, hasten with the brooklets
  onward;
For allure us yonder distant, richly-mantled mountain
  ranges.
Ever downwards, ever deeper, in meandering curves
  we water
First the meadow, then the pasture; then the garden
  round the house,
Marked by slender peaks of cypress, shooting clearly
  into ether
O'er the landscape and the waters and the fading line
  of shore.

A FOURTH PART.

Fare, ye others, at your pleasure; we will girdle and
  o'errustle
The completely-planted hillside, where the sprouting
  vines are green.
There at every hour the passion of the vintager is
  witnessed,
And the loving diligence, that hath so doubtful a
  result.
Now with hoe and now with shovel, then with hilling,
  pruning, tying,
Unto all the Gods he prayeth, chiefly to the Sun's
  bright god.
Small concern hath pampered Bacchus for his faithful
  servant's welfare,
But in arbors rests, and caverns, toying with the
  youngest Faun.
For his semi-drunken visions whatsoever he hath
  needed,
It is furnished him in wine-skins, and in amphoræ
  and vessels,
Right and left in cool recesses, cellared for eternal
  time.
But if now the Gods together, Helios before the others,
Have with breeze and dew and warmth and glow the
  berries filled with juice,
Where the vintager in silence labored, all is life and
  motion,

Every trellis stirs and rustles, and they go from stake
to stake.

Baskets creak and buckets rattle, groaning tubs are
borne on back,

All towards the vat enormous and the treaders' lusty
dance;

So is then the sacred bounty of the pure-born, juicy
berries

Rudely trodden; foaming, spirting, they are mixed
and grimly crushed.

Now the ear is pierced with cymbals and the clash of
brazen bosses,

For, behold, is Dionysos from his mysteries revealed!

Forth he comes with goat-foot Satyrs, whirling goat-
foot Satyresses,

While amid the rout Silenus' big-eared beast unruly
brays.

Naught is spared! The cloven hoofs tread down all
decent custom;

All the senses whirl bewildered, fearfully the ear is
stunned.

Drunkards fumble for the goblets, over-full are heads
and paunches;

Here and there hath one misgivings, yet increases thus
the tumult;

For, the fresher must to garner, empty they the ancient
skin!

[*The curtain falls.* PHORKYAS, *in the proscenium, rises
to a giant height, steps down from the cothurni,
removes her mask and veil, and reveals herself as*
MEPHISTOPHELES, *in order, so far as it may be
necessary, to comment upon the piece by way of
Epilogue.*]

ACT IV.

I.

HIGH MOUNTAINS.

*Strong, serrated rocky peaks. A cloud approaches,
pauses, and settles down upon a projecting ledge.
It then divides.*

FAUST (*steps forth*).

DOWN-GAZING on the deepest solitudes below,
I tread deliberately this summit's lonely edge,
Relinquishing my cloudy car, which hither bore
Me softly through the shining day o'er land and sea.
Unscattered, slowly moved, it separates from me.
Off eastward strives the mass with rounded, rolling
    march:
And strives the eye, amazed, admiring, after it.
In motion it divides, in wave-like, changeful guise;
Yet seems to shape a figure.—Yes! mine eyes not err!—
On sun-illumined pillows beauteously reclined,
Colossal, truly, but a godlike woman-form,
I see! The like of Juno, Leda, Helena,
Majestically lovely, floats before my sight!
Ah, now 't is broken! Towering broad and formlessly,
It rests along the east like distant icy hills,
And shapes the grand significance of fleeting days.
Yet still there clings a light and delicate band of mist
Around my breast and brow, caressing, cheering me.
Now light, delayingly, it soars and higher soars,
And folds together.—Cheats me an ecstatic form,
As early-youthful, long-foregone and highest bliss?
The first glad treasures of my deepest heart break
    forth;
Aurora's love, so light of pinion, is its type,
The swiftly-felt, the first, scarce-comprehended glance,
Outshining every treasure, when retained and held.
Like Spiritual Beauty mounts the gracious Form,
Dissolving not, but lifts itself through ether far,
And from my inner being bears the best away.

(*A Seven-league boot trips forward: another imme-
    diately follows.* MEPHISTOPHELES *steps out of them.
    The Boots stride onward in haste.*)

MEPHISTOPHELES.

I call that genuine forward-striding!
But what thou mean'st, I'd have thee own,
That in such horrors art abiding,
Amid these yawning jags of stone?

It was not here I learned to know them well;
Such was, indeed, the bottom-ground of Hell.

FAUST.

In foolish legends thou art never lacking;
Again thy store thou set'st about unpacking.

MEPHISTOPHELES (*seriously*).

When God the Lord—wherefore, I also know,—
Banned us from air to darkness deep and central,
Where round and round, in fierce, intensest glow,
Eternal fires were whirled in Earth's hot entrail,
We found ourselves too much illuminated,
Yet crowded and uneasily situated.
The Devils all set up a coughing, sneezing,
At every vent without cessation wheezing:
With sulphur-stench and acids Hell dilated,
And such enormous gas was thence created,
That very soon Earth's level, far extended,
Thick as it was, was heaved, and split, and rended!
The thing is plain, no theories o'ercome it:
What formerly was bottom, now is summit.
Hereon they base the law there's no disputing,
To give the undermost the topmost footing:
For we escaped from fiery dungeons there
To overplus of lordship of the air;—
A mystery manifest and well concealed,
And to the people only late revealed.

FAUST.

To me are mountain-masses grandly dumb:
I ask not, Whence? and ask not, Why? they come.
When Nature in herself her being founded,
Complete and perfect then the globe she rounded,
Glad of the summits and the gorges deep,
Set rock to rock, and mountain steep to steep,
The hills with easy outlines downward moulded,
Till gently from their feet the vales unfolded!
They green and grow; with joy therein she ranges,
Requiring no insane, convulsive changes.

MEPHISTOPHELES.

Yes, so you talk! You think it clear as sun;
But he knows otherwise, who saw it done.
For I was there, while still below was surging
The red abyss, and streamed the flaming tide,—
When Moloch's hammer, welding rocks and forging,
Scattered the mountain-ruins far and wide.
O'er all the land the foreign blocks you spy there;
Who solves the force that hurled them to their place?
The lore of learned men is all awry there;
There lies the rock, and we must let it lie there;
We've thought already—to our own disgrace.
Only the common, faithful people know,
And nothing shakes them in their firm believing:
Their wisdom ripened long ago,—
A marvel 't is, of Satan's own achieving.
On crutch of faith my traveller climbs the ridges,
Past Devil's Rocks and over Devil's Bridges.

FAUST.

Well,—'t is remarkable and new
To note how Devils Nature view.

MEPHISTOPHELES.

What's all to me? Her shape let Nature wear!
The point of honor is, the Devil was there!
We are the folk to compass grand designs:
Tumult, and Force, and Nonsense! See the signs!—
Yet now, with sober reason to address thee,
Did nothing on our outside shell impress thee?
From this exceeding height thou saw'st unfurled
The glory of the Kingdoms of the World.
Yet, as thou art, unsatisfied,
Didst feel no lust of power and pride?

FAUST.

I did! A mighty plan my fancy won:
Canst guess it?

MEPHISTOPHELES.

That is quickly done.
I'd take some town,—a capital, perchance,—

Its core, the people's need of sustenance;
With crooked alleys, pointed gables,
Beets, cabbage, onions, on the market-tables;
With meat-stands, where the blue flies muster,
And round fat joints like gourmands cluster:
There shalt thou find, undoubtedly,
Stench, always, and activity.
Then ample squares, and streets whose measure
Assumes an air of lordly leisure;
And last, without a gate to bar,
The boundless suburbs stretching far.
'T were joy to see the coaches go,
The noisy crowding to and fro,
The endless running, hither, thither,
Of scattered ants that stream together:
And whether walking, driving, riding,
Ever their central point abiding,
Honored by thousands, should be I.

FAUST.

Therewith I would not be contented!
One likes to see the people multiply,
And in their wise with comfort fed,—
Developed even, taught, well-bred,
Yet one has only, when all's said,
The sum of rebels thus augmented.

MEPHISTOPHELES.

Then I should build, with conscious power and grace,
A pleasure-castle in a pleasant place;
Where hill and forest, level, meadow, field,
Grandly transformed, should park and garden yield.
Before green walls of foliage velvet meadows,
With ordered paths and artful-falling shadows;
Plunge of cascades o'er rocks with skill combined,
And fountain-jets of every form and kind,
There grandly shooting upwards from the middle,
While round the sides a thousand spirt and piddle.
Then for the fairest women, fresh and rosy,
I'd build a lodge, convenient and cosey;
And so the bright and boundless time I should

Pass in the loveliest social solitude.
Women, I say; and, once for all, believe
That in the plural I the sex conceive!

FAUST.

Sardanapalus! Modern,—poor!

MEPHISTOPHELES.

Then might one guess whereunto thou hast striven ·
Boldly-sublime it was, I'm sure.
Since nearer to the moon thy flight was driven,
Would now thy mania that realm secure?

FAUST.

Not so! This sphere of earthly soil
Still gives us room for lofty doing.
Astounding plans e'en now are brewing:
I feel new strength for bolder toil.

MEPHISTOPHELES.

So, thou wilt Glory earn? 'T is plain to see
That heroines have been thy company.

FAUST.

Power and Estate to win, inspires my thought!
The Deed is everything, the Glory naught.

MEPHISTOPHELES.

Yet Poets shall proclaim the matter,
Thy fame to future ages flatter,
By folly further folly scatter!

FAUST.

All that is far beyond thy reach.
How canst thou know what men beseech?
Thy cross-grained self, in malice banned,
How can it know what men demand?

MEPHISTOPHELES.

According to thy will so let it be!
Confide the compass of thy whims to me!

FAUST.

Mine eye was drawn to view the open Ocean:
It swelled aloft, self-heaved and over-vaulting,
And then withdrew, and shook its waves in motion,
Again the breadth of level strand assaulting.
Then I was vexed, since arrogance can spite
The spirit free, which values every right,
And through excited passion of the blood
Discomfort it, as did the haughty flood.
I thought it chance, my vision did I strain;
The billow paused, then thundered back again,
Retiring from the goal so proudly won:
The hour returns, the sport's once more begun.

MEPHISTOPHELES (*ad spectatores*).

'T is nothing new whatever that one hears;
I've known it many a hundred thousand years.

FAUST
(*continuing impassionedly*).

The Sea sweeps on, in thousand quarters flowing,
Itself unfruitful, barrenness bestowing;
It breaks and swells, and rolls, and overwhelms
The desert stretch of desolated realms.
There endless waves hold sway, in strength erected
And then withdrawn,—and nothing is effected.
If aught could drive me to despair, 't were, truly
The aimless force of elements unruly.
Then dared my mind its dreams to over-soar:
Here would I fight,—subdue this fierce uproar!
And possible 't is!—Howe'er the tides may fill,
They gently fawn around the steadfast hill;
A moderate height resists and drives asunder,
A moderate depth allures and leads them on.
So, swiftly, plans within my mind were drawn:
Let that high joy be mine forevermore,
To shut the lordly Ocean from the shore,
The watery waste to limit and to bar,
And push it back upon itself afar!
From step to step I settled how to fight it:
Such is my wish: dare thou to expedite it!

(*Drums and martial music in the rear of the spectators,
from the distance, on the right hand.*)

MEPHISTOPHELES.

How easy, that!—Hear'st thou the drums afar?

FAUST.

Who's wise likes not to hear of coming war.

MEPHISTOPHELES.

In War or Peace, 't is wise to use the chance,
And draw some profit from each circumstance.
One watches, marks the moment, and is bold:
Here's opportunity!—now, Faust, take hold!

FAUST.

Spare me the squandering of thy riddle-pelf!
What means it, once for all? Explain thyself!

MEPHISTOPHELES.

Upon my way, to me it was discovered
That mighty troubles o'er the Emperor hovered:
Thou knowest him. The while we twain, beside him,
With wealth illusive bounteously supplied him,
Then all the world was to be had for pay;
For as a youth he held imperial sway,
And he was pleased to try it, whether
Both interests would not smoothly pair,
Since 't were desirable and fair
To govern and enjoy, together.

FAUST.

A mighty error! He who would command
Must in commanding find his highest blessing:
Then, let his breast with force of will expand,
But what he wills, be past another's guessing!
What to his faithful he hath whispered, that
Is turned to act, and men amaze thereat:
Thus will he ever be the highest-placed
And worthiest!—Enjoyment makes debased.

MEPHISTOPHELES.

Such is he not! He *did* enjoy, even he!
Meanwhile the realm was torn by anarchy,
Where great and small were warring with each other,
And brother drove and slaughtered brother,
Castle to castle, town 'gainst town arrayed,
The nobles and the guilds of trade,
The Bishop, with his chapter and congregation,—
All meeting eyes but looked retaliation.
In churches death and murder; past the gates,
The merchants travelled under evil fates;
And all grew bolder, since no rule was drawn
For life, but: Self-defence!—So things went on.

FAUST.

They went, they limped, they fell, arose again,
Then tumbled headlong, and in heaps remain.

MEPHISTOPHELES.

Such a condition no man dared abuse.
Each would be something, each set forth his dues;
The smallest even as full-measured passed:
Yet for the best it grew too bad at last.
The Capable, they then arose with energy,
And said: "Who gives us Peace, shall ruler be.
The Emperor can and will not!—Be elected
An Emperor new, anew the realm directed,
Each one secure and sheltered stand,
And in a fresh-constructed land
Justice and Peace be mated and perfected!"

FAUST.

Priest-like, that sounds.

MEPHISTOPHELES.

　　　　　　　Priests were they, to be sure;
They meant their well-fed bellies to secure;
They, more than all, therein were implicated.
The riot rose, the riot was consecrated,
And now our Emperor, whom we gave delight,
Comes hitherward, perchance for one last fight.

FAUST.

I pity him; he was so frank, forgiving.

MEPHISTOPHELES.

Come, we'll look on! There's hope while one is living!
Let us release him from this narrow valley!
He's saved a thousand times, if once he rally.
Who knows how yet the dice may fall?
If he has fortune, vassals come withal.

[*They cross over the middle range of mountains, and
view the arrangement of the army in the valley.
Drums and military music resound from below.*]

MEPHISTOPHELES.

A good position is, I see, secured them;
We'll join, then victory will be assured them.

FAUST.

What further, I should like to know?
Cheat! Blind delusion! Hollow show!

MEPHISTOPHELES.

No,—stratagems, for battle-winning!
Be steadfast for the grand beginning,
And think upon thy lofty aim!
If we secure the realm its rightful claimant,
Then shalt thou boldly kneel, and claim
The boundless strand in feoff, as payment.

FAUST.

In many arts didst thou excell:
Come, win a battle now, as well!

MEPHISTOPHELES.

No, *thou* shalt win it! Here, in brief,
Shalt thou be General-in-Chief.

FAUST.

A high distinction thou wouldst lend,—
There to command, where naught I comprehend!

MEPHISTOPHELES.

Leave to the Staff the work and blame,
Then the Field-Marshal's sure of fame!
Of War-Uncouncils I have had enough,
And my War-Council fashion of the stuff
Of primal mountains' primal human might:
He's blest, for whom its elements unite!

FAUST.

What do I see, with arms, in yonder place?
Hast thou aroused the mountain-race?

MEPHISTOPHELES.

No! But I've brought, like Peter Squence,
From all the raff the quintessence.

The Three Mighty Men appear.

MEPHISTOPHELES.

My fellows draw already near!
Thou seest, of very different ages,
Of different garb and armor they appear:
They will not serve thee ill when battle rages.

(*Ad spectatores.*)

Now every child delights to see
The harness and the helm of knightly action
And allegoric, as the blackguards be,
They'll only all the more give satisfaction.

BULLY

(*young, lightly armed, clad in motley*).

When one shall meet me, face to face,
My fisticuffs shall on his chops be showered;
And midway in his headlong race,
Fast by his flying hair I'll catch the coward.

HAVEQUICK

(*manly, well-armed, richly clad*).

Such empty brawls are only folly!
They spoil whate'er occasion brings.
In *taking*, be unwearied wholly,
And after, look to other things!

HOLDFAST

(well in years, strongly-armed, without raiment).
Yet little gain thereafter lingers!
Soon slips great wealth between your fingers,
Borne by the tides of Life as down they run.
'T is well to take, indeed, but better still to hold:
Be by the gray old churl controlled,
And thou shalt plundered be by none.
                    (They descend the mountain together.)

II.

ON THE HEADLAND.

Drums and military music from below. The EM-
PEROR'S *tent is pitched.*

EMPEROR. GENERAL-IN-CHIEF. LIFE-GUARDSMEN.

GENERAL-IN-CHIEF.

IT still appears the prudentest of courses
   That here, in this appropriate vale,
We have withdrawn and strongly massed our forces:
I firmly trust we shall not fail.

EMPEROR.

What comes of it will soon be brought to light;
Yet I dislike this yielding, semi-flight.

GENERAL-IN-CHIEF.

Look down, my Prince, where our right flank is
        planted!
The field which War desires hath here been granted:
Not steep the hills, yet access not preparing,
To us advantage, to the foe insnaring;
Their cavalry will hardly dare surround
Our strength half hid, on undulating ground.

EMPEROR.

My commendation, only, need I speak;
Now arm and courage have the test they seek.

GENERAL-IN-CHIEF.

Here, on the middle meadow's level spaces
Thou seest the phalanx, eager in their places.
In air the lances gleam and sparkle, kissed
By sunshine, through the filmy morning mist.
How darkling sways the grand and powerful square!
The thousands burn for great achievements there.
Therein canst thou perceive the strength of masses;
And thine, be sure, the foemen's strength surpasses.

EMPEROR.

Now first do I enjoy the stirring sight:
An army, thus, appears of double might.

GENERAL-IN-CHIEF.

But of our left I've no report to make.
Brave heroes garrison the rocky brake;
The stony cliffs, by gleams of weapons specked,
The entrance to the close defile protect.
Here, as I guess, the foemen's force will shatter,
Forced unawares upon the bloody matter.

EMPEROR.

And there they march, false kin, one like the other!
Even as they styled me Uncle, Cousin, Brother,
Assuming more, and ever more defying,
The sceptre's power, the throne's respect, denying;
Then, in their feuds, the realm they devastated,
And now as Rebels march, against me mated!
Awhile with halting minds the masses go,
Then ride the stream, wherever it may flow.

GENERAL-IN-CHIEF.

A faithful man, sent out some news to win,
Comes down the rocks; may he have lucky been!

FIRST SPY.

Luckily have we succeeded;
Helped by bold and cunning art,
Here and there have pressed, and heeded,
But 't is ill news we impart.

Many, purest homage pledging,
Like the faithful, fealty swore,—
For inertness now alleging
People's danger, strife in store.

EMPEROR.

They learn from selfishness self-preservation,
Not duty, honor, grateful inclination.
You do not think that, when your reckoning's shown,
The neighbor's burning house shall fire your own!

GENERAL-IN-CHIEF.

The Second comes, descending slowly hither;
A weary man, whose strength appears to wither.

SECOND SPY.

First with comfort we detected
What their plan confused was worth;
Then, at once and unexpected,
Came another Emperor forth.
As he bids, in ordered manner
March the gathering hosts away;
His unfolded lying banner
All have followed.—Sheep are they!

EMPEROR.

Now, by a Rival Emperor shall I gain:
That *I* am Emperor, thus to me is plain.
But as a soldier I the mail put on;
Now for a higher aim the sword be drawn!
At all my shows, however grand to see,
Did nothing lack: but Danger lacked, *to me.*
Though you but tilting at the ring suggested,
My heart beat high to be in tourney tested;
And had you not from war my mind dissuaded,
For glorious deeds my name were now paraded.
But independence then did I acquire,
When I stood mirrored in the realm of fire:
In the dread element I dared to stand;—
'T was but a show, and yet the show was grand.
Of fame and victory I have dreamed alone;
But for the base neglect I now atone!

(*The* HERALDS *are despatched to challenge the Rival
Emperor to single combat.*)

FAUST *enters, in armor, with half-closed visor.   The*
THREE MIGHTY MEN, *armed and clothed, as already
described.*

FAUST.

We come, and hope our coming is not chidden;
Prudence may help, though by the need unbidden.
The mountain race, thou know'st, think and explore,—
Of Nature and the rocks they read the lore.
The Spirits, forced from the level land to sever,
Are of the rocky hills more fain than ever.
Silent, they work through labyrinthine passes,
In rich, metallic fumes of noble gases,
On solving, testing, blending, most intent:
Their only passion, something to invent.
With gentle touch of spiritual power
They build transparent fabrics, hour by hour;
For they, in crystals and their silence, furled,
Behold events that rule the Upper World.

EMPEROR.

I understand it, and can well agree;
But say, thou gallant man, what's that to me?

FAUST.

The Sabine old, the Norcian necromancer,
Thy true and worthy servant, sends thee answer:
What fearful fate it was, that overhung him!
The fagots crackled, fire already stung him;
The billets dry were closely round him fixed,
With pitch and rolls of brimstone intermixed;
Not Man, nor God, nor Devil, him could save,—
The Emperor plucked him from his fiery grave.
It was in Rome.   Still is he bound unto thee;
Upon my path his anxious thoughts pursue thee;
Himself since that dread hour forgotten, he
Questions the stars, the depths, alone for thee.
Us he commissioned, by the swiftest courses
Thee to assist. Great are the mountain's forces:

There Nature works all-potently and free,
Though stupid priests therein but magic see.

EMPEROR.

On days of joy, when we the guests are greeting,
Who for their gay delight are gayly meeting,
Each gives us pleasure, as they push and pull,
And crowd, man after man, the chambers full;
Yet chiefly welcome is the brave man, thus,
When as a bold ally he brings to us
Now, in the fateful morning hour, his talents,
While Destiny uplifts her trembling balance.
Yet, while the fates of this high hour unfold,
Thy strong hand from the willing sword withhold,—
Honor the moment, when the hosts are striding,
For or against me, to the field deciding!
Self is the Man! Who crown and throne would claim
Must personally be worthy of the same.
And may the Phantom, which against us stands,
The self-styled Emperor, Lord of all our lands,
The army's Duke, our Princes' feudal head,
With mine own hand be hurled among the dead!

FAUST.

Howe'er the need that thy great work be finished,
Risked were thy head, the chances were diminished.
Is not the helm adorned with plume and crest?
The head it shields, that steels our courage best.
Without a head, what should the members bridle?
Let it but sleep, they sink supine and idle.
If it be injured, all the hurt confess in 't,
And all revive, when it is convalescent.
Then soon the arm its right shall reassert,
And lift the shield to save the skull from hurt:
The sword perceives at once its honored trust,
Parries with vigor, and repeats the thrust:
The gallant foot its share of luck will gain,
And plants itself upon the necks of slain.

EMPEROR.

Such is my wrath; I'd meet him thus, undaunted,
And see his proud head as my footstool planted!

HERALDS (*returning*).

Little honor was accorded;
We have met with scorn undoubted:
Our defiance, nobly worded,
As an empty farce they flouted:
"Lo, your Lord is but a vision,—
Echo of a vanished prime:
When we name him, says Tradition:
'He was—*once upon a time!*'"

FAUST.

It's happened as the best would fain have planned,
Who, firm and faithful, still beside thee stand.
There comes the foe, thy army waits and wishes;
Order attack! the moment is auspicious.

EMPEROR.

Yet I decline to exercise command.
   (*To the* GENERAL-IN-CHIEF.)
Thy duty, Prince, be trusted to thy hand!

GENERAL-IN-CHIEF.

Then let the right wing now advance apace!
The enemy's left, who just begin ascending,
Shall, ere the movement close, give up their place,
Before the youthful force our field defending.

FAUST.

Permit me, then, that this gay hero may
Be stationed in thy ranks, without delay,—
That with thy men most fully he consort,
And thus incorporate, ply his vigorous sport!
  (*He points to the* MIGHTY MAN *on the right.*)

BULLY (*coming forward*).

Who shows his face to me, before he turn
Shall find his cheekbones and his chops are shattered:
Who shows his back, one sudden blow shall earn,
Then head and pig-tail dangling hang, and battered!
And if thy men, like me, will lunge
With mace and sword, beside each other,

Man over man the foe shall plunge
And in their own deep blood shall smother!

[*Exit.*

GENERAL-IN-CHIEF.

Let then our centre phalanx follow slow,—
Engage with caution, yet with might, the foe!
There to the right, already overtaken,
Our furious force their plan has rudely shaken!

FAUST (*pointing to the middle one*).

Let also this one now obey thy word!

HAVEQUICK (*comes forward*).

Unto the host's heroic duty
Shall now be joined the thirst for booty;
And be the goal, where all are sent,
The Rival Emperor's sumptuous tent!
He shall not long upon his seat be lorded:
To lead the phalanx be to me accorded!

SPEEDBOOTY
(*sutleress, fawning upon him*).

Though never tied to him by priest,
He is my sweetheart dear, at least.
Our autumn 't is, of ripest gold!
Woman is fierce when she takes hold,
And when she robs, is merciless:
All is allowed, so forth to victory press!

[*Exeunt both.*

GENERAL-IN-CHIEF.

Upon our left, as was to be foreseen,
Their right is strongly hurled. Yon rocks between,
Ours will resist their furious beginning,
And hinder them the narrow pass from winning.

FAUST
(*beckons to the* MIGHTY MAN *on the left*).

I beg you, Sire, let this one also aid;
'T is well when even the strong are stronger made.

HOLDFAST (*coming forwards*).

Now let the left wing have no fear!
The ground is surely held, where I appear:

I am the Ancient you were told of:
No lightning splits what I keep hold of!

[Exit.

MEPHISTOPHELES
(*descending from above*).

And now behold, how, more remote,
From every jagged rocky throat
Comes forth an arméd host, increasing,
Down every narrow pathway squeezing,
With helm and harness, sword and spear,
A living rampart in our rear,
And wait the sign to charge the foemen!
(*Aside, to the knowing ones.*)
You must not ask whence comes the omen.
I have not been a careless scout,
But cleared the halls of armor round about.
They stood a-foot, they sat on horses,
Like Lords of Earth and real forces:
Once Emperors, Kings, and Knights were they,
Now empty shells,—the snails have crawled away.
Full many ghosts, arrayed so, have for us
Revamped the Middle Ages thus.
Whatever Devils now the shells select,
This once 't will still create effect.
(*Aloud.*)
Hark! in advance they stir their anger,
Each jostling each with brassy clangor!
The banner-rags of standards flutter flowing,
That restless waited for the breeze's blowing.
Here standeth ready, now, an ancient race;
In the new conflict it would fain have place.
(*Tremendous peal of trumpets from above: a percept-*
ible wavering in the hostile army.)

FAUST.
The near horizon dims and darkles;
Yet here and there with meaning sparkles
A ruddy and presaging glow;
The blades are red where strife is sorest,
The atmosphere, the rocks, the forest,
The very heavens the combat show.

MEPHISTOPHELES.

The right flank holds its ground with vigor:
There, towering over all, defiant,
Jack Bully works, the nimble giant,
And drives them with his wonted rigor.

EMPEROR.

I first beheld one arm uplifted,
But now a dozen tossed and shifted:
Unnatural such things appear.

FAUST.

Hast thou not heard of vapors banded,
O'er the Sicilian coasts expanded?
There, hovering in daylight clear,
When mid-air gleams in rarer phases,
And mirrored in especial hazes,
A vision wonderful awakes:
There back and forth are cities bending,
With gardens rising and descending,
As form on form the ether breaks.

EMPEROR.

Yet how suspicious! I behold
The tall spears tipped with gleams of gold:
Upon our phalanx' shining lances
A nimble host of flamelets dances:
Too spectral it appears to me.

FAUST.

Pardon me, Lord, those are the traces
Of spirits of the vanished races,—
The fires of Pollux and of Castor,
Whom seamen call on in disaster:
They here collect their final strength for thee.

EMPEROR.

But say, to whom are we indebted,
That Nature hath our plans abetted,
With shows of rarest potency?

MEPHISTOPHELES.

To whom, indeed, but that old Roman

Whose care for thee at last is proved?
By the strong menace of thy foemen
His deepest nature has been moved.
His gratitude would see thee now delivered,
Though his own being for thy sake be shivered.

EMPEROR.

They cheered my march, with every pomp invested;
I felt my power, I meant to see it tested;
So, carelessly, I found it well, as ruler,
To send the white beard where the air was cooler.
I robbed the Clergy of a pleasant savor,
And, truly, have not thus acquired their favor.
Shall I, at last, since many years are over,
The payment for that merry deed recover?

FAUST.

Free-hearted help heaps interest:
Look up, and cease to watch the foemen!
Methinks that *he* will send an omen:
Attend! the sign is now expressed.

EMPEROR.

An Eagle hovers in the heavenly vault:
A Griffin follows, menacing assault.

FAUST.

Give heed! It seems most favorable.
The Griffin is a beast of fable:
How dare he claim a rival regal,
And meet in fight a genuine Eagle?

EMPEROR.

And now, in circles wide extended,
They wheel involved,—then, like a flash,
Upon each other swiftly dash,
That necks be cleft and bodies rended!

FAUST.

Mark now the evil Griffin quail!
Rumpled and torn, the foe he feareth,

And with his drooping lion's-tail,
Plunged in the tree-tops, disappeareth.

EMPEROR.

E'ven as presaged, so may it be!
I take the sign, admiringly.

MEPHISTOPHELES (*towards the right*).

From the force of blows repeated
Have our enemies retreated;
And in fight uncertain, shifting,
Towards their right they now are drifting,
Thus confusing, by their courses,
All the left flank of their forces.
See! our phalanx, firmly driven,
Moves to right, and, like the levin,
Strikes them in the weak position.—
Now, like waves in wild collision,
Equal powers, with rage opposing,
In the double fight are closing.
Gloriously the weapons rattle;
We, at last, have won the battle!

EMPEROR

(*on the left, to* FAUST).

Look! it yonder seems suspicious;
For our post the luck's capricious.
Not a stone I see them throw there;
Mounted are the rocks below there,
And the upper ones deserted.
Now!—to one huge mass converted
Nearer moves the foe, unshaken,
And perchance the pass hath taken.
Such the unholy plan's conclusion!
All your arts are but delusion.
                    Pause.

MEPHISTOPHELES.

There come my ravens, croaking presage;
What nature, then, may be their message?
I fear we stand in evil plight.

EMPEROR.

What mean these fatal birds enchanted?
Their inky sails are hither slanted,
Hot from the rocky field of fight.

MEPHISTOPHELES (*to the Ravens*).

Sit at mine ears, your flight retarded!
He is not lost whom you have guarded;
Your counsel's logical and right.

FAUST (*to the* EMPEROR).

Thou hast, of course, been told of pigeons,
Taught to return from distant regions
To nests upon their native coast.
Here, differently, the plan's succeeded;
The pigeon-post for Peace is needed,
But War requires the raven-post.

MEPHISTOPHELES.

The birds announce us sore mischances.
See, yonder, how the foe advances
Against our heroes' rocky wall,
The nearest heights even now attaining!
Should they succeed the pass in gaining,
Our fortunes, then, were critical.

EMPEROR.

Defeat and cheat at last are on me!
Into your meshes you have drawn me:
I shudder, since they bind me fast.

MEPHISTOPHELES.

Courage! Not yet the die is cast.
Patience and knack, for knot-untying!
The close will be the fiercest stand.
Sure messengers for me are flying:
Command that I may give command!

GENERAL-IN-CHIEF
(*who has meanwhile arrived*).

To follow these hast thou consented;
Thence all the time was I tormented:

No fortune comes of jugglery.
The battle's lost, I cannot mend it;
'T was they began, and they may end it:
My baton I return to thee.

EMPEROR.

Retain it for the better season
Which Fortune still to us may send!
I dread the customers with reason,—
The ravens and their ugly friend.
                (*To* MEPHISTOPHELES.)
As for the baton, thou must leave it;
Thou 'rt not, methinks, the proper man.
Command the fight, canst thou retrieve it!
Let happen all that happen can!
        [*Exit into the tent with the* GENERAL-IN-CHIEF.

MEPHISTOPHELES.

The blunt stick still be his protection!
'T would naught avail in *our* direction;
There was a sort of Cross thereon.

FAUST.

What's to be done?

MEPHISTOPHELES.

                The thing is done!—
Now, my black cousins, speed upon your duties
To the mountain-lake! The Undines, watery beauties,
Entreat, the appearance of their floods to spare!
By female arts, beyond our sharpest seeing,
They can divide the Appearance from the Being,
And all will swear the Being's there!
                Pause.

FAUST.

Our ravens must, with flattery beladen,
Have sweetly coaxed each winsome water-maiden;
The trickling streams at once descend.
The bald and rocky shoulders of the mountains
Give birth to full and swiftly-flowing fountains;
Their victory is at an end.

HAVEQUICK.

No raven flies so swift as we.

SPEEDBOOTY.

O, how the treasure-piles extend!
Where shall I once begin? where end?

HAVEQUICK.

But all the space is full! And now
I know not what to take, I vow!

SPEEDBOOTY.

This carpet is the thing I need!
My couch is often hard indeed.

HAVEQUICK.

Here hangs a morning-star, so strong,
The like of which I've wanted long.

SPEEDBOOTY.

This crimson mantle, bound with gold,
Is like the one my dreams foretold.

HAVEQUICK (*taking the weapon*).

With this, a man is quickly sped;
One strikes him dead, and goes ahead.
Thou art already laden so,
And nothing right thy sack can show.
This rubbish, rather, here forsake,
And one of yonder caskets take!
The army's modest pay they hold,
Their bellies full of purest gold.

SPEEDBOOTY.

O what a murderous weight is there!
I cannot lift it, cannot bear.

HAVEQUICK.

Quick, bend and squat to take the pack!
I'll heave it on thy sturdy back.

SPEEDBOOTY.

O me!   Alack! the burden slips:
The weight has crushed my back and hips.
                    (*The chest falls and bursts open.*)

HAVEQUICK.

There lies the red gold in a heap!
Quick, rake and take what thou canst keep!

SPEEDBOOTY (*crouching down*).

Quick, let the booty fill my lap!
'T will still be quite enough, mayhap.

HAVEQUICK.

So! there's enough!   Now haste, and go!
                    (*She rises.*)
The apron has a hole, ah woe!
Wherever thou dost walk or stand,
Thou sowest treasure on the land.

GUARDSMEN (*of our* EMPEROR).

What seek ye here with wanton eyes?
Ye rummage the Imperial prize!

HAVEQUICK.

We hazarded our limbs for pay,
And now we take our share of prey.
In hostile tents 't is always so,
And we are soldiers too, you know.

GUARDSMEN.

Among our troops he comes to grief
Who's both a soldier and a thief:
Who serves our Emperor fair and **free,**
Let him an honest soldier be!

HAVEQUICK.

O yes! such honesty we know:
'T is *Contribution,*—call it so!
In the same mould you all are made.
"Give!" is the password of your trade.

(*To* SPEEDBOOTY.)

With what thou hast, the coast we'll clear:
As guests we are not welcome here.

[*Exeunt.*

FIRST GUARDSMAN.

Why didst thou not at once bestow
On the scamp's face a smashing blow?

SECOND.

I know not,—had not strength to strike;
They seemed to me so phantom-like.

THIRD.

Something there was disturbed my sight,—
A flash: I could not see aright.

FOURTH.

I, also, can declare it not:
The whole day long it was so hot,
So sultry, close, and terrible;
One man stood firm, another fell;
We groped and fought, with valor rash,
The foemen fell at every slash;
Before one's eyes there was a mist,
And something roared, and hummed, and hissed;
So to the end, and here are we,
And how it happened, cannot see.

(*The* EMPEROR *enters, accompanied by* FOUR PRINCES
The GUARDSMEN *retire.*)

EMPEROR.

Now fare he, as he may! For us is won the battle,
And o'er the plain the foe have fled like frightened
    cattle.
The trait'rous treasure, here, the empty throne, we've
    found,
That, hung with tapestry, contracts the space around.
Enthroned in honor we, true guardsmen us protecting,
The people's envoys are imperially expecting.
The messengers of joy arrive from every side,
And, loyal now to us, the realm is pacified.

Though in our fight, perchance, some jugglery was
    woven,
Yet, at the last, our own unaided strength we've proven.
True, accidents sometimes for combatants are good;
A stone may fall from heaven, on foes a shower of
    blood;
From rocky caves may ring tremendous strains of
    wonder,
That lift our hearts with faith, and drive the foe
    asunder.
The Conquered yielded, scourged by Scorn's immortal
    rod;
The Victor, as he boasts, exalts the favoring God;
And all responsive shout, unordered, unentreated:
"We praise Thee, God our Lord!" from million throats
    repeated.
Yet as the highest praise, so rarely else expressed,
I turn my pious glance on mine own grateful breast.
A young and lively Prince may give his days to
    pleasure;
Him teach the years, at last, the moment's use to
    measure.
Therefore, without delay, I call ye, for support,
Beside me, worthy Four, in realm and house and court.
            (*To the* FIRST.)
Thine was, O Prince! the host's arrangement, wise
    inspection,
Then, in the nick of time, heroic, bold direction:
Act now in peace, as Time thine offices may show!
Arch-Marshal shalt thou be: the sword I here bestow.

ARCH-MARSHAL.

Thy faithful host, till now employed for civil order,
Thee and thy throne secured, shall strengthen next
    thy border:
Then let us be allowed, when festal throngs are poured
Through thine ancestral halls, to dress for thee the
    board.
Before thee brightly borne, and brightly held beside
    thee,

Thy Majesty's support, the sword shall guard and
  guide thee!

 EMPEROR (*to the* SECOND).

He who as gallant man can also gracious be,
Thou,—be Arch-Chamberlain!—not light the place,
  for thee.
Thou art the highest now of all the house-retainers
Whose strife makes service bad,—the threateners and
  complainers:
Let thy example be an honored sign to these,
How they the Prince and Court, and all, should seek
  to please!

ARCH-CHAMBERLAIN.

To speed thy high design, thy grace is fair precursor:
The Better to assist, and injure not the Worser,—
Be frank, yet cunning not, and calm without deceit!
If thou but read my heart, I'm honored as is meet.
But let my fancy now to festal service hasten!
Thou goest to the board, I bear the golden basin,
And hold thy rings for thee, that on such blissful days
Thy hands may be refreshed, as I beneath thy gaze.

EMPEROR.

Too serious am I still, to plan such celebration;
Yet be it so! We need a glad inauguration.
            (*To the* THIRD.)
I choose thee Arch-High-Steward! Therefore hence-
  forth be
Chase, poultry-yard, and manor subject unto thee!
Give me at all times choice of dishes I delight in,
As with the month they come, and cooked with appe-
  tite in!

ARCH-HIGH-STEWARD.

A rigid fast shall be the penalty I wish,
Until before thee stands a goodly-savored dish.
The kitchen-folk shall join, and gladly heed my reasons
To bring the distant near and expedite the seasons.

Yet rare and early things shall not delight thee long:
Thy taste desires, instead, the simple and the strong.

EMPEROR (*to the* FOURTH).

Since here, perforce, we plan but feasts, and each is
    sharer,
Be thou for me transformed, young hero, to Cup-
    Bearer!
Arch Cup-Bearer, take heed, that all those vaults of
    mine
Richly replenished be with noblest taps of wine!
Be temperate thyself, howe'er temptation presses,
Nor let occasion's lure mislead thee to excesses!

ARCH CUP-BEARER.

My Prince, the young themselves, if trust in them be
    shown,
Are, ere one looks around, already men full-grown.
I at the lordly feast shall also take my station,
And give thy sideboard's pomp the noblest decoration
Of gorgeous vessels, golden, silver, grand to see;
Yet first the fairest cup will I select for thee,—
A clear Venetian glass, good cheer within it waiting,
Helping the taste of wine, yet ne'er intoxicating.
One oft confides too much on such a treasured store:
Thy moderation, though, High Lord, protects thee
    more.

EMPEROR.

What, in this earnest hour, for you have I intended,
From valid mouth confidingly you've comprehended.
The Emperor's word is great, his gift is therefore sure,
But needs, for proper force, his written signature:
The high sign-manual fails. Here, for commission
    needful,
I see the right man come, of the right moment heedful.
    (*The* ARCHBISHOP-ARCH-CHANCELLOR *enters.*)

EMPEROR.

If in the keystone of the arch the vault confide,
'T is then securely built, for endless time and tide.

Thou seest Four Princes here! To them we've just
  expounded
How next our House and Court shall be more stably
  founded.
Now, all the realm contains, within its bounds enclosed,
Shall be, with weight and power, upon Ye Five im-
  posed!
Your landed wealth shall be before all others splendid;
Therefore at once have I your properties extended
From their inheritance, who raised 'gainst us the hand.
You I award, ye Faithful, many a lovely land,
Together with the right, as you may have occasion,
To spread them by exchange, or purchase, or invasion:
Then be it clearly fixed, that you unhindered use
Whate'er prerogatives have been the landlord's dues.
When ye, as Judges, have the final sentence spoken,
By no appeal from your high Court shall it be broken:
Then levies, tax and rent, pass-money, tolls and fees
Are yours,—of mines and salt and coin the royalties.
That thus my gratitude may validly be stated,
You next to Majesty hereby I've elevated.

ARCHBISHOP.
In deepest thanks to thee we humbly all unite:
Thou mak'st us strong and sure, and strengthenest thy
  might.

EMPEROR.
Yet higher dignities I give for your fulfilling.
Still for my realm I live, and still to live am willing;
Yet old ancestral lines compel the prudent mind
To look from present deeds to that which looms behind.
I, also, in my time, must meet the sure Redresser;
Your duty be it, then, to choose me a successor.
Crowned, at the altar raise his consecrated form,
That so may end in peace what here began in storm!

ARCH-CHANCELLOR.
With pride profound, yet humbly, as our guise evinces,
Behold, before thee bowed, the first of earthly princes!
So long the faithful blood our living veins shall fill,
We are the body which obeys thy lightest will.

EMPEROR.

Now, to conclude, let all that we have here asserted,
Be, for the future time, to document converted!
'T is true that ye, as lords, have your possession free,
With this condition, though, that it unparcelled be;
And what ye have from us, howe'er ye swell the treas-
　　ure,
Shall to the eldest son descend in equal measure.

ARCH-CHANCELLOR.

On parchment I, at once, shall gladly tabulate,
To bless the realm and us, the statute of such weight:
The copy and the seals the Chancery shall procure us,
Thy sacred hand shall then validly assure us.

EMPEROR.

Dismissal now I grant, that you, assembled, may
Deliberate upon the great, important day.
　　　　(*The Secular Princes retire.*)

ARCHBISHOP

(*remains and speaks pathetically*).

The Chancellor withdrew, the Bishop stands before
　　thee:
A warning spirit bids that straightway he implores
　　thee!
His heart paternal quakes with anxious fear for thee.

EMPEROR.

In this glad hour what may thy dread misgiving be?

ARCHBISHOP.

Alas, in such an hour, how much my pain must greaten,
To find thy hallowed head in covenant with Satan!
True, to the throne, it seems, hast thou secured thy
　　right;
But, woe! in God the Lord's, the Holy Pontiff's spite.
Swift shall he punish when he learns the truth — the
　　latter:
Thy sinful realm at once with holy ban he'll shatter!
He still remembers how, amid thy highest state,

When newly crowned, thou didst the wizard liberate.
Thy diadem but made thy heart for Christians harden,
For on that head accurst fell its first beam of pardon.
Now beat thy breast, and from thy guilty stores, this
    day,
Unto the Sanctuary a moderate mite repay!
The spacious sweep of hills, where stood thy tent
    erected,—
Where Evil Spirits then, united, thee protected,—
Where late the Liar-Prince thy hearing did secure,—
Devote thou, meekly taught, to pious use and pure,
With hill and forest dense, far as they stretch extended,
And slopes that greenly swell for pastures never ended,
Then crystal lakes of fish, unnumbered brooks that flow
In foamy windings down, and braid the vale below;
The broad vale then, itself, with mead, and lawn, and
    hollow!
Thus penitence is shown, and pardon soon shall follow.

EMPEROR.

For this, my heavy sin, my terror is profound:
By thine own measure shalt thou draw the borders
    round.

ARCHBISHOP.

First be the spot profane, where sin was perpetrated
To God's high service soon and wholly dedicated!
With speed the walls arise to meet the mind's desire;
The rising morning sun already lights the choir;
The growing structure spreads, the transept stands
    exalted;
Joy of Believers, then, the nave is lifted, vaulted;
And while they press with zeal within the portals grand,
The first clear call of bells is swept across the land,
Pealed from the lofty towers that heavenwards have
    striven:
The penitent draws near, new life to him is given.
The consecration-day—O, may it soon be sent!—
Thy presence then shall be the highest ornament.

EMPEROR.

So great a work shall be my pious proclamation

To praise the Lord our God, and work mine expiation.
Enough! I feel, e'en now, how high my thoughts
    aspire.

ARCHBISHOP.

As Chancellor, next, the formal treaty I require.

EMPEROR.

A formal document,—the Church needs full requital!
Bring it to me, and I with joy will sign her title!

ARCHBISHOP

(*has taken leave, but turns back again at the door*).

At once unto the work devote, that it may stand,
Tithes, levies, tax,—the total income of the land,
Forever.   Much it needs, to be supported fairly,
And careful maintenance will also cost us rarely:
And, that it soon be built, on such a lonesome wold,
Thou 'lt from thy booty spare to us some little gold.
Moreover, we shall want—here, most, we claim assis-
    tance—
Lumber, and lime, and slate, and such like, from a
    distance.
The people these shall haul, thus from the pulpit
    taught;
The Church shall bless the man, whose team for her
    has wrought.

[*Exit.*

EMPEROR.

The sin is very sore, wherewith my soul is weighted:
Much damage unto me the Sorcerers have created.

ARCHBISHOP

(*returning once again, with profoundest genuflections*).

Pardon, O Prince! to him, that vile, notorious man,
The Empire's coast was given; but him shall smite the
    ban,
Unless thy penitence the Church's wrath relaxes
There, too, with tithes and gifts, and revenues and
    taxes.

EMPEROR (*ill-humoredly*).

The land doth not exist: far in the sea it lies.

ARCHBISHOP.

Who patient is, and right, his day shall yet arise.
Your word for us remains, and makes secure our
    trover!

[Exit

EMPEROR (*solus*).

I might as well, at last, make all the Empire over!

ACT V

I.

OPEN COUNTRY.

WANDERER.

YES! 't is they, the dusky lindens;
  There they stand in sturdy age:
And again shall I behold them,
After such a pilgrimage?
'T is the ancient place, the drifted
Downs, the hut that sheltered me,
When the billow, storm-uplifted,
Hurled me shoreward from the sea!
Here with blessing would I greet them,
They, my hosts, the helpful pair,—
Old, indeed, if now I meet them,
Since they then had hoary hair.
Pious folk, from whom I parted!
Be my greeting here renewed,
If ye still, as open-hearted,
Taste the bliss of doing good!

BAUCIS (*a little woman, very old*).

Gently, stranger! lest thou cumber
Rest, whereof my spouse hath need!
He but gains from longest slumber
Strength for briefest waking deed.

WANDERER.

Tell me, mother, art thou even

She, to whom my thanks I bear,—
I, the youth, whose life was given
By your kind, united care?
Art thou Baucis, who the coldly
Fading mouth refreshment gave?
    (*The Husband appears.*)
Thou, Philemon, who so boldly
Drew my treasure from the wave?
From your fire, so quickly burning,
From your silver-sounding bell,
Changed my doom, to fortune turning,
When the dread adventure fell.
Forth upon the sand-hills stealing,
Let me view the boundless sea!
Let me pray, devoutly kneeling,
Till my burdened heart be free!
    (*He walks forward upon the downs.*)

PHILEMON (*to* BAUCIS).
Haste, and let the meal be dighted
'Neath the garden's blooming trees!
Let him go, and be affrighted!
He'll believe not what he sees.
(*Follows, and stands beside the* WANDERER.)
Where the savage waves maltreated
You, on shores of breaking foam,
See, a garden lies completed,
Like an Eden-dream of home!
Old was I, no longer eager,
Helpful, as the younger are:
And when I had lost my vigor,
Also was the wave afar.
Wise lords set their serfs in motion,
Dikes upraised and ditches led,
Minishing the rights of Ocean,
Lords to be in Ocean's stead.
See the green of many a meadow,
Field and garden, wood and town!
Come, our table waits in shadow!
For the sun is going down.
Sails afar are gliding yonder;

Nightly to the port they fare:
To their nest the sea-birds wander,
For a harbor waits them there.
Distant now, thou hardly seëst
Where the Sea's blue arc is spanned,—
Right and left, the broadest, freest
Stretch of thickly-peopled land.

II.

IN THE LITTLE GARDEN.

THE THREE AT THE TABLE.

BAUCIS (*to the Stranger*).
ART thou dumb? Of all we've brought here,
In thy mouth shall nothing fall?

PHILEMON.
He would know the marvel wrought here:
Fain thou speakest: tell him all!

BAUCIS.
'T was a marvel, if there's any!
And the thought disturbs me still:
In a business so uncanny
Surely helped the Powers of Ill.

PHILEMON.
Can the Emperor's soul be perilled,
Who on him the strand bestowed?
Gave the mandate not the herald,
Trumpeting, as on he rode?
Near our downs, all unexpected,
Was the work's beginning seen,
Tents and huts!—but, soon erected,
Rose a palace o'er the green.

BAUCIS.
Knaves in vain by day were storming,

Plying pick and spade alike;
Where the fires at night were swarming,
Stood, the following day, a dike.
Nightly rose the sounds of sorrow,
Human victims there must bleed:
Lines of torches, on the morrow,
Were canals that seaward lead.
He would seize our field of labor,
Hut and garden, godlessly:
Since he lords it as our neighbor,
We to him must subject be.

PHILEMON.

Yet he bids, in compensation,
Fair estate of newer land.

BAUCIS.

Trust not watery foundation!
Keep upon the hill thy stand!

PHILEMON.

Let us, to the chapel straying,
Ere the sunset-glow has died,
Chime the vespers, kneel, and, praying,
Still in our old God confide!

III.

PALACE.

SPACIOUS PLEASURE-GARDEN: BROAD, STRAIGHTLY-CUT
CANAL.

FAUST (*in extreme old age, walking about, meditative*).

LYNCEUS, THE WARDER
(*through the speaking-trumpet*).

THE sun goes down, the ships are veering
To reach the port, with song and cheer:
A heavy galley, now appearing

On the canal, will soon be here.
The gaudy pennons merrily flutter,
The masts and rigging upward climb:
Blessings on thee the seamen utter,
And Fortune greets thee at thy prime.
        (*The little bell rings on the downs.*)

FAUST (*starting*).

Accurséd chime! As in derision
It wounds me, like a spiteful shot:
My realm is boundless to my vision,
Yet at my back this vexing blot!
The bell proclaims, with envious bluster,
My grand estate lacks full design:
The brown old hut, the linden-cluster,
The crumbling chapel, are not mine.
If there I wished for recreation,
Another's shade would give no cheer:
A thorn it is, a sharp vexation,—
Would I were far away from here!

WARDER (*from above*).

With evening wind and favoring tide,
See the gay galley hither glide!
How richly, on its rapid track,
Tower chest and casket, bale and sack!
(*A splendid Galley, richly and brilliantly laden with
the productions of Foreign Countries.*)

MEPHISTOPHELES. THE THREE MIGHTY MEN.

CHORUS.

Here we have landed:
Furl the sail!
Hail to the Master,
Patron, hail!
(*They disembark: the goods are brought ashore.*)

MEPHISTOPHELES.

We've proved our worth in many ways,
Delighted, if the Patron praise!

We sailed away with vessels twain,
With twenty come to port again.
Of great successes to relate,
We only need to show our freight.
Free is the mind on Ocean free;
Who there can ponder sluggishly?
You only need a rapid grip:
You catch a fish, you seize a ship;
And when you once are lord of three,
The fourth is grappled easily;
The fifth is then in evil plight;
You have the Power, and thus the Right.
You count the *What*, and not the *How:*
If I have ever navigated,
War, Trade and Piracy, I vow,
Are three in one, and can't be separated!

THE THREE MIGHTY MEN.

No thank and hail?
No hail and thank?
As if our freight
To him were rank!
He makes a face
Of great disgust;
The royal wealth
Displease him must.

MEPHISTOPHELES.

Expect no further
Any pay;
Your own good share
Ye took away.

THE MIGHTY MEN.

We only took it
For pastime fair;
We all demand
An equal share.

MEPHISTOPHELES.

First, arrange them

In hall on hall,—
The precious treasures,
Together all!
If such a splendor
Meets his ken,
And he regards it
More closely then,
A niggard he
Won't be, at least:
He'll give our squadron
Feast on feast.
To-morrow the gay birds hither wend,
And I can best to them attend.
(*The cargo is removed.*)

MEPHISTOPHELES (*to* FAUST).
With gloomy gaze, with serious brow,
Of this great fortune hearest thou.
Crowned is thy wisest industry,
And reconciled are shore and sea;
And from the shore, to swifter wakes,
The willing sea the vessels takes.
Speak, then, that here, from thy proud seat,
Thine arm may clasp the world complete.
Here, on this spot, the work was planned;
Here did the first rough cabin stand;
A little ditch was traced, a groove,
Where now the feathered oar-blades move.
Thy high intent, thy servants' toil,
From land and sea have won the spoil.
From here—

FAUST.
Still that accursed *Here!*
To me a burden most severe.
To thee, so clever, I declare it,—
It gives my very heart a sting;
It is impossible to bear it!
Yet shamed am I, to say the thing.
The old ones, there, should make concession;
A shady seat would I create:

The lindens, not my own possession,
Disturb my joy in mine estate.
There would I, for a view unbaffled,
From bough to bough erect a scaffold,
Till for my gaze a look be won
O'er everything that I have done,—
To see before me, unconfined,
The masterpiece of human mind,
Wisely asserting to my sense
The people's gain of residence.
No sorer plague can us attack,
Than rich to be, and something lack!
The chiming bell, the lindens' breath,
Oppress like air in vaults of death:
My force of will, my potence grand,
Is shattered here upon the sand.
How shall I ban it from my feeling!
I rave whene'er the bell is pealing.

MEPHISTOPHELES.

'T is natural that so great a spite
Thy life should thus imbitter quite.
Who doubts it? Every noble ear,
Disgusted, must the jangle hear;
And that accurséd bim-bam-booming,
Through the clear sky of evening glooming,
Is mixed with each event that passes,
From baby's bath to burial-masses,
As if, between its *bam* and *bim*,
Life were a dream, in memory dim.

FAUST.

Their obstinate, opposing strain
Darkens the brightest solid gain,
Till one, in plague and worry thrust
Grows tired, at last, of being just.

MEPHISTOPHELES.

Why be annoyed, when thou canst well despise them?
Wouldst thou not long since colonize them?

FAUST.

Then go, and clear them out with speed!
Thou knowest the fair estate, indeed,
I chose for the old people's need.

MEPHISTOPHELES.

We'll set them down on other land;
Ere you can look, again they'll stand:
When they've the violence outgrown,
Their pleasant dwelling shall atone.
           (*He whistles shrilly.*)

THE THREE *enter.*

MEPHISTOPHELES.

Come, as the Master bids, and let
The fleet a feast to-morrow get!

THE THREE.

Reception bad the old Master gave:
A jolly feast is what we crave.

MEPHISTOPHELES
    (*ad spectatores*).

It happens as it happed of old:
Still Naboth's vineyard we behold!

IV.

DEAD OF NIGHT.

LYNCEUS, THE WARDER
(*singing on the watch-tower of the Palace*).

FOR seeing intended,
   Employed for my sight,
The tower's my dwelling,
The world my delight.
I gaze on the Distant,
I look on the Near,—
The moon and the planets,

The forest and deer.
So see I in all things
The grace without end,
And even as they please me,
Myself I commend.
Thou fortunate Vision,
Of all thou wast 'ware,
Whatever it might be,
Yet still it was fair!

Pause.

Not alone that I delight me,
Have I here been stationed so:—
What a horror comes, to fright me,
From the darksome world below!
Sparks of fire I see outgushing
Through the night of linden-trees;
Stronger yet the glow is flushing,
Fanned to fury by the breeze.
Ah! the cabin burns, unheeded,
Damp and mossy though it stand:
Quick assistance here is needed,
And no rescue is at hand!
Ah, the good old father, mother,
Else so careful of the fire,
Doomed amid the smoke to smother!—
The catastrophe how dire!
Now the blackening pile stands lonely
In the flames that redly swell:
If the good old folk be only
Rescued from the burning hell!
Dazzling tongues the crater launches
Through the leaves and through the branches;
Withered boughs, at last ignited,
Break, in burning, from the tree:
Why must I be thus far-sighted?
Witness such calamity?
Now the little chapel crashes
'Neath a branch's falling blow;
Soon the climbing, spiry flashes
Set the tree-tops in a glow.
Down to where the trunks are planted

Burn they like a crimson dawn.
                    Long pause.   Chant.
What erewhile the eye enchanted
With the centuries is gone.

FAUST
     (*on the balcony, towards the downs*).
Above, what whining lamentation?
The word, the tone, too late I heed.
My warder wails: I feel vexation
At heart, for this impatient deed.
Yet be the lindens extirpated,
Till half-charred trunks the spot deface,
A look-in-the-land is soon created,
Whence I can view the boundless space.
Thence shall I see the newer dwelling
Which for the ancient pair I raise,
Who, my benign forbearance feeling,
Shall there enjoy their latter days.

MEPHISTOPHELES AND THE THREE (*below*).
We hither come upon the run!
Forgive! not happily 't was done.
We knocked and beat, but none replied,
And entrance ever was denied;
Of jolts and blows we gave good store,
And broken lay the rotten door;
We called aloud, with direst threat,
But still no hearing could we get.
And, as it haps, with such a deed,
They would not hear, they would not heed;
But we began, without delay,
To drive the stubborn folks away.
The pair had then an easy lot:
They fell, and died upon the spot.
A stranger, who was there concealed,
And fought, was left upon the field;
But in the combat, fierce and fast,
From coals, that round about were cast,
The straw took fire. Now merrily
One funeral pile consumes the three.

FAUST.

Deaf unto my commands were ye!
Exchange I meant, not robbery.
The inconsiderate, savage blow
I curse! Bear ye the guilt, and go!

CHORUS.

The proverb old still runs its course:
Bend willingly to greater force!
If you are bold, and face the strife,
Stake house and home, and then—your life!

[Exeunt.

FAUST (on the balcony).

The stars conceal their glance and glow,
The fire sinks down, and flickers low;
A damp wind fans it with its wings,
And smoke and vapor hither brings.
Quick bidden, and too quick obeyed!—
What hovers hither like a shade?

V.

MIDNIGHT.

Four Gray Women enter.

FIRST.

MY name, it is Want.

SECOND.

And mine, it is Guilt.

THIRD.

And mine, it is Care.

FOURTH.

Necessity, mine.

THREE TOGETHER.

The portal is bolted, we cannot get in:
The owner is rich, we've no business within.

WANT.

I shrink to a shadow.

GUILT.

I shrink unto naught.

NECESSITY.

The pampered from me turn the face and the thought.

CARE.

Ye Sisters, ye neither can enter, nor dare;
But the keyhole is free to the entrance of Care.
(CARE *disappears.*)

· WANT.

Ye, grisly old Sisters, be banished from here!

GUILT.

Beside thee, and bound to thee, I shall appear!

NECESSITY.

At your heels goes Necessity, blight in her breath.

THE THREE.

The clouds are in motion, and cover each star!
Behind there, behind! from afar, from afar,
He cometh, our Brother! he comes, he is — — —
— — — Death!

FAUST (*in the Palace*).

Four saw I come, but those that went were three;
The sense of what they said was hid from me,
But something like *"Necessity"* I heard;
Thereafter, *"Death,"* a gloomy, threatening word!
It sounded hollow, spectrally subdued:
Not yet have I my liberty made good:
If I could banish Magic's fell creations,
And totally unlearn the incantations,—
Stood I, O Nature! Man alone in thee,
Then were it worth one's while a man to be!
Ere in the Obscure I sought it, such was I,—
Ere I had cursed the world so wickedly.

Now fills the air so many a haunting shape,
That no one knows how best he may escape.
What though One Day with rational brightness beams,
The Night entangles us in webs of dreams.
From our young fields of life we come, elate:
There croaks a bird: what croaks he? Evil fate!
By Superstition constantly insnared,
It grows to us, and warns, and is declared.
Intimidated thus, we stand alone.—
The portal jars, yet entrance is there none.
                    (*Agitated.*)
Is any one here?

CARE.
Yes! must be my reply.

FAUST.
And thou, who art thou, then?

CARE.
                    Well,—here am I.

FAUST.
Avaunt!

CARE.
I am where I should be.

FAUST
(*first angry, then composed, addressing himself*).
Take care, and speak no word of sorcery!

CARE.
Though no ear should choose to hear me,
Yet the shrinking heart must fear me:
Though transformed to mortal eyes,
Grimmest power I exercise.
On the land, or ocean yonder,
I, a dread companion, wander,
Always found, yet never sought,
Praised or cursed, as I have wrought!
Hast thou not Care already known?

FAUST.

I only through the world have flown:
Each appetite I seized as by the hair;
What not sufficed me, forth I let it fare,
And what escaped me, I let go.
I've only craved, accomplished my delight,
Then wished a second time, and thus with might
Stormed through my life: at first 't was grand, com-
        pletely,
But now it moves most wisely and discreetly.
The sphere of Earth is known enough to me;
The view beyond is barred immutably:
A fool, who there his blinking eyes directeth,
And o'er his clouds of peers a place expecteth!
Firm let him stand, and look around him well!
This World means something to the Capable.
Why needs he through Eternity to wend?
He here acquires what he can apprehend.
Thus let him wander down his earthly day;
When spirits haunt, go quietly his way;
In marching onwards, bliss and torment find,
Though, every moment, with unsated mind!

CARE.

Whom I once possess, shall never
Find the world worth his endeavor:
Endless gloom around him folding,
Rise nor set of sun beholding,
Perfect in external senses,
Inwardly his darkness dense is;
And he knows not how to measure
True possession of his treasure.
Luck and Ill become caprices;
Still he starves in all increases;
Be it happiness or sorrow,
He postpones it till the morrow;
To the Future only cleaveth:
Nothing, therefore, he achieveth.

FAUST.

Desist! So shalt thou not get hold of me!

I have no mind to hear such drivel.
Depart! Thy gloomy litany
Might even befool the wisest man to evil.

CARE.

Shall he go, or come?—how guide him?
Prompt decision is denied him;
Midway on the trodden highway
Halting, he attempts a by-way;
Ever more astray, bemisted,
Everything beholding twisted,
Burdening himself and others,
Taking breath, he chokes and smothers,
Though not choked, in Life not sharing,
Not resigned, and not despairing!
Such incessant rolling, spinning,—
Painful quitting, hard beginning,—
Now constraint, now liberation,—
Semi-sleep, poor recreation,
Firmly in his place insnare him
And, at last, for Hell prepare him!

FAUST.

Ill-omened spectres! By your treatment strays
A thousand times the human race to error:
Ye even transform the dull, indifferent days
To vile confusion of entangling terror.
'T is hard, I know, from Dæmons to escape;
The spirit's bond breaks not, howe'er one tries it;
And yet, O Care, thy power, thy creeping shape,
Think not that I shall recognize it!

CARE.

So feel it now: my curse thou 'lt find,
When forth from thee I've swiftly passed!
Throughout their whole existence men are blind:
So, Faust, be thou like them at last!
(*She breathes in his face.*)

FAUST (*blinded*).

The Night seems deeper now to press around me,

But in my inmost spirit all is light;
I rest not till the finished work hath crowned me:
The master's Word alone bestows the might.
Up from your couches, vassals, man by man!
Make grandly visible my daring plan!
Seize now your tools, with spade and shovel press!
The work traced out must be a swift success.
Quick diligence, severest ordering
The most superb reward shall bring;
And, that the mighty work completed stands,
One mind suffices for a thousand hands.

VI.

GREAT OUTER COURT OF THE PALACE.

Torches.

MEPHISTOPHELES (*in advance, as Overseer.*)
COME here, come here! Come on, come on!
   Ye Lemures, loose-hung creatures!
Of sinew, ligament, and bone
Your knitted semi-natures!

LEMURES (*in Chorus*).
Without delay are we at hand,
And half 't is our impression
That this concerns a spacious land,
Whereof we'll have possession.
The pointed stakes, we bring them all,
The measuring-chain, for distance;
But we've forgotten why the call
Was made for our assistance.

MEPHISTOPHELES.
Here is no need of your artistic zeal:
Proceed as you may think it best!
Your tallest lay full length, from head to heel,
And lift the turf around him, all the rest!
As for our fathers made, prepare

To excavate a lengthened square!
From palace to the narrow house transferred,
Such is, at last, the issue most absurd.

LEMURES

(*digging with mocking gestures*).
In youth when I did love, did love,
Methought it was very sweet;
When 't was jolly and merry every way,
And I blithely moved my feet.

But now old Age, with his stealing steps,
Hath clawed me with his crutch:
I stumbled over the door of a grave;
Why leave they open such?

FAUST

(*comes forth from the Palace, groping his way along
the doorposts*).
How I rejoice, to hear the clattering spade!
It is the crowd, for me in service moiling,
Till Earth be reconciled to toiling,
Till the proud waves be stayed,
And the sea girded with a rigid zone.

MEPHISTOPHELES (*aside*).
And yet, thou 'rt laboring for us alone,
With all thy dikes and bulwarks daring;
Since thou for Neptune art preparing—
The Ocean-Devil—carousal great.
In every way shall ye be stranded;
The elements with us are banded,
And ruin is the certain fate.

FAUST.

Overseer!

MEPHISTOPHELES.
          Here!

FAUST.
                    However possible,
Collect a crowd of men with vigor,

Spur by indulgence, praise, or rigor,—
Reward, allure, conscript, compel!
Each day report me, and correctly note
How grows in length the undertaken moat.

MEPHISTOPHELES (*half aloud*).
When they to me the information gave,
They spake not of a moat, but of—*a grave.*

FAUST.
Below the hills a marshy plain
Infects what I so long have been retrieving;
This stagnant pool likewise to drain
Were now my latest and my best achieving.
To many millions let me furnish soil,
Though not secure, yet free to active toil;
Green, fertile fields, where men and herds go forth
At once, with comfort, on the newest Earth,
And swiftly settled on the hill's firm base,
Created by the bold, industrious race.
A land like Paradise here, round about:
Up to the brink the tide may roar without,
And though it gnaw, to burst with force the limit,
By common impulse all unite to hem it.
Yes! to this thought I hold with firm persistence;
The last result of wisdom stamps it true:
He only earns his freedom and existence,
Who daily conquers them anew.
Thus here, by dangers girt, shall glide away
Of childhood, manhood, age, the vigorous day:
And such a throng I fain would see,—
Stand on free soil among a people free!
Then dared I hail the Moment fleeing:
"Ah, still delay—thou art so fair!"
The traces cannot, of mine earthly being,
In æons perish,—they are there!—
In proud fore-feeling of such lofty bliss,
I now enjoy the highest Moment,—this!

(FAUST *sinks back: the* LEMURES *take him and lay
him upon the ground.*)

MEPHISTOPHELES.

No joy could sate him, and suffice no bliss!
To catch but shifting shapes was his endeavor:
The latest, poorest, emptiest Moment—this,—
He wished to hold it fast forever.
Me he resisted in such vigorous wise,
But Time is lord, on earth the old man lies.
The clock stands still—

CHORUS.

        Stands still! silent as midnight, now!
The index falls.

MEPHISTOPHELES.

      It falls; and it is finished, here!

CHORUS.

'T is past!

MEPHISTOPHELES.

      —Past! a stupid word.
If past, then why?
Past and pure Naught, complete monotony!
What good for us, this endlessly creating?—
What is created then annihilating?
"And now it's past!" Why read a page so twisted?
'T is just the same as if it ne'er existed,
Yet goes in circles round as if it had, however:
I'd rather choose, instead, the Void forever.

SEPULTURE.

LEMUR. *Solo.*

Who then hath built the house so ill,
With shovel and with spade?

LEMURES. *Chorus.*

For thee, dull guest, in hempen vest,
It all too well was made.

LEMUR. *Solo.*

Who then so ill hath decked the hall?
No chairs, nor table any!

LEMURES. *Chorus.*

'T was borrowed to return at call:
The creditors are so many.

MEPHISTOPHELES.

The Body lies, and if the Spirit flee,
I'll show it speedily my blood-signed title.—
But, ah! they've found such methods of requital,
His souls the Devil must oft abstracted see!
One now offends, the ancient way;
Upon the new we're not yet recommended:
Once, I alone secured my prey,
But now by helpers need to be befriended.
In all things we must feel the spite!
Transmitted custom, ancient right,—
Nothing, indeed, can longer one confide in.
Once with the last breath left the soul her house;
I kept good watch, and like the nimblest mouse,
Whack! was she caught, and fast my claws her hide in!
Now she delays, and is not fain to quit
The dismal place, the corpse's hideous mansion;
The elements, in hostile, fierce expansion,
Drive her, at last, disgracefully from it.
And though I fret and worry till I'm weary,
When? How? and *Where?* remains the fatal query:
Old Death is now no longer swift and strong;
Even the *Whether* has been doubtful long.
Oft I beheld with lust the rigid members:
'T was only sham; Life kindled from its embers.
   (*Fantastic, whirling gestures of conjuration.*)
Come on! Strike up the double quick, anew,
With straight or crooked horns, ye gentlemen infernal!
Of the old Devil-grit and kernel,
And bring at once the Jaws of Hell with you!
Hell hath a multitude of jaws, in short,
To use as suiteth place and dignity;
But we, however, in this final sport,

Will henceforth less considerate be.
 (*The fearful Jaws of Hell open, on the left.*)
The side-tusks yawn: then from the throat abysmal
The raging, fiery torrents flow,
And in the vapors of the background dismal
I see the city flame in endless glow.
Up to the teeth the breakers lash the red arena;
The Damned, in hope of help, are swimming through;
But, caught and mangled by the fell hyena,
Their path of fiery torment they renew.
In every nook new horrors flash and brighten,
In narrow space so much of dread supreme!
Well have you done, the sinners thus to frighten;
But still they'll think it lie, and cheat, and dream!
 (*To the stout Devils, with short, straight horns.*)
Now, paunchy scamps, with cheeks so redly burning!
Ye glow, so fat with hellish sulphur fed;
With necks thick-set and stumpy, never turning,—
Watch here below, if phosphor-light be shed:
It is the Soul, the wingéd Psyche is it;
Pluck off the wings, 't is but a hideous worm:
First with my stamp and seal the thing I'll visit,
Then fling it to the whirling, fiery storm!
The lower parts be well inspected,
Ye Bloats! perform your duty well:
If there the Soul her seat selected
We cannot yet exactly tell.
Oft in the navel doth she stay:
Look out for that, she thence may slip away!
 (*To the lean Devils, with long, crooked horns.*)
Ye lean buffoons, file-leaders strange and giant,
Grasp in the air, yourselves no respite give!
Strong in the arms, with talons sharp and pliant,
That ye may seize the fluttering fugitive!
In her old home discomforted she lies,
And Genius, surely, seeks at once to rise.
  (*Glory from above, on the right.*)

THE HEAVENLY HOST.
Envoys, unhindered,
Heavenly kindred,

Follow us here!
Sinners forgiving,
Dust to make living!
Lovingest features
Unto all creatures
Show in your swaying,
Delaying career!

MEPHISTOPHELES.

Discords I hear, a harsh, disgusting strumming,
Flung from above with the unwelcome Day;
'T is that emasculate and bungled humming
Which Pious Cant delights in, every way.
You know how we, atrociously contented,
Destruction for the human race have planned:
But the most infamous that we've invented
Is just the thing their prayers demand.
The fops, they come as hypocrites, to foòl us!
Thus many have they snatched, before our eyes:
With our own weapons they would overrule us;
They're also Devils—in disguise.
To lose this case would be your lasting shame;
On to the grave, and fortify your claim!

CHORUS OF ANGELS (*scattering roses.*)
Roses, ye glowing ones,
Balsam-bestowing ones!
Fluttering, quivering,
Sweetness delivering,
Branching unblightedly,
Budding delightedly,
Bloom and be seen!
Springtime declare him,
In purple and green!
Paradise bear him,
The Sleeper serene!

MEPHISTOPHELES (*to the Satans*).
Why do ye jerk and squat? Is this Hell's rule?
Stand to your ground, and let them sprinkle!
Back to his place each gawky fool!

They think, perhaps, with such a flowery crinkle,
As if 't were snow, the Devils' heat to cool:
Your breath shall make it melt, and shrink, and
    wrinkle.
Now blow, ye Blowers!—'T is enough, enough!
Before your breath fades all the floating stuff.
Not so much violence,—shut jaws and noses!
Forsooth, ye blow too strongly at the roses.
The proper measure can you never learn?
They sting not only, but they wither, burn!
They hover on with flames of deadly lustre:
Resist them ye, and close together cluster!—
Your force gives out; all courage fails you so:
The Devils scent the strange, alluring glow.

ANGELS.

    Blossoms of gratitude,
    Flames of beatitude,
    Love they are bearing now,
    Rapture preparing now,
    As the heart may!
    Truth in its nearness,
    Ether in clearness,
    Give the Eternal Hosts
    Everywhere Day!

MEPHISTOPHELES.

O curse and shame upon such dolts be sped!
Each Satan stands upon his head!
In somersaults the stout ones whirl and swerve,
And into Hell plunge bottom-uppermost.
Now may your bath be hot as you deserve!
But I remain, unflinching, at my post.
    (*Beating off the hovering roses.*)
Off, will-o'-the-wisps! Bright as ye seem to be,
When caught, the vilest clinging filth are ye.
Why flutter thus? Off with you, quick!—
Like pitch and sulphur on my neck they stick.

CHORUS OF ANGELS.
What not appertaineth

To you, cease to share it!
What inwardly paineth,
Refuse ye to bear it!
If it press in with might,
Use we our stronger right:
Love but the Loving
Leads to the Light!

MEPHISTOPHELES.

My head, heart, liver, by the flames are rent!
An over-devilish element!—
Sharper than Hell's red conflagration!
Thence so enormous is your lamentation,
Unfortunate Enamored! who, so spurned,
Your heads towards the sweethearts' side have turned.
Mine, too! What twists my head in like position?
With them am I not sworn to competition?
The sight of them once made my hatred worse.
Hath then an alien force transpierced my nature?
I like to see them, youths of loveliest stature;
What now restrains me, that I dare not curse?
And if I take their cozening bait so,
Who else, henceforth, the veriest fool will be?
The stunning fellows, whom I hate so,
How very charming they appear to me!—
Tell me, sweet children, ere I miss you,
Are ye not of the race of Lucifer?
You are so fair, forsooth, I'd like to kiss you;
It seems to me as if ye welcome were.
I feel as comfortable and as trustful,
As though a thousand times ere this we'd met!
So surreptitiously catlike-lustful:
With every glance ye're fairer, fairer yet.
O, nearer come,—O, grant me one sweet look!

ANGELS.

We come! Why shrink? Canst not our presence
    brook?
Now we approach: so, if thou canst, remain!
(*The* ANGELS, *coming forward, occupy the whole
        space.*)

MEPHISTOPHELES
(*who is crowded into the proscenium*).
Us, Spirits damned, you brand with censure,
Yet you are wizards by indenture;
For man and woman, luring, you enchain.—
What chance the curst adventure brings me?
Is this Love's chosen element?
The fire o'er all my body stings me;
My neck I scarcely feel, so hotly sprent.—
Ye hover back and forth; sink down and settle!
Move your sweet limbs with more of worldly mettle!
The serious air befits you well, awhile,
But I should like, just once, to see you smile;
That were, for me, an everlasting rapture.
I mean, as lovers look, the heart to capture;
About the mouth a simper there must be.
Thee, tall one, as enticing I'll admit thee;
The priestly mien does not at all befit thee,
So look at me the least bit wantonly!
You might be nakeder, and modest made so:
Your shirts' long drapery is over-moral.—
They turn!—and, from the rear surveyed so,
With their attraction there's no need to quarrel!

CHORUS OF ANGELS.
Love still revealing,
Flames, become clearer!
All, cursed with error,
Truth be their healing!
Glad self-retrieval
Free them from Evil,
In the all-folding Breast,
Blessed, to rest!

MEPHISTOPHELES (*collecting himself*).
How is 't with me?—Like Job, the boils have cleft me
From head to foot, so that myself I shun;
Yet triumph also, when my self-inspection's done,—
When self and tribe I have confided in.
The noble Devil-parts, at least, are left me!
This love-attack's a rash upon the skin.

Burned out already are the scurvy fires,
And one and all I damn you, as the case requires!

CHORUS OF ANGELS.
Hallowed glories!
Round whom they brood,
Wakes unto being
Of bliss with the Good.
Join ye, the Glorified,
Rise to your goal!
Airs are all purified,—
Breathe now the Soul!
(*They rise, bearing away the immortal part of* FAUST.)

MEPHISTOPHELES (*looking around him*).
But how?—at once I find them failing!
This race of minors takes me by surprise!
They with their booty heavenwards are sailing;
Thence on this grave they cast their greedy eyes!
My rare, great treasure they have peculated:
The lofty soul, to me hypothecated,
They've rapt away from me in cunning wise.
But unto whom shall I appeal for justice?
Who would secure to me my well-earned right?
Tricked so in one's old days, a great disgust is;
And I deserve it, this infernal spite.
I've managed in a most disgraceful fashion;
A great investment has been thrown away:
By lowest lust seduced, and senseless passion,
The old, case-hardened Devil went astray.
And if, from all this childish-silly stuff
His shrewd experience could not wrest him,
So is, forsooth, the folly quite enough,
Which, in conclusion, hath possessed him.

VII.

MOUNTAIN-GORGES, FOREST, ROCK, DESERT.

HOLY ANCHORITES,

Divided in ascending planes, posted among the ravines.

CHORUS AND ECHO.

FORESTS are waving grand,
   Rocks, they are huge at hand,
Clutching, the roots expand,
Thickly the tree-trunks stand;
Foaming comes wave on wave;
Shelter hath deepest cave;
Lions are prowling dumb,
Friendly where'er we come,
Honoring the sacred place,
Refuge of Love and Grace!

PATER ECSTATICUS
(hovering up and down).

Endless ecstatic fire,
Glow of the pure desire,
Pain of the pining breast,
Rapture of God possessed!
Arrows, transpierce ye me,
Lances, coerce ye me,
Bludgeons, so batter me,
Lightnings, so shatter me,
That all of mortality's
Vain unrealities
Die, and the Star above
Beam but Eternal Love!

PATER PROFUNDUS.
(Lower Region.)

As at my feet abysses cloven
Rest on abysses deep below;
As thousand severed streams are woven
To foamy floods that plunging go;
As, up by self-impulsion driven,
The tree its weight sustains in air,
To Love, almighty Love, 't is given
All things to form, and all to bear.
Around me sounds a savage roaring,
As rocks and forests heaved and swayed,
Yet plunges, bounteous in its pouring,
The wealth of waters down the glade,

Appointed, then, the vales to brighten;
The bolt, that flaming struck and burst,
The atmosphere to cleanse and lighten,
Which pestilence in its bosom nursed,—
Love's heralds both, the powers proclaiming,
Which, aye creative, us infold.
May then, within my bosom flaming,
Inspire the mind, confused and cold,
Which frets itself, through blunted senses,
As by the sharpest fetter-smart!
O God, soothe Thou my thoughts bewildered,
Enlighten Thou my needy heart!

PATER SERAPHICUS.
(*Middle Region.*)
What a cloud of morning hovers
O'er the pine-trees' tossing hair!
Can I guess what life it covers?
They are spirits, young and fair.

CHORUS OF BLESSED BOYS.
Tell us, Father, where we wander;
Tell us, Kind One, who are we.
Happy are we; for so tender
Unto all, it is, To Be.

PATER SERAPHICUS.
Boys, brought forth in midnights haunted,
Half-unsealed the sense and brain,
For the parents lost when granted,
For the angels sweetest gain!
That a loving heart is nigh you
You can feel: then come to me!
But of earthly ways that try you,
Blest ones! not a trace have ye.
Enter in mine eyes: enjoy them,
Organs for the earthly sphere!
As your own ye may employ them:
Look upon the landscape here!
(*He takes them into himself.*)
Those are trees, there rocks defend us;

Here, a stream that leaps below,
And with plunges, wild, tremendous,
Shorteneth its journey so.

BLESSED BOYS (*from within him*).
To a vision grand we waken,
But the scenès too gloomy show;
We with fear and dread are shaken:
Kindest Father, let us go!

PATER SERAPHICUS.
Upward rise to higher borders!
Ever grow, insensibly,
As, by pure, eternal' orders,
God's high Presence strengthens ye!
Such the Spirits' sustentation,
With the freest ether blending;
Love's eternal Revelation,
To Beatitude ascending.

CHORUS OF BLESSED BOYS

(*circling around the highest summit*).

Hands now enring ye,
Joyously wheeling!
Soar ye and sing ye,
With holiest feeling!
The Teacher before ye
Trust, and be bold!
Whom ye adore, ye
Him shall behold.

ANGELS

(*soaring in the higher atmosphere, bearing the immortal part of* FAUST).

The noble Spirit now is free,
And saved from evil scheming:
Whoe'er aspires unweariedly
Is not beyond redeeming.
And if he feels the grace of Love

That from On High is given,
The Blessed Hosts, that wait above,
Shall welcome him to Heaven!

THE YOUNGER ANGELS.

They, the roses, freely spended
By the penitent, the glorious,
Helped to make the fight victorious,
And the lofty work is ended.
We this precious Soul have won us;
Evil ones we forced to shun us;
Devils fled us, when we hit them:
'Stead of pangs of Hell, that bit them,
Love-pangs felt they, sharper, vaster:
Even he, old Satan-Master,
Pierced with keenest pain, retreated.
Now rejoice! The work's completed!

THE MORE PERFECT ANGELS.

Earth's residue to bear
Hath sorely pressed us;
It were not pure and fair,
Though 't were asbestus.
When every element
The mind's high forces
Have seized, subdued, and blent,
No Angel divorces
Twin-natures single grown,
That inly mate them:
Eternal Love, alone,
Can separate them.

THE YOUNGER ANGELS.

Mist-like on heights above,
We now are seeing
Nearer and nearer move
Spiritual Being.
The clouds are growing clear;
And moving throngs appear
Of Blessed Boys,
Free from the earthly gloom,

In circling poise,
Who taste the cheer
Of the new spring-time bloom
Of the upper sphere.
Let them inaugurate
Him to the perfect state,
Now, as their peer!

THE BLESSED BOYS.

Gladly receive we now
Him, as a chrysalis:
Therefore achieve we now
Pledge of our bliss.
The earth-flakes dissipate
That cling around him!
See, he is fair and great!
Divine Life hath crowned him.

DOCTOR MARIANUS
(*in the highest, purest cell*).

Free is the view at last,
The spirit lifted:
There women, floating past,
Are upward drifted:
The Glorious One therein,
With star-crown tender,—
The pure, the Heavenly Queen,
I know her splendor.

(*Enraptured.*)

Highest Mistress of the World!
Let me in the azure
Tent of Heaven, in light unfurled,
Here thy Mystery measure!
Justify sweet thoughts that move
Breast of man to meet thee,
And with holy bliss of love
Bear him up to greet thee!
With unconquered courage we
Do thy bidding highest;

But at once shall gentle be,
When thou pacifiest.
Virgin, pure in brightest sheen,
Mother sweet, supernal,—
Unto us Elected Queen,
Peer of Gods Eternal!
  Light clouds are circling
  Around her splendor,—   **5**
  Penitent women
  Of natures tender,
  Her knees embracing,
  Ether respiring,
  Mercy requiring!
Thou, in immaculate ray,
Mercy not leavest,   **3**
And the lightly led astray,
Who trust thee, receivest!
In their weakness fallen at length,
Hard it is to save them:
Who can crush, by native strength,
Vices that enslave them?
Whose the foot that may not slip
On the surface slanting?
Whom befool not eye and lip,
Breath and voice enchanting?
(*The* Mater Gloriosa *soars into the space.*)

   Chorus of Women Penitents.
   To heights thou 'rt speeding
   Of endless Eden:
   Receive our pleading,
   Transcendent Maiden,
   With Mercy laden!

  Magna Peccatrix (*St. Luke,* vii. 36.)
By the love before him kneeling,—
Him, Thy Son, a godlike vision;
By the tears like balsam stealing,
Spite of Pharisees' derision;
By the box, whose ointment precious
Shed its spice and odors cheery;

By the locks, whose softest meshes
Dried the holy feet and weary!—

MULIER SAMARITANA. (*St. John*, iv.)
By that well, the ancient station
Whither Abram's flocks were driven;
By the jar, whose restoration
To the Saviour's lips was given;
By the fountain, pure and vernal,
Thence its present bounty spending,—
Overflowing, bright, eternal,
Watering the worlds unending!—

MARIA ÆGYPTIACA. (*Acta Sanctorum.*)
By the place, where the Immortal
Body of the Lord hath lain;
By the arm, which, from the portal,
Warning, thrust me back again;
By the forty years' repentance
In the lonely desert-land;
By the blissful farewell sentence
Which I wrote upon the sand!—

THE THREE.
Thou Thy presence not deniest
Unto sinful women ever,—
Liftest them to win the highest
Gain of penitent endeavor,—
So, from this good soul withdraw not—
Who but once forgot, transgressing,
Who her loving error saw not—
Pardon adequate, and blessing!

UNA PŒNITENTIUM

(*formerly named Margaret, stealing closer*).

Incline, O Maiden,
With Mercy laden,
In light unfading,
Thy gracious countenance upon my bliss!
My loved, my lover,

His trials over
In yonder world, returns to me in this!

BLESSED BOYS
(approaching in hovering circles).
With mighty limbs he towers
Already above us;   ·
He, for this love of ours,
Will richlier love us.
Early were we removed,
Ere Life could reach us;
Yet he hath learned and proved,
And he will teach us.

THE PENITENT
(formerly named Margaret)
The spirit-choir around him seeing,
New to himself, he scarce divines
His heritage of new-born Being,
When like the Holy Host he shines.
Behold, how he each band hath cloven,
The earthly life had round him thrown,
And through his garb, of ether woven,
The early force of youth is shown!
Vouchsafe to me that I instruct him!
Still dazzles him the Day's new glare.

MATER GLORIOSA.
Rise, thou, to higher spheres! Conduct him,
Who, feeling thee, shall follow there!

DOCTOR MARIANUS
(prostrate, adoring).
Penitents, look up, elate,
Where she beams salvation;
Gratefully to blessed fate
Grow, in re-creation!
Be our souls, as they have been,
Dedicate to Thee!
Virgin Holy, Mother, Queen,
Goddess, gracious be!

CHORUS MYSTICUS.

All things transitory
But as symbols are sent:
Earth's insufficiency
Here grows to Event:
The Indescribable,
Here it is ,done:
The Woman-soul leadeth us
Upward and on!

MODERN LIBRARY COLLEGE EDITIONS

The Best of the World's Best Books
COMPLETE LIST OF TITLES IN
THE MODERN LIBRARY

*A series of handsome, cloth-bound books, formerly
available only in expensive editions.*

MODERN LIBRARY

MISCELLANEOUS

MODERN LIBRARY GIANTS

A series of sturdily bound and handsomely printed, full-sized library editions of books formerly available only in expensive sets. These volumes contain from 600 to 1,400 pages each.

THE MODERN LIBRARY GIANTS REPRESENT A
SELECTION OF THE WORLD'S GREATEST BOOKS

MODERN LIBRARY GIANTS